Adolescent Coping

Adolescent Coping

ALICE E. MORIARTY, PH.D.

POVL W. TOUSSIENG, M.D.

with a Foreword by
Gardner Murphy and Lois Barclay Murphy

GRUNE & STRATTON

A Subsidiary of Harcourt Brace Jovanovich, Publishers

New York □ San Francisco □ London

Moriarty, Alice Ewell, 1917-
  Adolescent coping.

  Bibliography: p.
  Includes index.
  1. Adolescent psychology. 2. Personality.
I. Toussieng, Povl W., joint author. II. Title.
BF724.3.P4M67   155.5   76-13452
ISBN 0-8089-0942-8

Grune & Stratton, Inc.
111 Fifth Avenue
New York, New York 10003

Library of Congress Catalog Card Number 76-13452
International Standard Book Number 0-8089-0942-8
Printed in the United States of America

To Lois Murphy
who started and inspired this research,
and to the dedicated young people and
their families who made it possible

Contents

1. CENSORS AND SENSERS   1

Adolescents differ in how they perceive their experiences. Some limit or reduce direct experience, resulting in coping styles which are essentially traditionalistic. We have termed these adolescents the "Censors." The Censors are also subdivided into the "Obedient Traditionalists," or those who quietly adopt parental standards without question, and the "Ideological Conservatives," or those who more vigorously develop and defend a conservative stance.

More frequently, midwestern adolescents choose to modify parental viewpoints on the basis of their own sensory intake. We have termed these adolescents the "Sensers," and they are subdivided into the "Cautious Modifiers" and the "Passionate Renewers." Of the "Cautious Modifiers" need or wish to respond to what they perceive in their world, and modify their own behavior moderately or cautiously. The "Passionate Renewers" raise more questions, take little for granted, and following rethinking of traditional values, are more likely to adopt behavioral styles which differ from those of their traditional environment.

2. THE OBEDIENT TRADITIONALISTS   11

Description and behavioral examples of characteristic deportment; self-presentation; attitudes toward family, peers, religion, sex, and social issues; aspirations and plans for their future. Factors contributing to the choice of this coping style are discussed.

3. HARRIET: AN OBEDIENT TRADITIONALIST   21

4. THE IDEOLOGICAL CONSERVATIVES   37

Description and behavioral examples of characteristic deportment; self-presentation; attitudes toward family, peers, religion, sex, and social issues; aspirations and plans for their future. Factors contributing to the choice of this coping style are discussed.

5. CALVIN: AN IDEOLOGICAL CONSERVATIVE   47

6. THE CAUTIOUS MODIFIERS   59

Description and behavioral examples of characteristic deportment; self-presentation; attitudes toward family, peers, religion, sex, and social issues; aspirations and plans for their future. Factors contributing to the choice of this coping style are discussed.

7. VICTOR, FAITH, AND FLOYD: CAUTIOUS MODIFIERS   71

8. THE PASSIONATE RENEWERS   103

Description and behavioral examples of characteristic deportment; self-presentation; attitudes toward family, peers, religion, sex, and social issues; aspirations and plans for their future. Factors contributing to the choice of this coping style are discussed.

9. EVELYN: A PASSIONATE RENEWER   115

10. A QUIET RENEWAL   131

Midwestern coping styles, as compared to and different from adolescent coping as seen by other investigators, notably Erikson and Keniston.

11. ADOLESCENCE IN A TIME OF TRANSITION   139

Discussion of the finding of accelerated development, as seen in our data and in other investigations. Coping styles as behavioral adaptation in relation to personal assets and liabilities and environmental demands.

12. SO WHAT?   153

Summary, emphasizing implications for parents and those who work professionally with adolescents.

APPENDICES

Foreword

This is a brilliant empirical study and depth analysis of contemporary youth seen in part from a psychoanalytic and specifically Eriksonian viewpoint. The danger is that this conception will be regarded as the final "last word" on such a mode of viewing youth at a given time in a given setting, or, by contrast, as a simplistic tour de force. Rather, it is an ingenious, refreshingly realistic and revealing way of letting depth psychology come to terms with the social and developmental psychology of adolescence.

In attempting a historical approach to a contemporary problem, the authors themselves do not fully grasp the need of a broad historical perspective on concepts of adolescence; turning back the leaves of history more than half a century there would, for example, appear Stanley Hall's classic on adolescence, McDougall's profound statement on the "self-regarding sentiment," and Piaget's and Lerner's methodologically unique interview approach to the study of children's moral development. The depth aspects of adolescent development are carried further here, and are so much richer in social science perspective that one must regard this volume as an important step forward into that region of "sociological" applied psychoanalysis with which Erikson is preeminently identified.

The attempt to make sense of the turmoil and reorientation of American youth in the 50s and 60s has found many psychologists and social scientists trying to combine (1) the classical conception of the biology of adolescence, (2) the cross-cultural viewpoint associated with Ruth Benedict and Margaret Mead, and (3) a "situational" perspective as presented by such psychiatrists as Harry Stack Sullivan. What has usually been missing is a rich empirical base in individualized studies of quasi-clinical material documenting the individual conflicts and resolutions observable in the life — both behavioral and subjective — of the preadolescent and adolescent years in the specific boys and girls in a fully specified social environment in a definable historical period.

This is here supplied by a thoughtful integration of Povl Toussieng's in-depth interviews and Alice Moriarty's psychological examinations with the intensive interdisciplinary records on these children. These include the incredibly detailed observations on the behavior of these children as infants with their mothers; and the independent records by a pediatrician, psychiatrist, and each of several psychologists in formal and natural life settings. These records were made at preschool, latency, and preadolescent phases. A statement about the "sensitivity" of a child, for instance, is thus a distillation from an enormous body of data. Each of the empirical studies based on these records focuses on one or another special aspect of the children's coping experiences. This study by Moriarty and Toussieng is the only one oriented to the larger question of the outcomes of varying coping patterns of the group of young people in a given time and place setting.

In our judgment, what we have called a "situational" approach involving a confrontation of individual with specific economic and social conditions at a given time is generally inadequately worked through. Much social science thinking has been concerned with the intrinsic moral conflict between the world as represented to youth and the actual world they confront. There needs to be a volume such as this which would illustrate the interaction between biological givens, the social context, and the child's ways of dealing with the challenges experienced by him and her. These experiences, even in a given town, will vary greatly with the range of exposure allowed in each family. For instance, this Topeka group included Catholic and Protestant children growing up in a coherent environment bounded by home, church, neighborhood and nearby school. With no TV in their early years, and not being allowed to go to movies, they were not exposed until adolescence to the racial and economic conflicts endemic in their growing-up years.

The professional orientation of the authors is, of course, apparent in a book so abundantly rich in professional insights. We can only hope that the reader will bring to bear, as he reads, his own bias of time, place, and special interests, for it is in the intersection of all these realities that the living individual exists. Finally, we hope that the reader will note that the longitudinal aspect of this series of Menninger studies supplies both the social viewpoint and the research thrust of this study of adolescence. It is, of course, only a beginning as a research approach, but in our judgment it is an important pioneer effort to integrate longitudinal records in a given subculture at a given time.

It is hoped that this volume will be used as an intimate reflection of a new and promising modality of multi-disciplinary research and a clinically challenging way of looking at processes of human growth.

Gardner Murphy
Director of the Research
Department of the Menninger Foundation
over the period of this research.

Lois Barclay Murphy
Director of Developmental Studies
over the same period.

Chapter 1

Censors and Sensers

> A sense of continous selfhood always demands a
> balance between the wish to hold onto what one
> has proven to be and the hope to be renewed.
> Erikson[1]

In many contemporary writings, and especially in the news media, adolescence is referred to as a time of breaking away from old ties, of change, and of rebellion. Yet, psychoanalytic writers, notably Erikson, have consistently shown adolescence to be a period of continuity rather than discontinuity, a time when one crystallizes what one truly is and has so far experienced oneself to be, which may or may not include a self that likes to play with new ideas or try different adaptive styles. Nesselroade and Baltes[2] have recently impressively documented that personality development also is heavily influenced by the era, even the year, in which development takes place.

What we shall describe in this book fits these ideas. We belong to a team which under the inspiring leadership of Dr. Lois Murphy has studied the coping styles of 54 midwestern children from early childhood to adulthood.[3] The part of the study to be discussed here concerns the adolescent phase, particularly the time just before our subjects graduated from high school. Having been at each phase of growth interested in the continuities and changes in the coping patterns and styles of these young men and women, we were intrigued by the fact that coping styles in adolescence had become orchestrated around some of the burning questions in this country in the last half of the

1

1960s — the time when we were interviewing and testing our subjects again. Thus, we want to discuss not merely our observations and thoughts about coping styles, but also how these coping styles were functionally adaptive in relation to the specific time and place in which these young people were approaching adulthood.

We observed our subjects in their late teens fitting their chosen coping styles and identity into the historical setting at that time — a setting which focused on tradition versus renewal. Our group of subjects divided itself clearly and easily along this dimension, so that there was a distinct traditional group, as well as a distinct group of young people who emphasized renewal. However, these two groups really fitted along a qualitative spectrum or continuum, which will become apparent when we describe the two subgroups into which we were able to divide each of these groups.

The spectrum ranged from those holding on to established values, whether unquestioningly or passionately, to those seeking renewal, whether cautiously or with abandon. In studying this polarity more closely, we found that it was related to whether the person derived his sensory experience from his value system or developed his value system out of his sensory experiences. Because of the values they were committed to, some of our subjects restricted their sensory input accordingly. For this reason, we came to call them the "censors."

The censors represented 28 percent of the total sample. Within this group, we distinguished between two relatively equally often observed coping styles, which we called the "obedient traditionalists" and the "ideological conservatives." The "sensers" made up 72 percent of the total sample, and they were subdivided into a large group, the "cautious modifiers," and a smaller group we called the "passionate renewers." Although this may be a rather arbitrary classification, we found that we were able, independently, to subdivide our subjects into these four subgroups with a high degree of agreement. At the outset, we want to emphasize that we are talking about distinct styles of coping, and not about four different personality types. Therefore, it would be entirely possible, although unlikely, for a person to move from one group into another at any time in his life by choosing to emphasize his senses differently which, as we have already stressed, is the main characteristic that differentiates the four coping styles.

The obedient traditionalists (13 percent of the total sample) tend to see little or no value in developing their own senses. They perceive the world, as well as their own feelings, through a filtering screen that insures perception of only what they have come to believe is sanctioned and expected in their traditional culture. The ideological conservatives (15 percent of the total sample) allow themselves a relatively freer use of their senses within certain ideologically sanctioned areas, while blocking out anything beyond those areas. In other words, within the sphere where they allow themselves to use their senses, perception is guided heavily by certain convictions, which their perceptions then support and verify. The cautious modifiers (46 percent of the total sample) allow themselves considerably more freedom in the use of their senses, and sometimes also allow their opinions and behavior to be modified or changed outright on the basis of sensory input. The passionate renewers (26 percent of the total sample) constantly seek new input from their senses and frequently use this input to question or modify any and all of their views as well as their overt behavior.

For example, the four groups differ distinctly in sources of self-respect. The obedient traditionalists discount their own judgment and base their self-respect on the extent to which they are able to make themselves rely on the values and behavior codes handed down by their elders and get approval from these elders. The ideological conservatives value and respect their own judgments more highly, but they do so with definite and self-imposed limits. Outside these boundaries, they proudly and militantly promote those community and parental standards they have adopted as the only solution to all problems.

The cautious modifiers base their self-respect predominantly on their own strength and gain further self-confidence from engaging in a fair range of experimentation. However, they keep these experiments within certain definite boundaries, and at times they seek outside reinforcement and support from peers, parents, or both to maintain these boundaries. Moving beyond the boundaries appears to threaten them with loss of self-esteem. The passionate renewers base their self-respect on the amount of boldness and courage with which they make forays in all directions, preferably into previously unexplored territory. It is important to their self-esteem to have as accurate, extensive, and intensive a picture as they can possibly get of themselves, of others, and of the world in general, and to change themselves as that picture changes.

Another distinguishable difference in the four coping styles lies in the quality of the object relationships these young people tend to establish. The obedient traditionalists more or less ritualize even their closest object relationships and thus keep them quite impersonal and superficial. For these reasons, their interpersonal ties often appear to be relatively free of conflict or anxiety. The ideological conservatives and passionate renewers actively seek stronger and more personalized relationships with others, but these relationships are in continuous competition (and, particularly in the renewers, sometimes in conflict) with whatever quests the individuals in these two groups are committed to at any given time. The cautious modifiers, having no particular axe to grind, are open to make stronger attachments and commitments to other people.

The quality of object ties also to some degree depends on the kind of perception the young people cultivate. The obedient traditionalists base love relationships on feelings of conscientiousness, appropriateness, and duty; they want frequent feedback from others that the loved one is proper and acceptable to other important people in their lives. Thus, they cultivate dependence on relatives, friends, and life partners who are "approved" since they possess appropriate social credentials; personal characteristics are for them unimportant. The ideological conservatives are interested in friends and partners who will share their views and thus be an asset in achieving their often high personal goals. They, too, are less interested in the actual personal characteristics of these allies than in their standards of self-controlled behavior. The cautious modifiers are interested in the actual personal characteristics of people and are relatively unbiased about them. For this reason, they can and do establish strong ties to a variety of people, even ones outside their own ideological and cultural groups. However, they tend to romanticize family ties, friendships, and marriage bonds. By superimposing their fantasies on friends and loved ones, they often fail to see them as they are. The passionate renewers cultivate accurate perception of all the "real" aspects of people they are involved with or move close to, often to such a degree that little or no room remains for romantic feelings in the midst of catalogs of every wart, blemish, and quirk. Hence, the passionate renewers have limited interest in establishing more permanent symbolic ties, such as rings or official marriage bonds.

To explain the differences we have described, we have examined closely the experiences our subjects have had with their parents. This brought some surprising findings. One hundred percent of the obedient traditionalists had controlling or distant mothers, whereas only seven percent of the passionate renewers had such mothers. Eighty-six percent of the obedient traditionalists had fathers who were physically or emotionally unavailable, whereas all the passionate renewers had fathers who were close. The ideological conservatives frequently had both controlling or distant mothers and unavailable fathers, whereas the cautious modifiers nearly always had close relationships with mothers and grew up with fathers who were much involved in their upbringing. (For further details, see Appendix.) Particularly because of the small size of our subgroups, we want to evaluate these findings cautiously. Therefore, we do not want to claim that these particular parameters caused our subjects to choose one coping style rather than another. Moreover, we want to warn against generalization from these findings, as interesting as they are, but we do find them at least suggestive of the importance of early relationships, with the father as well as the mother.

Another intriguing finding appears to link the choice of coping style to the sex of the subject. Of the censors, 80 percent were boys; of the sensers, 59 percent were girls. We do not know the full significance of this finding, but the high percentage of males among the censors may be related to the unavailability of their fathers. It may be that boys who do not have a father with whom they can interact closely instead identify with prevailing value systems in the community, or that in the absence of fathers they have greater needs to excel for mothers who also suffer from missing or uninvolved fathers.

In the same way, we cannot assess the full significance of the fact that the mothers of 4 of the 8 girls among the passionate renewers either had postpartum depressions or died in the children's early childhood. As with the previous findings, all we feel entitled to say from our small sample is that our data suggest that the availability and quality of the relationships to parents are contributing factors in determining the coping styles chosen and developed.

Comparing the censors and sensers along other dimensions, we found no clearly differentiating factors in the usual estimates of intelligence, mental health, or social experiences. For example, there were no significant differences in intelligence level, as measured on the Wechsler Adult Intelligence Scale.[5] The traditional criteria for mental health also failed to separate the two groups, a finding we consider significant since in this respect none of the four subgroups can be said to represent a less "healthy" (i.e., less valid) choice. Vulnerabilities and risks are associated equally with each coping style, but these differ in nature from group to group. We cannot definitely identify these liabilities because most of our subjects were in reasonably good mental health when we saw them just before they graduated from high school. Few if any of our young people's choices appeared to have been influenced by reading or television. Schools and teachers definitely played no role whatsoever in the subjects' choices of coping styles. By and large, the choices of these young people originated within themselves rather than in response to seeds planted by the peer group. Although peer relationships of our subjects had many conventional aspects, the peer groups also provided a sounding board and a source of further information. Peers were used to test one's views, refine them, and seek what Sullivan called "consensual validation."[6]

Besides the parts played by availability of fathers and the dominance of mothers, there is no question that the parents' value systems influenced the coping style our subjects chose. All of the obedient traditionalists and the ideological conservatives had parents with strong traditional views, whereas many but by no means all of the passionate renewers had parents with less traditional views. All the parents of the cautious modifiers adhered to traditional views. Thus, the great majority of the parents brought up their children according to the conservative standards prevailing in the northeastern part of Kansas for generations. For precisely these reasons, it is all the more surprising that most of the children adopted a more or less nontraditional stance.

An obvious conclusion might be that this was evidence of adolescent rebellion, which has been assumed to be a normal characteristic of adolescence since time immemorial. Twenty-four hundred years ago, Socrates lamented about the bad manners, contempt of authority, and disrespect for elders exhibited by the youth of his time. In the late 1960s, the news media and many people in society referred to the hippie movement, the drug problems among young people, youthful protests, and riots as the "youth revolt" — in other words, a particularly pernicious type of adolescent rebellion.

The views our sensers developed resembled to a remarkable degree the views expressed by militant young people elsewhere, particularly those described by Simmons and Winograd[7] and by Keniston[8] making it even more probable that the underlying motive for changing their views was rebellion. However, our sensers did not show the slightest trace of interest in revolution, or even in a mild rebellion. They were not against anyone; they talked freely and openly with their parents, with us, and with other adults, and they planned to live their lives in the same community in which they had grown up. At the same time, with quiet determination, they were planning their college, vocational, and life careers on the basis of their new values. These values had for the most part already been extensively integrated into their self-images.

What characterized the sensers was that they did not see themselves as moving away from something, but as moving toward goals that had become important to them. After falling in love, as it were, with new views and attitudes, they saw no need to reject or hate the views and attitudes they left behind. They had outgrown them — and this fact in itself was no big deal to them. The changes they had made, as important as they were to these young people as individuals, to them had no ideological overtones. They wanted to change themselves, and did, but did not find it necessary to change anyone or anything else. Most of these young people recalled having been rebellious in their junior high school years, but thought the rebellion was overcome by the ninth grade. Thus, as in Offer's[9] and Douvan and Adelson's[10] subjects, the period of adolescent rebellion had occurred earlier and did not overlap with the period when our subjects developed their new views. At the same time, none of Offer's or Douvan and Adelson's subjects, studied at approximately the same time as our subjects, were reported to express nontraditional contemporary concerns, as so many of our subjects did.

The relative serenity with which over half of our subjects changed their values may well be evolutionary, with roots in the persistence in their families of a farm culture. This was particularly true of mothers, many of whom had grown up in areas where floods and tornadoes had been taken in stride as facts of life. Farm life in the first half of this century involved a good deal of hardship, including these acts of nature and the Great Depression, from which there was no escape and which could not be coped with by denial. Survival in the farm culture necessitated facing these stresses squarely and realistically, unemotionally, actively, and to the best of one's ability. Thus, mothers, as the dominant parent in the child care provided in most of our families, and as the more active parent in setting values for the children, may well have brought this heritage to their children.

The rapid, unpredictable, and major changes our world is undergoing, changes which were already in the works in the 1960s, to many people present a stress comparable to natural disaster (see, for example, Toffler[11]). Although the mothers themselves, as far as we knew, were continuing to live as they always had — that is, characteristically accepting the way things were — they, too, may have been developing some different ways of coping with the new situation. Lack of funds prevented us from interviewing the parents as we were interviewing their children in their adolescence, so we do have no direct data on this. However, from our subjects' reports, most of the mothers tolerated, and in some instances even respected, new views and life styles in their youngsters, even while they regretted or were made uncomfortable by the changes.

Contributing to the mothers' tolerance may have been the fact that people on farms are thoroughly familiar with seeing creatures of all kinds grow up, multiply, and be useful in their particular way. In our experience rural parents, as a group, are less concerned with suppressing their children's accurate and idiosyncratic perception than parents coming from an urban background. In the same way, parents in a rural culture tend to show remarkable ease in accepting individual developmental patterns in all growing creatures, including their own children, without feeling the need to force these patterns. Because of this rural heritage, the parents of our sensers (who characteristically stubbornly clung to their own senses) may have intervened less than they might have done if they had been products of a long-standing urban tradition.

Furthermore, even in urban Kansas, the pioneer tradition is still strong. In this tradition it is customary to allow early autonomy in the children, within wide but definite and rigidly enforced limits. Within these limits, the children are free to move and to express themselves, and they can expect to be respected. As preschool children our subjects overwhelmingly saw themselves as valued human beings.[12] Those who showed vigorous individuality were particularly respected by the adults around them. However, when we saw the children again at prepuberty, the limits set by their parents were clearly being narrowed a great deal, and heavier demands were being made on them for obedience and conformity. The ensuing struggle with parental demands around and after puberty apparently determined whether the youngsters would hold on to their own perceptions and views of themselves and the world, possibly with the help of peers, or whether they would yield and conform to parental pressures.

The outcome, then, depended primarily on factors in the youngsters themselves: their strengths and weaknesses, the degree of their relative vulnerability and ability to cope, their determination, and their inclination and ability to solicit support from the peer group. In addition, the overall context in which they grew up, both their heritage and ongoing social changes, provided important direction and behavioral content for whatever choice of coping style was being made. Again, having made a choice does not preclude making other entirely different choices in the future. However, since coping styles remained constant in many of our subjects as we followed them from early childhood, we do not anticipate that many of them will change their choices fundamentally. For this reason our subdivisions continue to have relevance to our understanding of adolescence and, in our judgment, merit more detailed description in subsequent chapters.

Notes:

[1] Erikson Erik H: *Dimensions of a New Identity.* New York, W. W. Norton & Company, 1974, p 100.

[2] Nesselroade JR, Baltes P: *Monographs of the Society for Research in Child Development,* vol. 39, no. 1, serial no. 154, 1974.

[3] In the years 1947-1951 (USPHS Grant MH-27), Drs. Sibylle Escalona and Mary Leitch collected predominantly observational data on a group of 128 infants, who were free of known physical, neurological, or emotional impairment. In this study, 8 boys and 8 girls were examined at each 4-week age level from 4 through 32 weeks of age. This nonnormative study, conducted at the Menninger Foundation, proposed to assess early personality development, with special focus on the range of normal behavior. Results of this study are reported in Escalona SK, Leitch M, et al.: Early phases of personality development: a nonnormative study of infant behavior. *Monographs Social Research Child Development,* 17 (no. 1), 1-72, 1952.

Dr. Murphy's coping studies, also carried on at the Menninger Foundation (1952-1969) with USPHS support (Grant M680, M4093, PH43-65-41, MH09236-01, 5R12MH09236-02, 5R12MH09236-03), followed some of these infants in their preschool, latency, prepuberty, and adolescent years. The sequence of studies, although independently planned and assessed by a changing interdisciplinary staff, was longitudinal insofar as samples from the original Escalona population were studied at successive age levels. Each phase was completed before review of the earlier data. Dr. Murphy's studies shared the common aim of assessing aspects of mental health and ego strength in relation to children's spontaneous efforts to cope with expectable stresses in the vicissitudes of growth. Among the numerous publications coming out of this series of studies are Escalona and Heider's *Prediction and Outcome,* Gardner and Moriarty's *Personality Development at Preadolescence,* Heider's *Vulnerability in Infants and Young Children,* Moriarty's *Constancy and IQ Change,* Murphy's *Widening World of Childhood,* Murphy and Moriarty's *Development Vulnerability and Resilience.*

[4] Classification, made independently by the two authors on the basis of clinical interviews and test data obtained in individual sessions with subjects, agreed closely. We obtained a contingency coefficient of 0.80 and a Pearson coefficient of 0.88. This suggested an objective reality to our conception of differential coping styles, and pressed us to ask what factors were involved in the development of traditional coping styles by roughly a quarter (28 percent) of our sample, while roughly three-quarters (72 percent)

had adopted less traditional coping styles. Also intriguing was the fact that 80 percent of those demonstrating traditional coping styles were boys, whereas 59 percent of those exhibiting less traditional or evolving coping styles were girls. We shall present our thinking about these issues after describing and illustrating the four coping styles.

[5]We should probably point out, however, that insofar as there is apparently a difference in the perceptual styles of censors and sensers that there could be constitutional bases for these differences. Our data are not such that we can explore this possibility. Hence, we must conclude that we have evidence for no measurable differences in intellectual functioning. We do suggest that there is a difference in how perceptual skills, at whatever level they exist, are mobilized. Whether group differences result totally from differences in parental limitations, demands, and expectations, or are also influenced by inherent capacities in the child we cannot say.

[6]Sullivan HS: *The Interpersonal Theory of Psychiatry.* New York: W. W. Norton & Company, 1953.

[7]Simmons JL, Winograd B: *It's Happening.* Santa Barbara, California: Marc Laird Publications, 1966.

[8]Keniston Kenneth: *The Uncommitted.* New York: Dell Publishing Co., 1960. Keniston Kenneth. *Young Radicals.* New York: Harcourt Brace Jovanovich, 1968.

[9]Offer Daniel: *The Psychological World of the Teen-Ager.* New York: Basic Books, Inc., Publishers, 1969.

[10]Douvan Elizabeth, Adelson Joseph: *The Adolescent Experience.* New York: John Wiley & Sons, 1966.

[11]Toffler Alvin: *Future Shock.* New York: Random House, 1970.

[12]The integrity and spontaneity of most of our subjects as preschoolers is described in detail in Murphy's *Widening World of Childhood.*

Chapter 2

The Obedient Traditionalists

In their bearing and grooming, their characteristic deportment and self-presentation, the obedient traditionalists are entirely wholesome and free of guile. Of all the youths we saw, they expressed the viewpoints most directly reflecting the traditional value systems of parents they highly respect and of the community in which they live. For example, Eleanor told us, "I hardly ever disagree with my parents, I mean on things that really matter. . . . What matters is that I still appreciate them and respect them and respect what they ask me to do. . . . I see my parents as very wonderful people who are understanding and kind."

This respect for parents and tradition is extended, with remarkable consistency, even to their inner life and to their own senses. In order to avoid looking at or questioning traditional viewpoints in any way, these young people have estranged[1] themselves totally from their own experiences. This estrangement is so complete that they are unable to experience, in an idiosyncratic way, major events in their lives, whether they be triumphs or tragedies[2] Their descriptions of events they observed or participated in, such as family vacation trips, consequently lack detail and color, even though many of these young people are highly intelligent. They talk about their experiences in a brief, stereotyped way which at all times conveys their concern about looking at and accepting or rejecting everything as they believe their parents would do. Nor are any of these young people able to identify the high and low points in their lives. Everything is as it ought to be, and this precludes emotional ups and downs.

Always trim and neat in dress, they choose conservative hair styles and attire because they are aware of the impact of good grooming. Eleanor explained here, "I rely just as much on my inner self as I do on my outer self, but I mean I like to make a good first impression." That is, she chose to dress carefully in order to please adults, to fit their standards, and to compete for status with peers, particularly in athletic skills and leadership roles in clubs and social events in school.

Seeing these pursuits as valuable, the obedient traditionalists usually are actively involved and successful in sports, which they regard as healthful recreation, as an opportunity to meet appropriate friends (Horace commented, "In high school, I mostly hung around with guys that were in sports, but not necessarily the ones I was in."), and as a means of achieving self-control. (Barney confided, "I am usually doing something in sports, so I don't have time to go around raising trouble.")

Quite clearly, too, these youths welcome competition and savor their own excellence. (Horace: "I like to compete with someone and I like to try to do better than they do, and so I work at it. I work at golf and at bowling and I try to do my best in order to beat someone else.") At the same time, they are unpretentiously modest about their own accomplishments and particularly strive to avoid bragging, as Eleanor made clear: "Everybody tells me that I am very good, but I don't know. I don't like to say 'Here I am; I am great.' That's not the way to go about it. . . . it seems kind of conceited going up and saying, 'Well, I am here now; you can all clap.' I don't like that at all . . . sports have been a big thing all the way through school. I just like being active in sports. It gives you physical activity that I like. It is fun." It is as though they need to compete for the sake of being active and to gain an established position with their peer group. Tony said, "To get over the feeling of being lost, I tried to, as much as I could, be active as I could. I wasn't ever outstanding in basketball."

Conscientious, responsible youth, the obedient traditionalists have learned the value of hard work and responsibility, and thus adequately meet home and school demands, as well as the requirements of the experimenters, with little need for reminder or praise, encouragement to persist, or external disciplinary control. They take for granted that they should do their homework, help with household chores, and be at least partially self-supporting. They do all of these things with minimal grumbling because they feel their parents are essentially fair, not overly harsh, and ordinarily right in their demands and limits. In fact, they are grateful for some control and for structure, which they regard as fortunate, and helpful behavioral models. Expressing his sincere respect and appreciation of his parents and his sense of responsibility to them, Tony said, "They gave me a few things, but I still had to earn a lot. They gave me a sense of value....That will probably help me later in my life, too. I'm not going to get anything given to me later on."

Tony, typical of the obedient traditionalists, hoped and expected to match parental achievement, seeing this as suitable and as a guide for daily personal behavior. The traditionalists plan to live in their home town, in homes much like those of their parents, to raise their children with similar disciplinary controls, based on religious precepts and standards of ethical and sexual morality. For these youths, "Sex is reserved for marriage." Persons choosing to engage in more permissive activities are, if not openly condemned, at least disapproved of insofar as such persons are not acceptable personal companions. Eleanor explained, "It's none of my business really and I don't make it a practice to go around and ask people about their personal lives, but it's not for me. I think I am pretty much against new morality....Kids that I run around with, the ones who are my better friends, aren't like that."

Compatible with these standards is their almost total rejection of the use of alcohol, tobacco, or drugs. Lionel might have been a spokesman for the traditionalists as he said, "I don't go for alcohol. I like sports and stuff like that and that stuff slows you down, and so I had better lay off of it....smoking is a messy habit. Even if I wasn't in sports, I wouldn't do it. Most teenagers just do it to think they are grown up, or their friends do it and they think they have to do it to be cool. I don't go along with it though. Besides, I wouldn't want to get into trouble with my mom....I don't see why you need drugs and why anybody would want to use them....I wouldn't touch them with a 10-foot pole."

Horace, as the only one of the traditionalists who smoked, justified himself by saying that his parents smoked and left the option to smoke or not to smoke to him. "My parents said I could if I wanted to....It was just something to do, I guess — rather than sit there and do nothing,

I guess. Or maybe it was since everybody else was doing it, I may as well do it, too." He felt less constraint about drinking, saying, "Drinking is all right. But I wouldn't say that going out and getting drunk every night is okay — but to go out and have a few beers — but I don't think drinking to excess is right. . . .I was drunk once and I just about passed out and I never — I haven't done it since, and I doubt if I ever will. . . .I realized it was something that was important to my parents and they knew what was best for me. . . .I knew what we could do, and I respected my parents enough to not drink. . . .it really isn't a big thing and it doesn't make any difference."

Such standards are reinforced not only by parental example, but also by unquestioning loyalty to the church and by personal habits of long duration. Horace pointed out that religion is "one of the most important things that we've got because we are Catholics. I think it's a kind of binding together force. . . .I think it is right to do this because — well, we really can't live without some criterion for judgment of what is right and what is wrong. I'll probably go to mass this afternoon because I think it is important — because if it wasn't — they wouldn't have it."

Tony valued his Protestant religious upbringing primariiy because going to church every Sunday was a family activity, an opportunity to meet people socially, and a behavioral guide. He described himself as "pretty religious. . . .you can meet and talk to more people. . . .I haven't ever read the Bible or anything like that. I am kind of sorry for that and I don't know why it happened. . . .so many things that come out of the Bible deal with everyday life. The Bible just has to be one of the most handy things around because you can just take passages out of it and just fit it to the things that happen to you in life. . . .sometimes the sermons are kind of over your head. . . .but probably the basic things, like the Ten Commandments, they are pretty much what you should follow and that is what my parents tried to teach. . . .I learned more from what my parents said, a whole lot more, than I did from the church. But now I am finding out that it is pretty much the same, what they taught me and what the church has to say. . . .church is church and I like to go and I will probably always go."

Thus, traditional youths follow parental and religious standards because they feel they are right, comfortable, and an asset in establishing a reputation for moral decency. They see no reason to question any of these standards[5] or to move outside of tradition to experience solely for the sake of experiencing.

dicated, likely to choose friends who share their interests in activity. They are less likely to seek or to feel comfortable with special closeness or depth of feeling. In fact, they protect themselves from intense feelings of enthusiasm or ecstacy, as well as from disappointment or sadness in the event of loss. For instance, Lionel, whose father's career as a civil servant necessitated frequent moves, described explicitly how he avoided closeness to forestall likely emotional loss. "You find somebody you like, but you both realize that you will be moving pretty soon anyway, so you don't get really close. . . .There was this one boy I liked really well. We were both due to move soon, so we stopped hanging around together because we knew we would have to get used to not seeing each other. We would see each other maybe once a week, but we would never visit very long with each other."

Obedient traditionalists are willing and able to make some personal commitments to friendships, church, or deferred marriage because such commitments are expected of normal healthy individuals, but they prefer neutral relationships. This preference for relatively impersonal relationships was also apparent in their relationships with us.[8]

The characteristic lack of affective closeness and range in the obedient traditionalists was repeatedly reflected during our interviews in comments that they were rarely unusually angry, excited, exhilarated, or depressed and found it hard to identify high or low spots in their lives. For example, Horace remarked, "I try to keep as level as I can. I don't try to be antagonistic and I try to keep my temper." Eleanor could not remember ever being unhappy, or for that matter experiencing anything that had created unusual excitement in her.

Not feeling a need for closeness or for participating in the relationships such feelings involve, they seem reluctant if not totally unwilling to admit that they have any part in shaping their own lives. Often they express a "wait and see" attitude. In this regard, Lionel spoke for the group when he said, "I hope to control my own life, but fate can help out any way it can and I won't object. . . .I hope I run fate. . . .I am not sure." He added later, "You almost have to be happy to succeed and it takes money to succeed. . . .But I wouldn't fight for it. . . .You can't always tell what will happen. . . .And you can't really do anything about it." In other words, the obedient traditionalists are hard workers, dedicated to following in their parents' footsteps, but they do so quietly, without militancy, sometimes tentatively, and with modulated feelings.

Contributing to our subjects' stance were responsible parents who

provided adequate material care, and who had often weathered adversity and gently nudged their children to pursue education and seek
good jobs. Believing wholeheartedly that one can be whatever one
chooses, the parents urged their children to set moderate goals and
to abide by traditional standards. In responding to these admonitions,
the children, with considerable complacency and no defiance, were
like their parents emotionally controlled. They avoided extremes in
all aspects of their behavior and considered themselves unusually
well-settled teenagers.

Notes:

[1] For example, we noted that the obedient traditionalists frequently spoke in the
third rather than in the first person, and that they rarely identified friends or acquaintances
by name. In this respect, they appeared to depersonalize or to be impersonal in all
of their relationships.

[2] This is particularly well illustrated in the case study on Harriet (see Chapter 3),
who could not recall anything in her life that had been especially upsetting or which
gave her intense pleasure. She, like all of her obedient traditionalist peers, chose to
restrict the range of her feelings to such a degree that she and they appeared always
to be socially contained and emotionally bland.

[3] The lack of need for discipline stood out both in current subject reports and in
earlier interviews with parents. For example, Eleanor told us, "I remember only one
time in my whole life that I ever even got spanked, and that wasn't even bad. I guess
they taught me by example — I don't know. . . .I just don't steal and I don't lie and
I just don't cheat." Several years earlier, her mother had said much the same thing:
"She didn't have to be punished very often. . . .There never was any trouble in enforcing
rules. We don't have a lot of rules — at least it doesn't seem to me like we have a
lot of rules. Everything goes fairly well without having to lay any rules down. . . .We
used to take away privileges, but it has been so long since we have taken anything
away that I can't remember. . . .We have taught her by example."

[4] All but one of this group paid for their clothing out of their own earnings.

[5] As we shall see in succeeding chapters, the ideological conservatives more rigorously
define and defend their personal standards; the cautious modifiers more often question
but rarely overtly defy parental standards in their own behavior; the passionate renewers
irreverently probe all issues and beliefs and more often engage in experimental behavior.

[6] In this respect, the obedient traditionalists differ markedly from the ideological
conservatives, who with driving ambition hope to excel in high-level prestigious positions
in the arts and sciences.

[7] The emphasis on money was understandable in 5 of the 7 obedient traditionalists
whose parents had struggled to achieve economic stability in the face of limited
educational and vocational skills or seasonal unemployment. In the other 2 subjects,
these pressures were one generation removed.

[8] As compared with other subjects, particularly the cautious modifiers and the
passionate renewers, they were less interested in the purposes and uses of the material
we were gathering. They had more difficulties in keeping appointments, often complain-

ing that their many activities kept them too busy. They were less interested in returning for the final "wrap-up" session, in which we offered to go over test results, presumably helpful in planning their own education and vocational futures. It was also significant that they often did not recall staff members from one session to the next and were disinclined to use the psychiatric interviews to discuss immediate concerns.

Chapter 3

Harriet: An Obedient Traditionalist

At 18 years, pretty, dark-haired Harriet, a recent high school graduate, was socially poised, physically healthy, and casually dressed. Appropriately attentive and politely cooperative, she greeted the interviewer in a friendly, outgoing fashion. Characteristically, she explained that she had kept the appointment despite some personal inconvenience. She had a busy academic schedule and many sorority commitments and spent a good deal of time with a steady boyfriend. She had adjusted her schedule to meet our demands because she felt a responsibility to the longitudinal project and because her mother encouraged her to come.

She presented herself as one who was satisfied with a fairly sheltered life in which her fair and lenient parents had given her almost everything she wanted, so that her own efforts and wishes had met with few frustrations: "I never questioned their authority at all. . . .They've never really had to discipline because they don't think I've ever, you know, done anything that — you know — [was] outstandingly bad. But I mean, if I ever needed disciplining, they [the parents] were the ones that did it."

Academically and socially successful, interested and capable in sports, a member of a family who had over the years enjoyed vigorous physical activities and numerous camping trips together, she felt fortunate for having grown up in an emotionally stable, economically comfortable family who had given her protection, support, and considerable self-confidence. Considering the hypothetical option for changing her life, she could imagine little that she would want to change; she was content with herself and her world. She remarked that she had not really thought much about, and certainly had never been deeply worried or unhappy about, her lot in life. When she was questioned on specific points, she answered in generally positive terms, reflecting the unimportance to her of subtleties and of thoughts about why or how she had come to believe and feel as she did. To her it was meaningless to deal with the question of whether she had a part in shaping her own life. In fact, requested discussion of personal experiences made her uncomfortable, as manifested by a moderate physical restlessness when such discussions were initiated by the project staff.

Harriet saw herself as "fairly good looking, pretty outgoing, kind of a leader," as one who expected college to be fun although also demanding study, as one who anticipated marriage and a family, preferably in her own home town. She could remember nothing that had aroused emotions of a high pitch. She had never been more than briefly ecstatic, unhappy, or angry. She had never had a reason "really to get worried about anything." She listened to newscasts, but she did not wish to take sides on controversial political or social issues. "I just sort of sit back and watch what happens." In fact, she could not imagine feeling strongly enough about any community or personal issues to lead to experiences of emotional tumult, disequilibrium, or strong discharge of feelings. She was unlikely to protest, unlikely to fight for change of any kind "unless something really, really, you know, I was really. . . .felt real strongly about something, or I thought, you know, it was really wrong." A believer in the status quo, she treasured traditional middle class standards. Her goals in life were focused on personal achievement and self-advancement toward stability and respectability. Compared with most teenagers, she was remarkably settled, stable, and content.

Harriet's conscientious, careful, responsible handling of her life was impressive. This was also true of her cooperation in dealing with the demands of our interviews. Yet she carefully limited her participation, keeping her responses brief[1] and without a great deal of personal or spontaneous involvement or enthusiasm about the aims and the potential usefulness of the longitudinal project. She asked few questions about our findings, was not curious about other subjects, and did not inquire about publication plans or how we hoped to use the data. Therefore, her participation was based exclusively on an intellectual interpretation of what she saw as her duty in our sessions.

It became clear that introspective or reflective self-analysis was meaningless to Harriet. She was convinced that she already knew what were for her the correct and proper ways to behave so that there was no need to give further thought to them. Intellectually capable and academically efficient, she was perceptually alert, and she used her skills to help her meet standards which were appropriate to her social status, and which she had learned in her family. She was in her adolescence a younger edition of her mother, not through active identification but rather through meticulous imitation of the mother's decorous, ladylike, affable but self-absorbed, emotionally controlled behavioral style, which Harriet obviously had observed quite accurately during her growing years? The mild depressive trends and latent creativity, hinted at in the projective tests, were not strong enough to force her to struggle for deeper satisfactions than those she found in her safe, secure world. She was inimitably adjusted to her environment, easily and respectfully meeting its demands and enjoying the recognition she gained from her social and academic successes. She did so with calm self-possession, never seeming to need to experience the emotional ups and downs or intensity of feeling of many of our teenage subjects.

When we saw Harriet just after she had graduated from high school, she was planning to enter a small nearby college in the fall, partly because her boyfriend was a student there. She agreed with her parents that "if you have ability and capability you should go on to college." Although she had not definitely determined her major, she was attracted to physical education. This was a provisional choice influenced by her skills and experienced success in athletics, by some vaguely formulated preferences from personal experiences, and by her mother's professional experiences in working with children.

"Well, my mother influenced me quite a bit but I have already enjoyed working with children. I like the real small ones and yet I like high school age because I feel, you know, I can realize what they are going through and what their problems are because I've experienced them and so I'm not sure. . . .I'll just have to wait and see." In other words, her choice of a major was logical in terms of her background and personal competence, but characteristically she remained tentative about choices that might bring her experiences her mother had not had.

Harriet preferred a small school close to home, purportedly because she enjoyed her dependency on her parents and was not yet emotionally ready to break these ties. "If I were turned out into the world right now, I think I'd have a hard time because I know I am dependent on my parents, and I'd feel a little lost." She had depended on their authority in her growing years. "I never, you know, resented them for their strictness or anything like that." She felt that she continued to need their authority in her late adolescence. She admitted that in the interim period, particularly during her sophomore year in high school, she had felt her parents were unreasonable in the time limits they set on dates. In retrospect, she saw these restraints as appropriate. She said, "When I was a sophomore, I'd think, you know, they were so terrible and they were just so cruel, but really when I look back now, I mean it seems like such a little thing that I'd get upset at ....I wouldn't throw a fit or anything. I'd start crying and saying, 'Well, so and so can do this, you know, why can't I?' and in the end, I'd get over it, you know. . . .They never spanked me. They just made me feel bad. . . .I think it was pretty effective, man!"

Harriet admired and respected both of her parents, differing from their views only in regard to some aspects of participation in religious activities. By her junior year in high school, she had stopped going to Sunday school "because I didn't feel like I was really getting that much out of it." But she usually attended church services because "I've always gone and I do enjoy it." She saw herself as "sort of a rainy day Christian, I guess, but I'll admit this, and I'm trying, and I hope I change when I grow older and mature, but I think — I don't know how to say it, but I mean I just feel like it's not that much a part of my life yet." Still, "I just feel sort of empty — I mean on Sunday — it just wouldn't seem right if I didn't go to church. . . .it probably is habit, and I do get something out of it."

In other words, Harriet's views about college and about religion were sincere, but they were formulated indistinctly and they seemed to be based more on habit and family examples than on her own feelings. Her views bore witness to long-standing habits of conscientious and obedient adoption of very definite parental standards. They were also reinforced, of course, by the high degree of social recognition she had gained from peers and teachers. Having tried out for cheerleading in her sophomore year "mainly because all my friends were trying out," she had by her senior year become head cheerleader. She was recognized by teachers through their designation of her as a senior leader in her physical education classes. She was honored by the student body through their election of her to an honorary office. Even so, she saw herself only as "fairly popular, I guess."

In addition to making a conscientious effort to be a successful student and a leader, she had worked responsibly in a clerical job that gave her spending money to extend her wardrobe. Her commitment to all of these things was intellectual rather than emotional, an automatic adjustment to her environment rather than an active shaping of her own life. She enjoyed being busy and in fact relied on activity to avoid boredom.

Harriet seemed — at some inner level never quite openly expressed — to sense a gap in her experiences, perhaps recognizing a certain amount of superficiality or lack of closeness in her interpersonal relationships. She said this indirectly as she described athletic and club activities and her social leadership role: "If I didn't have these activities, I don't think I'd know what to do. I would be so bored ....I don't think I'm a real strong leader — not that I can't persuade people, but I don't know, I'm not sure what I mean." Here she seemed to be saying that she needed activities because she lacked the deep lasting relationships that might have provided other sources of involvement.

Harriet had many acquaintances but few close attachments. Neither by inclination nor by personal style was she one who demanded the closeness that pushes some adolescents to behave as the crowd behaves. She did not seek advice from girl friends and had in fact spent less time with her girl friends during her senior year in high school after she began going steady. Harriet double dated infrequently, and her social activities with other girls tended to be in terms of casual get-togethers during school hours rather than planned evening or weekend activities. She was not emotionally close, even to her steady boyfriend. This relationship, like so many of her life experiences, had become a comfortable habit, and incidentally a relationship socially approved by her parents. She explained, "We had good times together ....Well, he's athletic and we have the same interests and we enjoy — well, we must enjoy being together....He's a good talker with mom and dad....They admire him....and think he's a real fine boy ....I think I carry a lot by myself....I do think I keep a lot of things to myself."

Harriet had not had any serious arguments with her boyfriend. Although she declared she was in love, she could pinpoint no period of falling in love, nor could she foresee a major disruption in her life if he were to break off the relationship. "I'm sure it would shake me. . . .But I'd find — you know — I just wouldn't fall apart and I think I'd find something else to go to."

Neither had she in her senior high school year been very close to her siblings. This was true of her older brother of whom she said first, "We have a real good relationship," and then later added, "We weren't real close." In fact, she saw very little of him. She rarely joined him in social activities, nor did she share her feelings with him. "He wasn't really home that much and I was always on the go, so. . . .he had his friends and I had mine." Whereas in her earlier years she had a special place as a favorite butt of her brother's teasing, she was in late adolescence no longer singled out in this way. She admired her brother for his academic and athletic excellence ("He was quite upstanding.") and followed in his footsteps without consciously formulated competitiveness or jealousy. ("I didn't even think about it.")

Her relationship with her younger sister had little meaning because of age difference and little communality of interest. Her relationship with her other sister, who is closer to Harriet in age, was also one of quiet acceptance, following some relatively minor or at least temporary upsurges of conflict. She said, "We get along pretty good on the whole. . . .but she's different than I am. I mean, she just, the activities she participates in and doesn't participate in are just different than what I've ever done." Her sister was less serious than Harriet about her involvement in school activities, but like Harriet she was a good student. Harriet had been taught that individuals differ in their interests and in their personality, and she therefore logically believed her parents had been too harsh in their attempts to mold the sister in Harriet's image. Yet Harriet was critical of her sister and for a time felt distinctly alienated from and disappointed in her. Later, she came to accept these behavioral differences, or at least managed to avoid open conflicts with her sister. She was then less outspoken in her criticisms, although she continued to disapprove privately, of open display of affection between the sexes and of drinking and smoking — behavior which she knew was acceptable to and typical of her sister's crowd. This she condemned as "bad," yet she felt she should not condemn behavior that was common in many of her acquaintances. "I know a lot of kids in high school now that do drink and smoke. The majority of kids do in my school, and a lot of my friends do, but my close friends don't. And I don't look down on people — I don't think that I do, because I know I just don't care; well, I'm not going to do it, though I just, you know, don't have that much in common with them. . . .Well, I've just never gone to parties where it goes on."

Harriet's conflict between her intellectual appreciation of tolerance and her strong disapproval of her sister's behavior, as well as that of some of her acquaintances, produced some mildly experienced frustration or confusion in her thinking. "Sometimes I get sort of frustrated. I mean, you're not — and then when you start to think about things you — I mean — you can get pretty confused." This she dealt with primarily by ignoring it, by setting high standards of personal behavior for herself, and by quietly eliminating from her associations those acquaintances who engaged in these activities. "I myself would never smoke or drink. I can see myself maybe holding hands in some places, but I don't think it looks too nice. Well, some of them have changed and we [she and her boyfriend] don't run around with them anymore."

Nor was she, aside from social status and social recognition, more committed to things and ideas than she appeared to be to people. For instance, despite an avowed interest in reading and in keeping abreast of current events through TV, she was hard pressed to think of any favorite books or TV programs. She did not align herself with a political party or political activities, nor did she take a definite stand on international affairs. "I just sort of sit back and watch what happens . . . .I can see good on both sides." She was not especially concerned about racial tensions because she felt these issues would not affect her much. She denied being prejudiced insofar as she would not "hold anything against Negroes because they have a different color skin," but she set limits as to how much she would care to associate with blacks. "I know I would never marry a colored person. . . .and I hate to say this, but I mean, I think it would be hard to run around socially with a colored person. . . .If a colored person moved in next door to me. . . .you know you say, 'Oh, I don't care,' you know, but I think maybe I would." More comfortable with familiar and expected social activities in her own crowd, she was impressed with rush week and anticipated sorority life as a lot of fun. Yet even with this positive commitment, she was tentative and temperate about her plans, "I'll probably join a sorority, I guess."

Harriet's moderate enthusiasm and commitment were part of her lifestyle, reflected also in the mildness of her stated emotional reactions to most situations. For instance, she indicated that she had little temper, rarely got mad, and could not imagine being loud or becoming verbally abusive. At the most, Harriet said, "I might raise my voice or something at home sometime." She remembered having questioned parental authority only once in relation to the time she had to be home from dates. Likewise, she expressed only rare and mild feelings of rebelliousness in school. If she had felt misjudged by teachers, she would possibly have inquired into the situation, but she granted teachers the final word. In other words, she was not prone to become angry, and if she were angry, she was not inclined to express her anger forcefully. She lived within the reality of her own life and was not one to attempt to change the reality of a situation by her own perceptions, feelings, judgments, or insights.

Overtly, Harriet was content with her lot, and in many ways considered herself fortunate to have been given many material advantages, to have established herself with little obvious pressure from her parents, and to have achieved considerable recognized success academically and in athletics. She also indicated that she enjoyed her feminine role, insisting that "I wouldn't give up being a girl for anything," and conceding only under pressure from the psychiatrist the vague possibility that she might on rare occasions have felt mild envy of her brother. She denied having skill, interest, or experience in homemaking tasks and she was vague and indefinite about how capable she was in most areas. "I think potentially, I think I couldn't — I think I could be maybe smarter than I am; I think I'd feel a little lost" — if she were really independent; "I'm fairly popular, I guess; I don't think I'm a real strong leader; I wasn't real outstanding" — in swimming. Thus, despite considerable demonstrated competence and social recognition, she was quite humble about her assets and skills.

This modulated or muted way of experiencing and expressing feelings extended to the full range of her feelings. She could not, for example, immediately think of any great disappointments in her life because she felt "I've had so many things, you know." She could recall no outstandingly happy period of her life because "There are a lot of things that are — they seem happy. . . .and at the time they are the happiest. . . .you just can't say because there are so many happy times and then there are equally some sad times." Pressed to describe some of these happy times or sad times, she could think of no concrete examples. Harriet was not unwilling to communicate her feelings; she seemed literally unaccustomed to identifying any of her feelings.

The one possible exception to this generalization was the combined anger toward her mother and sympathy for her father expressed as she described her parents' lack of shared social activities. Explaining how dull she saw her parents' lives, she remarked, "Mom has her friends. She belongs to bridge clubs and things such as this, but dad — she and dad — just don't go out together and I mean, I feel sorry for him because I think this is, I mean, you can, I mean when you get married, that doesn't mean your fun stops. I mean you can. . . .I think you should, you know, go out and do things together. . . .so they sit home at night and watch TV." Then, depressively as she considered her own likely reaction to marriage and family responsibilities, she added, "I'll probably be doing it too. . . .it's usually the way it is. I mean usually you'll plan all the things you'll do but you turn out the same as them." This fatalistic depression about her own future came out also in the final session with the psychologist (AM) 7 months later when Harriet was enrolled at a nearby college.

After an interview focused primarily on how she had experienced school in the past 12 years, Harriet was asked to take our standard battery of structured and projective tests. She agreed to do this, performing competently but with limited interest, keeping her responses brief, factual, and relatively impersonal. She admitted that she had found the projective tests difficult ("I couldn't pick out too much"), and that some of the abstract ideas we had asked her to discuss were "pretty hard to define." Unlike most of our subjects, she did not take the opportunity to review test findings to compare them with her own understanding of herself or to discuss her plans for her future.

Speaking first about college, Harriet said that she very much enjoyed sorority life, which she saw as a mark of social prestige. She was also pleased that her boyfriend belonged to a popular fraternity and that he had acquired some status and recognition in athletics.

Academically, she was successful and anticipated no difficulties with classwork. She was planning to major in physical education which she felt would prepare her to work if she decided to do so after graduating from college. She had chosen this course as insurance against the unlikely possibility that she might not marry, but she did not expect to teach and had not formulated any distinct personal philosophy about education. She was content with her success and happy to have found a niche that was compatible with her social status and family back- ground. As to her own future, she was clear that she wanted security, probably in an economically stable marriage. Ten years hence, "I think I'd like to be married. . . .I'd like to live in a fairly nice home. . . .I'd like to have kids, but....I don't know if I'd teach or not....I like certain aspects of physical education. I don't think I'd enjoy teaching it."

In the same way, she looked back on her high school experiences in a generally positive way because she had enjoyed the many activities in which she had engaged. It was clear that she had associated with a large number of students, but she identified none by name as particularly meaningful to her as individuals. She could think of only one teacher she had disliked because this teacher had not maintained discipline in the classroom. She pointed out that teachers should have "a fairly dominant personality and be able to control their classes." Secondarily, she believed teachers should be "really interested in children." She was unable to say how this interest could be developed or demonstrated.

In describing herself, Harriet assessed herself as "one who is conforming....I don't like to sit down and think — well, why I'm doing this. I don't do that sort of thing." Nor, even when she was encouraged to think about herself, was she able to come up with strong interests or preferences, or to recall situations that aroused her to extremes of positive or negative feelings. She made concise remarks and was not prone to document, elaborate, or clarify. This was equally true in the interview with her and in her performance while taking the usual test battery.

An individual of moderately superior intelligence, Harriet showed good retention of what she had been taught but was not inclined toward deductive or inductive thinking. That is, she was unlikely to need or want to explain how she had reached conclusions or to elaborate on details of her thinking. She had mastered computational skills in math, but she could not explain how to apply these skills. She saw her reading, largely restricted to classroom assignments, as pleasant, but she did not try to apply it to her own thinking. She seemed to like structure and to enjoy following directions more than she liked setting up her own structure. She spoke softly, using a relatively good but not very differentiated or unusual vocabulary. She was well coordinated, neat, and fairly persistent in everything she did.

She was politely interested and entirely cooperative in the tests. It was clear that she wanted to do well, insofar as she technically met test demands, by complying with what she felt was expected of her, and by concentrating wholly on the specific requirements of the intellectual tasks posed. For a girl of her intellectual potential, she gave relatively few and very brief answers. She did not use the tests to perceive idiosyncratically or to express distinct or personal feelings. Nor did she seem interested in or able to elaborate on and to organize her thinking precisely. She dealt with both structured and projective tests competently, logically, without originality. In no way did Harriet expect or openly want to protest, nor if she had would she have expected to be heard or to modify outcomes. In her eyes, mothers and teachers were always right, and they never let anybody forget it.

Nevertheless, on rare occasions Harriet passively defied a few cues in the projective tests simply by not paying attention. Thus, her thematic stories were predominantly realistic descriptions of the given scenes, leading to logical outcomes associated with bland but generally positive feelings. This was true even when she twice projected a story of suicide. With this hint of depression, Harriet stopped short, interrupted the finality of suicide, and ended up by saying that the heroine "realized there was something good in life somewhere and that she could find it." Literally, Harriet preferred not to think about defiance, misconduct, or misery, and she diluted depressive feelings just as she had her entire range of feelings. Harriet seemed to have little urge to think about herself, or even to find out who she was.

In her responses to the Rorschach test, Harriet limited content almost entirely to animals that were mild, unthreatening, and unaggressive. Human responses were rare and were when present seen as immobile. She remarked about color, but did not use it in her percepts. She concentrated on usual large details and shape rather than on broadly integrated whole answers. She found most of the popular answers and did not look for unusual answers. She set out to do well but did not press for achievement beyond what came to her easily. Relatively comfortable in her life as she experienced it, she did not question how or why she behaved as she did.

Her responses to the Strong Vocational Interest Blank added little new information but again emphasized her preferred factually oriented and modulated style of responding to any situation. She filled in the test blank appropriately but showed little intellectual curiosity about the possible meanings of her responses. She answered every question, doing so neatly and quickly, rarely feeling a need to balance or weigh contingencies. Quite a few vocational choices were acceptable to her, but none aroused great eagerness. She was clear that she wanted to be physically active, that she disliked introspective and integrative thinking, and that she was not attracted to creative or artistic pursuits.

From the examples we have given of her verbal replies, the reader can sense the vague and undifferentiated quality of the perceptions reported by this bright girl. Even in talking about activities and accomplishments she valued, such as her election to honorary office in high school, Harriet could not describe her excitement before the election result was announced. Instead, she quoted the other candidates. When given repeated opportunities to elaborate further, her reactions were primarily those of surprise and muted pleasure: "I mean it never entered my mind and so I was really surprised. . . .[being elected] was pure joy, I think. . . .It was [fun]. It's something I'll always remember, I know." Harriet said she loved camping and had camped out with her family all over the continent. Yet in describing these experiences, she limited her comments to saying that Kansas was "too dirty" to make camping pleasant and that Canada was "really beautiful." It was impossible for her to give any specific details that explained these judgments, and in this respect she was representative of the youths whom we classified as the obedient traditionalists.

HARRIET'S EARLIER LIFE

Looking backward into Harriet's earlier life, we found a number of factors apparently contributing to her coping style. Harriet was generally robust, well coordinated and alert, but she was not particularly sensitive to or curious about sensory or interpersonal experiences.

She was a contented, self-sufficient baby without strong drives or preferences. As an undemanding baby, she was responsive to her mother's meticulous, organized style of care and was disinclined to protest. Having been breast fed and rocked to sleep for the first 10 days, she protested only moderately when these procedures were discontinued. Nor did she seem to have a preference, insofar as she did not cry or drink less when the bottle was propped rather than held. From the time she was 2 months old, she slept through the night and awoke cheerfully, staying contentedly in her crib without needing the mother's immediate attention. In the same way, at 3 months, she made an easy adjustment to solid foods, although her appetite was small.

At 6.5 months, she appeared unable to differentiate between the several professional observers, but she was more vigorous, especially in vocalization, when she was in direct contact with her mother. She followed objects and movements and seemed to listen deliberately to verbal or musical sounds. She rarely startled and was not particularly sensitive to pain, shock, or position or temperature changes. When observed trying to creep, she several times lost her balance, falling in a way that looked painful. Each time, she did not cry and simply tried again.

One serious illness[5] in her early infancy apparently fixed her temperamental inclination to adjust to rather than change her environment, and this illness fortified her mother's need to provide her child with a smooth, protected life. Thus, in both infancy and early childhood, there were no reported sleep or feeding problems, no difficulties in weaning or toilet training, and little need for disciplinary control or punishment. Her mother's confident plan of child rearing and her high standards for child behavior were definitely formulated and consistently followed, and Harriet's even temper, generally good health, and lack of decided preferences contributed to her ability to meet her mother's expectations of a ladylike, well-behaved child. Furthermore, this carefully organized and serene family living style was promoted by the responsible, hard-working father who quietly supported his wife's viewpoints, and by the fact that the extended family neither chose nor were available to alter or modify the nuclear family's living style.

Distinctly shy in her preschool years and reserved in emotional contacts throughout her life, Harriet chose to restrict her experiences, contain her feelings, and relate to others in a predominantly impersonal way. We saw this reflected in her efficient responsible adjustment to school, her energetic but noncontentious play with peers, the casual relationships she developed with all members of our staff, and her appropriate but restrained responsiveness to our tests and interviews.

In her middle years, Harriet was busy with church activities and numerous lessons to develop her physical skills in sports and dancing, and in all of these she was proficient yet unpretentiously modest. According to her mother, Harriet was demurely pleased with her successes but not particularly desirous of praise or likely to seek it.

In her own family, where environmental stress[6] was minimal, Harriet was perceived by her mother as a congenial, refined child with few emotional ups and downs. She was less likely to display affection than either of her sisters, but she idealized her father and was rewarded or controlled by minimal cues of his pleasure or displeasure. On rare occasions, when she was drawn into bickering with her siblings, she exhibited no bitterness and accepted as just her punishment (usually isolation) along with the others. She responded to peers in the same noncontentious fashion, energetically engaging in activity, but avoiding conflict and staying somewhat emotionally aloof.

Hence, there appeared to be some early temperamental predispositions for conformity, and these were undoubtedly fostered and further developed by the family environment. Harriet's mild and infrequent protests were put down easily by her mother's definite and consistent standards to raise a competent, ladylike child, by parental unity in pursuing these clear-cut goals, and by their successful efforts to minimize failure and stress of all kinds.[7] This reflected the parents' love for their children and their wish to give them appropriate, responsible care in accordance with these aims. Had Harriet been more forceful or vigorous in expressing herself or wanted more direct sensory experience, or had family life been less well organized and organizing, she might have been more inclined to seek idiosyncratic sensory experiences, to extend her emotional range, and to develop more distinct individuality.[8] However, after the first 6 months, when behavior patterns were already well established, the wish for such striving had apparently disappeared.

In summing up, Harriet lived quietly, undemonstratively. She was overtly and consciously gratified and content with parental controls and felt fortunate for having been given stability. Thus, she coped realistically and successfully with school demands, enjoyed an active but not emotionally close social life, and was less influenced by the peer culture than many teenagers. She saw no need for change or reform. She approached any kind of deviance from her own standards by avoiding undesirable people and by refraining from thinking about new or different ideas. By her choice, her convictions had never been tempered in the furnace of direct experience and lacked the depth of feelings such encounters might have raised. Consequently, she needed and appreciated reinforcement of her convictions and continued to rely on her parents, their values, and their methods of child rearing.

Finding introspection unnecessary, Harriet did not know herself well, and her relationships with others were based on social convention and recognition rather than on personalized feelings. She saw no need to take an active part in shaping her own life, nor to seek warm close involvement or commitment to people, things, or ideas. She faultlessly imitated maternal behavior without true introjection of maternal values. The extent to which she kept herself organized and controlled was illustrated by her inability to recall any major disappointments, sadness, or special happiness. With her boyfriend, she found love on the basis of habit and social appropriateness; she thus avoided the glories and pains of falling in love and could not imagine herself being very upset if this relationship were terminated. She presented herself as a moderate, temperate individual with few decided preferences, and as one who by choice kept her thinking tentative and indefinite. In all of these ways, Harriet seemed to us to be the epitome of the obedient traditionalist.[2]

Notes:

[1]The perceptive reader will note that there are fewer quotations in this chapter describing the obedient traditionalists than in descriptions of other coping styles. The reason for this is that obedient traditionalists gave so many short and tentative answers: "I mean when you accept responsibility, I mean, if you didn't, I mean, well?"

[2]The description of the mother by the observers in Harriet's infancy fitted Harriet almost perfectly when we saw her as a young adult. She even moved and talked exactly like her mother. The degree to which she imitated her mother rather than identified with her is illustrated by the following remark. "It makes you feel good when your parents show that they approve."

[3]See Appendix A for a description of test procedures.

[4]Over time, as reported by many observers of different professional backgrounds and in a variety of situations imposing various demands, the obedient traditionalists were unlikely to explore or respond to refined nuances of perceptual or social-emotional experience. This was true of their responses to people and things, feelings and ideas, as well as in their search for self-definition.

[5]At 6 weeks of age, Harriet was close to death. Subsequently, she was remarkably healthy, and in the 18 years we knew her, she was rarely ill and recovered rapidly from the few usual childhood diseases she suffered. She had no accidental injuries and no dental problems. In her entire life, she had never even needed to have one tooth filled.

[6]According to the mother, the mild jealousy of an older brother and some maternal illnesses had little effect on Harriet's positive development. In case of family distress, the family were likely to turn to prayer, to stress their independence, and to recognize but discourage help from relatives or friends. Like Harriet, her mother was totally unwilling or unable to communicate anything that might have implied dissatisfaction with her life.

[7]From earliest infancy, all of the obedient traditionalists appeared to be temperamentally predisposed to conform and to have little urgency, ability, or willingness to protest. Quite clearly, such predispositions were fostered and reinforced by mothers who were the dominant parents in these families, and who were in their interpersonal transactions emotionally controlled and somewhat distant and aloof.

[8]Along with such temperamental predispositions, it seems entirely possible, although beyond the scope and capacity of the present research, that constitutional factors were also involved. This would then account for individual differences between siblings raised in objectively similar environments.

[9]We believe that choice of coping style is multiply determined and is, in the total

interactive context of the environment and the temperamental-constitutional predisposi-tions of the child, psychically economic and behaviorally adaptive. In the obedient traditionalists, this results in censorship of sensory intake, overtly inhibited behavior, and total unquestioning adoption of traditional viewpoints.

Chapter 4

The Ideological Conservatives

The ideological conservatives are impressively practical, organized, enterprising young people[1] who characteristically strive for self-improvement toward definite high-level vocational goals with a tenacity that brooks no interference or distraction. They resemble the obedient traditionalists insofar as they adopt from their parents predominantly traditional viewpoints about most topical issues. In their own functioning they are likely to shut out or censure behavior they consider too permissive or irresponsible. Paul expressed this stance when he told us, "I don't get myself in a position where I cross the point of no return. I will stay away from the edge of the cliff."

They differ from the obedient traditionalists in the extent to which they vigorously develop and defend their chosen stance. They define their points of view more rigorously, pursue their goals with more determination, and are more often openly critical of views different from their own. Having forged definite credos out of their own logical thinking and personal convictions, they are able to offer more refined justifications for their beliefs, which are vitally and internally a part of their being. Consciously unambivalent, they hold their opinions to be uncontroversial, absolute, and unquestionably right. Therefore, they often appear to be dogmatic, unspontaneous, and highly judgemental of persons who have less determination or self-control in personal behavior, or who are less clear about their own values. Douglas explained, "I'm afraid I can't respect anyone who puts in half a performance. . . .I have goals that I think are tremendously high. . . .I hold against many forms of compromise. . . .I don't think I should have to change for anybody."

In order to maintain such an uncompromising stance, the ideological conservatives have to curb and make special use of their often keen senses. If they allow themselves to observe all the facts, they may have difficulty in being as sure of what they believe as they regularly are, and wish to be. They have to use their perception — both of themselves and of others — in a highly selective fashion, so that nothing will disturb their inner serenity. Thus, large areas of perception are blacked out completely, even when overwhelming evidence foists itself on them. Douglas mused, "That is the strange thing, I've felt grown for the last 5 years." Within the areas where they allow themselves to use their senses, the senses are subordinated to their ideological needs. Their senses have to — and do — confirm the beliefs and views so vitally important to these proud, aggressive young people. John stated, "Necessity, I am using that word an awful lot, aren't I?"

Seeing themselves as self-sufficient and confident that their abilities give them considerable control over their own future, the ideological conservatives are more consciously self-assured than their obedient traditionalist peers. For instance, in assessing his intelligence, Avery said with embarrassment, "I think I am a little bit above average because. . . .I can see things and see how they fit together. . . .How to put my knowledge into action." At a more concrete level, George described in detail how he had been able to improve his grades by seeking a teacher's help, while simultaneously broadening his mechanical skills and achieving economic independence from his parents in a series of close to full time jobs. (Since his sixth-grade year, he had paid for his own clothing, and in his senior year, he purchased a car which he serviced himself.) Very proud of these achievements, he felt that his future was in his own hands: "It will be mostly up to me. . . .You have to show that you can."

Sharing high self-confidence and self-expectation, the ideological conservatives aspire to future community leadership roles, prestige, and economic gains. This Peter planned to achieve by seeking political office after graduating from law school; with total sincerity and dedication, he asked, "Don't you think every kid would like to be President?" Douglas planned to and had already begun to compose classical music.

Earl fantasied himself a second Schweitzer. Others, with somewhat less formal plans, anticipated graduate work in the arts and sciences or in business administration. All, with driving ambition, chose to work toward their goals with consuming energy and dedication. For Douglas, this meant "A constant demand for maximization of my potential with absolute intolerance of less than perfection in my behavior." Not surprisingly, the ideological conservatives condemn with equal vigor anyone who does not seize on the opportunities for self-advancement, which they believe are available to everyone in our democratic society.

Setting priorities compatible with these ambitious goals, they limit current participation in sports and social activities, and are slow to develop heterosexual contacts. They delay dating until the junior or senior year in high school and then restrict frequency of dating, partly for economic reasons. Preferring to keep these relationships informal and without too intense emotional involvement, they avoid physical contacts and choose friends of the other sex who are wholesome and morally strict. Several remarked that they kept a light touch in relationships with girls by joking and kidding a good deal. For instance, Simon said, "If I get embarrassed — well I don't let it get to me. I make a joke of it and it is easily put off." They are as a group completely against premarital sex and hope to establish themselves economically before marriage. Douglas said, "It is very hard to learn to take care of someone else when you are still trying to learn to take care of yourself. . . .very basically I hope before I get married to be pretty well settled — to have some good income and hopefully some money saved up." Avery said directly, "I wouldn't want to be that close." He added, as he recalled maternal demands for household help, "The only reason I would really like to get married is so my wife can do all the housework."

Our ideological conservatives had no philosophical objections to military service nor to the war in Vietnam, although they differed in what they thought were effective ways to end the war. None considered burning their draft cards or becoming conscientious objectors. None proposed to dodge service responsibility or to use college enrollment for deferment purposes, but all were mildly upset that they might be asked to delay their educational plans. In the event of draft, they were agreed that they would seek officer status. Peter commented, "I hope it won't interfere with my schooling. If I am drafted, I will try for Officer Candidate School." Avery added, "If you have to go, you have to go. I will make the best of it. . . .I won't dodge it just to be dodging it. . . .if I can keep my grades high enough, I may be able to stay out of it legally."

The ideological conservatives also choose to avoid social situations, ideas, or people that distract them from achieving their long-term goals. For example, Avery said that he had discontinued cross-country running because it was time consuming and fatiguing and "Kind of ruined my studies there for a while, so I decided I hadn't better go out for it this year." In the same way, Earl, although continuing a modified sports program to keep himself in shape, declared, "My education comes before all other needs, personal or otherwise. . . .you have to give up something in your life."

Applying these standards to their personal lives, the ideological conservatives as a group carefully pick friends who demonstrate equal moral rectitude and high achievement drives.[3] In this position they sometimes appear intolerant and self-absorbed, although they profess to like people. Douglas said, "Some people I can meet very readily but there are some I can't. . . .I don't know. . . .I am tolerant I guess. A couple of kids come to mind at school whom I can't say that I really like, nor do I dislike them. I always try to have a 'Hi' for them, and a 'How are you?' and 'How is your life kid?' There is a gray in between. I have no qualms about associating with those people in this group. It is those other people on the other side in the black, that I don't care for, that I associate with really only out of necessity."

As a special aspect of their self-absorption, the ideological conservatives make it clear that they, unlike the obedient traditionalists, sometimes like to be alone — to think, to organize themselves, to control their tempers, or just to relax in the outdoors. Simon remarked, "Well sometimes I just have to sit there and talk to myself a while." (If he were angry or frustrated.) He added, "I like the outdoors very much. . . .On a real nice day, I like to go out and just sit on the bank, not necessarily just to fish. . . .but I like to relax where it is real quiet. I like some place with a lot of trees around, where it is real quiet and still. . . .Listen to the birds sing. . . .I don't like the big crowds, you know."[4]

The ideological conservatives as a group disapprove of smoking, drinking, and the use of drugs for reasons which usually include their observations of damage to the body, interference with their ambitions, needless expense, conflict with religious and parental injunctions, and occasionally unwillingness to participate in illegal activities. For example, Simon reported, "Mainly the reason I don't smoke is because my Dad smokes and has since he was 13 years old and wishes he hadn't. . . .He doesn't like to wrestle me because he will go with me maybe 30 seconds and then he has to quit — no air. I can just see plainly that it isn't good for your health. . . .My father used to drink barrels of it until one day he got into a fight with his best friend. This was a long time ago, but they still aren't as good friends as they used to be." Albert said, "Number one, it is too expensive for me. Number two, it is stupid to drink for you've got too much else to do and then your mind becomes numb and you can't really think. . . .I had rather do other things 'cause there is a lot to see and observe. . . .And my parents don't approve. . . .I think tobacco is disgusting. . . .And I would get lung cancer. . . .I would rather spend the money on a book, or some clothes or dates." Earl added, "If you hang around with a bunch of alcoholics. . . .Or with a bunch of kids who have LSD or marijuana, even though you are not one, you can be tagged with the same name. . . .I've got a clean police record, and I just want to keep it that way."

In disapproving of certain kinds of behavior, the ideological conservatives tend to come up with practical reasons for their disapproval,[5] particularly stressing damage to themselves. For instance, in discussing premarital sex, Earl said, "You might get the girl in trouble — and yourself, of course. That would throw us in an outcast situation. . . .And I don't want to have that on my shoulders."

In commenting on racial issues, Earl said, "I feel that you should respect all minority groups because someday they just may very well be the majority groups. I feel that a colored person down the street is just as good as a white person up the street — as long as neither one of them do anything to me that would bother me, or hurt me, or hurt my family, or cause conflict." George, who lived near some Negro families and occasionally invited Negro boys to work on cars with him said, "Some of them have some funny kind of ways you know. . . .Some of them look down on us. . . .Some of them like to make trouble."

The ideological conservatives are as a group opposed to student or racial militancy and choose to avoid active participation in political activity. Douglas described himself as an "Ole middle of the roader, I guess." He suggests that he does not want to be tied to a political party or be associated with a political stance. At some future date, he might want to have limited involvement in civic activities, but now while focusing on his academic achievements, he prefers "Just to kind of sit back and listen." In that way, he can "hear both sides of the topic and if I do choose to argue about it later, I will know much more about it." He also strongly disavows nationwide strikes as directly harmful to national economy, and indirectly detrimental to his own economic future.

Ideological conservatives do not consider themselves prejudiced against racial minorities, although they are strongly opposed to interracial dating and consider interracial marriage an outrage. They are convinced that minorities could improve their status by their own efforts if they applied themselves. Douglas said, "It is a very ticklish question. . . .There are 300 years of slavery to be undone. . . .There seems to me to be an awfully lot of good white kids and a few bad kids. I mean the good kids are in the majority, and it seems to be just the other way around with the Negroes? I don't know — maybe that is the result of slavery. . . .It does force us to socially right that and morally we have the obligation to correct the error." However, he added, "I do get rather disenchanted with those cases of welfare people who take the welfare and then go out and spend it all on six packs and leave the family for that."

In their values, the ideological conservatives are strongly identified with parental standards of responsibility and achievement, even though they competitively propose to surpass their parental models. For example, George remarked that the happiest time of his life was "in junior high school when I started up rassling and took first in the city. Then that was a pretty big thing because nobody in our family had ever before won first in anything."

The ideological conservatives attribute a good deal of their drive for self-improvement to their mothers' urging, prodding, and encouragement, especially for academic excellence, for making something of themselves by preparing for high level jobs. Fathers apparently are seen as quietly agreed, being less active in discipline, at least in the early years because they were busy with their jobs? They are likely to be stoically accepting of the reality of fathers' emotional distance, yet at times they are wistful over the limited time available from fathers. Simon spoke for the group in saying, "It didn't make me feel terribly bad, but I would have liked to do more stuff with my Dad. I understand that it wasn't really his fault or anything. I just had to take it as it was." Here again, we see how these youths differ from the obedient traditionalists who would be unlikely to raise the issue.

Despite their emphasis on the practical value of schooling and their own generally excellent achievement, ideological conservatives are often bitingly critical of their schools. For them, a good teacher is a strong disciplinarian and one who is thoroughly versed in the subject matter. Douglas said, "Mrs. Brown was rough and tough and also honest and fair and it was a very good combination." Albert related his perception of inadequacy in many public school teachers to lack of community interest in raising teaching standards and pay scales. "It is very difficult to get good dedicated high school teachers. The pay is lousy. . . .Some of the teachers are slobs and they can't be anything else, so they become teachers. . . .In fact, you often find out that you know more about the subject already than the teacher does and it becomes nothing but a farce. . . .You come out of high school and out of college with a real bitterness and become poor citizens."

For the ideological conservatives, an important source of support and control is a strong religious background in these families. Earl expressed the value of religion for the group in saying, "The human being is a funny animal. It must have a God to look up to. Even the Barbarians had to have a maker or a creator. . . .I feel I need somebody to express all thoughts to, or all doubts, all innermost needs, because you can't tell any one person every problem of your life. . . .I believe in God the Father, the Son and the Holy Ghost. . . .You can't be an atheist. You have to set your heart into something and you have to believe in it."

Simon saw his religious beliefs as a refuge and a strength, a comfort and a source of ideals. "Well, it has put my standards high and I keep myself out of trouble and from doing wrong things and stuff. . . .I have often wondered what I would be like if I hadn't gotten into a youth group. . . .It's an inner joy actually and a peace. Well, when I have something that just didn't go right and it really bothered me, well, I can pray and it will calm me down. It just relaxes me. . . .I can pray for forgiveness and grace and it seems to just change things right there. My slate is clean and I have no more guilt for anything." With these views, it is not surprising that he planned to be a counselor for boys.

Although religion clearly is important to ideological conservatives — as it is to the obedient traditionalists — the former are less constant in attending church and performing religious ritual and are less likely to use their religion habitually for social outlets or for parental approval than the latter. They differ from the cautious modifiers and the passionate renewers insofar as they never question or criticize religious viewpoints or traditions. Peter explained, "I don't go to church every Sunday, but I believe God is within me. I do believe He is alive. I don't go along with the people who think He is dead. . . .I think most people prefer a minister who lives in the present. They are aware of both the past and the future, but you have to concentrate on the now and not on being saved in the future." In their feelings about religion, as about most important issues, there is a practical personal return, a support, and a control.

Many of the behavioral traits and the expressed viewpoints of the ideological conservatives, as we have described them, are apparent in the psychological tests, where the intellectual intensity, efficiency, and competency of these youths are impressive. Striving for exactness and clarity, these youths often question the demands of the tests in order to be assured that they are responding accurately. They want to give the best of themselves and at the same time be reassured that their position and their personal integrity are appreciated. Having a rather broad range of interests and information, they are as a group quick to understand what is expected of them, and they make sober efforts to be logical and practical. They often try to explain their reasoning by enumerating the bases for their answers.

On the structured tests, they are inclined to have a broad range of general information, to be especially alert to details, and to be good at organizing the facts as they see them. They carefully consider their answers and are unlikely to respond impulsively. They are very clear about what they know or do not know and are disinclined to guess.

The ideological conservatives generally accept the projective tests as a challenge, although they make every effort to come up with realistic percepts, and seek to support or justify with multiple details the large number of whole answers they find. They are more able to use fantasy than the obedient traditionalists, yet they always take care to point out that they are totally alert to distinctions between fantasy and reality. Content is varied, almost always including the usual popular answers and a few carefully delineated or original percepts. Answers are not restricted to form, but when color or perspective are added, they need to fit the context of the whole. They are likely to reverse figure and ground, suggesting intellectual opposition or self-assertive competitiveness. One could say that the results of the Rorschach test support our observation and interview data insofar as they reflect high drive for achievement, careful reality testing, lack of impulsivity, and considerable critical commentary. That the lack of structure in the Rorschach is to some degree more difficult than the intelligence tests is suggested by the fact that the ideological conservatives are likely to insert or add factual information associated with their percepts.

On the Thematic Tests, predominant themes are appreciation for families and controls, personal responsibility, and winning or losing or striving to overcome disadvantages or hardships. Most stories end happily or with the conclusion that if they put forth effort, everything will come out well, as it is supposed to do.[8] After perceiving a grueling chase by a prehistoric monster, Douglas remarked, "Through my rose-colored view of the world, he has to escape, naturally." They do this by remaining alert, striving for clarity, taking advantage of every opportunity offered to them, and occasionally integrating subtle, pithy, facetious or sarcastic humor. (As, for example, Albert's response to the blank card: "Well, it is a snowstorm with a polar bear eating a vanilla ice cream cone.") They seek to make optimally effective use of their time, their money, and their abilities.

Contributing to the coping style of the ideological conservatives are high sensory sensitivity in infancy,[9] high desire for self-advancement,[10] and careful control of emotional involvement and expression throughout childhood. Consciously, the ideological conservatives attribute much of their ambition to their mothers, who are demanding and sometimes prodding, but also very proud and supportive of their youngsters. The ideological conservatives are generally responsive to these maternal behaviors, but can on occasion defy some maternal injunctions they see as inconsequential.[11] Perhaps also significant is the fact already mentioned that in all cases the fathers were in some respects removed (by divorce, death, or emotional passivity) or relatively less involved than the mothers in the upbringing of these children. In a way, these youngsters are competing with fathers for the sake of making up to their mothers for fathers' lack of academic or vocational success. In emphasizing self-advancement, the ideological conservatives are self-restricting, censoring both thoughts and feelings, resulting in reduced emotional closeness. However, they are practical, realistic, determined, opportunistic youths dedicated to achievement, and in their high school years, they are likely to be savoring their rewards of self-assurance and high self-esteem.

Notes:

[1]Of special interest to us was the fact that no girls were classified as ideological conservatives. Although in our small sample, this could have been a finding arising totally by chance, it occurred to us that a constellation of social or environmental factors may have been involved. In the Midwest, girls are less frequently pushed to achieve academically and are not ordinarily expected to pursue or excel in professional or administrative positions. In fact, they are more likely to be encouraged to accept the traditionally submissive role of women and to attend college with the specific aim of associating with upstanding, responsible, and potentially marriageable young men. Their task is then to gain vicarious social position and economic security through their successful husbands. Given and accepting a traditional orientation, they are thus more likely to assume the conforming, supportive role of the obedient traditionalists than to seek the more competitive self-actualizing role of the ideological conservatives.

[2]Like the obedient traditionalists, they enjoy athletics, but ordinarily participate less. Both tend to defer heterosexual contacts and condemn premarital sex, but the obedient traditionalists do so primarily out of moralistic concerns, whereas the ideological conservatives do so because of concentration on academic and vocational advancement.

[3]The ideological conservatives are like the obedient traditionalists in their careful choice of friends. However, they differ in their reasons for their choices. The obedient traditionalists select friends with whom they can share social or sports activities; the ideological conservatives choose friends (including adults) who can help them, or at least not interfere with the achievement of their academic and vocational goals.

[4]The obedient traditionalists seem always to prefer peer companions. Being alone is boring and uncomfortable.

[5]The obedient traditionalists are more likely to stress the immorality of the behavior.

[6]The reader will notice the inconsistency here. Although theoretically willing to consider some responsibility on the part of whites, Douglas also says that the majority of blacks are natively undisciplined, and in general that people on welfare are irresponsible.

[7]Three of the fathers were absent through death or divorce. In these cases, stepfathers resembled natural fathers in allowing the mothers the dominant role in child rearing.

[8]Significantly, all of the ideological conservatives responded to the blank card with stories of peaceful family or pastoral scenes or with successful competition.

[9]As a group, the ideological conservatives were from infancy much more differentiated in perceptual intake and responsiveness than the obedient traditionalists. (See case study of Calvin for documentation.)

[10]In the ideological conservatives, drive to achieve seems to be native insofar as they are from infancy avid learners. This characteristic was of course reinforced by mothers' efforts to encourage self-sufficiency and by the commendation given for the children's developing skills. It is probably also important that in each of the ideological conservatives, mothers regard this particular child as in some ways outstanding or superior to siblings.

[11]This is illustrated in the case study of Calvin, who although usually abiding by maternal standards, chose to engage in Sunday sports despite his mother's objection. In this respect, they differ from the obedient traditionalists who rarely if ever act in opposition to any parental limit.

Chapter 5

Calvin: An Ideological Conservative

Seventeen-year-old Calvin was a stocky, snappily dressed, cheerful, bright high school senior who was ambitious for economic success. Having grown up in a large, highly religious, traditional, and often economically hard-pressed family, he pursued these aims with great responsibility and conscientiousness. Like Harriet, he almost totally took over parental values, which were compatible with his predispositions and defensive needs. He differed from Harriet insofar as he more definitely formulated and actively adopted his value system, rather than imitating an observed set of values.

He had strong convictions about what was right and wrong, and he was in every respect intensely dedicated to following his beliefs. Through self-direction and firm self-control, and with little ambivalence, he kept himself within the bounds he set. In his ambitious pursuit of the life he desired, he had little time or need for close personal attachments or social activities, was not easily influenced by his peers, and in fact was proud of his own moral rectitude.This position was well stated in his own words, "I try and stand my ground if there is ever a disagreement or something, but I try and see their point of view and not shun them if I don't agree with them....I don't try to get too close or too attached to them....because if they ever get to doing something I don't think is right, I would like to say no. I wouldn't want to go along with them, and if I got too attached with them I am afraid that if they get to doing something, I might go ahead and join in 'cause they are my friends and I would like to be with them and things like that....I try to be real friendly and make as good friends as I can without being influenced....I try and avoid trouble if I can....and I try to stand for what I believe."

Calvin's success in maintaining this position was impressive. Despite having been one of the youngest in his class and simultaneously having held a close to full time job, he was academically in the top 25 percent of his graduating class. He did this by setting definite priorities, carefully scheduling his activities, and limiting his pursuit of knowledge to those subjects he considered practical and which would directly contribute to personal advancement and to later economic security in his chosen field. For example, he studiously maintained a straight A average in math, selectively relaxing his high standards somewhat in subjects such as English, which he saw as less immediately relevant. However, aware of the urgency for communication as a professional person, he forced himself to take a course in public speaking. He gave up participation in sports[1] as a concession to his wish to excel in math. He did not seek to explore broad intellectual concepts nor to engage in social activities for their own sake. He was proud of his accomplishments in having largely met his standards, but was critically evaluative in feeling that he might have done better had he found more time for study.

Having made these choices, he was gratified that he had been able to keep up payments and insurance and to make repairs on a secondhand sports car and to squeeze out time for dating his steady girl friend of 17 months. Characteristically, he had chosen her because she was quiet and ladylike, appreciated his inability to spend money lavishly, and generally shared his viewpoints. He disapproved of movies, dancing, smoking, drinking, and the decline in sexual morality. These things he felt resulted from going along with the crowd or from a desire to show off. Having decided that these behaviors were inappropriately personally, he refrained from association with those who had these habits, and disclaimed his responsibility to modify their behavior. Justifying his position, he remarked, "I look at it this way. If they want to mess up their lives, then let them go ahead. I'd rather them not, but if they make up their mind that they are going to, I can't do anything to stop them....Well, I think mainly kids do it just to show their age. They want to show everybody that they are old enough to do it, too. Mainly, it is just to show off. I don't see much sense in it myself....I try not to run around with them privately because the temptation would be there." Through this comment there ran a feeling of self-commendation for his strength to be different and to resist temptation. He dealt with threatening ideas by turning away from them, by choosing his associates carefully, and by setting self-restricting limits on his own behavior. He felt that his views were his own, but he agreed that his parents had influenced his standards: "Well, they aren't as strict as most − I mean some. Some are real strict. My parents are stricter than some and not as strict as some. I like it that way, 'cause you aren't scared to go to them, but you aren't so loose that you do anything 'cause you know you can get by with it."

Calvin was strongly opposed to premarital sex because he felt that "If they try to control themselves, then they could. I don't know why they do it. There are so many girls that get into trouble and get bad names and everything because of the boys." On the other hand, he felt that some girls "sort of ask for it. They have as much to do with it as the boys do. I think those are the kind of girls that should be punished....A lot of girls probably are afraid that if they don't do it, they will lose their boy friend or something like that. I think some of the boys really pressure the girls by saying things like 'prove your love.'" He felt that the practical way to avoid such problems would be to delay dating until 16 or 17 years of age. In his eyes, this would also have an economic advantage: the boys would be "old enough to get a job and get your own money." Beyond these practical considerations, he was not interested in examining the reasons behind premarital sexual behavior in his peers, nor did he wish to take responsibility to try to stop it. He saw the world as disappointingly bad, and preferred to separate himself from it.

He regarded his own steady girl friend as a friend and confidante more than as a sex object. He explained that this was possibly because, "She goes to the same church I do, that's where I met her, and we go along with about the same things. So it helps to have a girl that goes to the same church. You can talk over your problems and things like that and not be ashamed and wonder what she will think of you for saying things like that. She will think the same about you, I hope."

He said that his parents had never talked to him about sex, and had given him relatively little factual information. His parents had given him a book to read, but most of what he knew he had learned from friends. He was inclined to believe that he would handle the situation with his own future family much as his father had done. He commented, "I don't know. I think that is partly what would be embarrassing for him (that is, his future son) because you don't know when to talk to him or when he is thinking about things like that. It would probably be when he is around the eighth or ninth grade. He will be starting and there is a lot more talk about that stuff in high school than in junior high. There is enough in junior high. I think really he should hear some of it from the outside before, so he will have sort of an interest in it before you talk to him. I don't feel that you should rush it in any way....He wouldn't know anything about it if you started in the sixth or seventh grade probably, so I think if you wait until he does know a little bit about it, then he will be more interested in learning about it and will pay more attention and hopefully it will do more good." Once again, we saw Calvin's dislike for and disinterest in looking at change, his insistence on moving at his own pace, and his tendency to handle potentially stressful situations by avoidance. He was one of a small number of our subjects who believed sex education had no place in early childhood.

Calvin reported that he had never gone to a movie or attended a dance. Nor did he feel any conscious interest in doing so, although he admitted he might be interested at some later time. In this stance, he followed family prohibitions, and saw no inconsistency with the fact that it was permissible to watch movies on television. He proposed to impose similar restrictions on his own children. He did, however, mildly protest against several other maternal injunctions. For instance, he remarked, "I think that is saying too much that you can't read Sunday newspapers." In regard to participation in and observation of Sunday sports where his own interests were stronger, he overroad his mother's objections, saying, "I don't see anything wrong with it, so I go ahead and do it anyway."

Calvin largely accepted his parental standards, was able to deny or minimize inconsistencies of which he was aware, did not appear to be conflicted, and only rarely — when it was in line with his own interests as in the case of Sunday sports — set up new standards for himself. He had taken over family religious indoctrination, and, like his parents, found the church a major social outlet and an emotional support. In speaking about his religious feelings, he said, "When I was younger I didn't want to go to church too often. I think everybody goes through that stage when they are about 13 or 14. When they start junior high school, they think they are big people and don't need church....I think it only lasts about a year or two and then you start realizing that it isn't so bad after all....my parents made me go....Now, I go to church every Sunday."

There was no doubt about his sincerity, but the unquestioning definiteness with which he knew he was right and his lack of tolerance for any dissension made him appear more rigid and conservative in these viewpoints than most of his contemporaries. Furthermore, his religious beliefs did not lead to humanistic appreciation of social ills or sympathy for human weaknesses.

Like his parents, Calvin objected to foreign aid and welfare projects and expressed strong approval of private enterprise as more appropriate than governmental control. He felt that he had been strengthened by never having had an allowance as a child and was convinced that it is necessary to earn privileges and advantages. "I don't like getting something for nothing myself, and it made us work for what money we did get." By analogy, he applied these standards to the poor, to minority groups, and to all groups who demonstrated against society. Speaking of blacks and civil rights issues, he said, "Negroes are just like whites; there are good and bad ones. There are a few bad ones that give the whole colored race a bad name — the demonstrators ....If they were nice, I wouldn't mind living next door, but if they were rough and tough, then I had just as soon that they stay away ....It isn't their fault that they are that way — that they are colored. ...They aren't really that particular about the houses they have." He meant to struggle for personal advancement and economic security and believed that everyone can better himself if he works hard and uses the opportunities open to him. Having attained his own goals, he could entertain the possibility of helping others. "If I had a good stand and was pretty good in my work, and I could make enough to where I could help somebody like that, I would. I would have to get started first." He had satisfied himself that these views were sound and thus saw no reason for further questioning.

Since both of his older brothers had served in Vietnam, Calvin felt less urgency to fulfill this responsibility. He hoped for acceleration and termination of the Vietnamese war before he became of draft age. He meant to assume his responsibilities without protest, but he hoped that his youthfulness might gain him a year or two to advance his career before being drafted. He stated his position as follows: "I don't particularly want to go, but I don't disagree by burning my draft card and things like that. I will go along peacefully but I would rather not go. I would rather have a college education and get started." Like most of our teenage subjects, he disapproved of war; he differed from many in basing his disapproval on resentment against the delay of his own progress educationally and vocationally rather than on ideological considerations. He was not sympathetic toward those who dissented on idealistic grounds. In fact, he saw them as troublemakers and implied his superiority to them by not participating in overt protests. He commented, in speaking of protestors, "I guess it is their own choice, but I wouldn't act that way. All they do is cause a bigger situation here in America. We have enough to worry about in other places and not in our own country."

Barring the possibility of the draft, Calvin felt confident of his own future, which he believed he could determine. He said, "It is time for adulthood and time for you to start making decisions of your own. . . .If you are a good student, you want to be a good student. Your parents don't have to make you. . . .If there is something to do, I force myself to get up and get going. . . .I hope I will be pretty prosperous. I just hope I am successful. I think I will be 'cause I am interested in the field I want to go into. . . .If somebody is interested in it and willing to work, I don't see what can stop him if he has the ability. . . .Most of it is my own self. As bad as I want to be, then that is what I will be. I will be as much as I want to work for. But chance does have something to do with it because maybe there will be thousands graduating in my field, and at the same time I am, and maybe there won't be a demand for it that much."

Although somewhat critical of his teachers, Calvin was generally positive about his high school experiences. He felt that some teachers were cold and distant and not primarily interested in helping students. He felt school spirit was low, but he was not overly concerned about this because he saw school as a stepping stone to a secure future; he planned to work his way through college. He hoped to attend a large school because he had gone to a small high school. He remarked that the larger school, in addition to having more academic opportunities, could promote concentration on studies. He thought, "It would be nice not to know everybody." In choosing math as a major field of endeavor, he had enjoyed a good deal of success, and at the same time found a socially acceptable and potentially economically profitable field. Looking ahead to college, he was considering working 1 year before enrolling to save money for tuition. He was not resentful that his parents could offer little help. It seemed clear that he meant to surpass his father's educational and vocational achievements, as well as those of his two older brothers whose behavior fell somewhat short of Calvin's high moral and academic standards.

Realistic and practical about the necessity to struggle for success, he vigorously and persistently engaged in this struggle without resentment and with a good deal of commitment and effort. He felt that he had a good life with particular advantages as the middle boy in the family of five children, and he energetically exerted himself to maintain and enhance these advantages. Moving at his own pace and setting his sights high, he consciously and consistently tried to control his temper, avoid temptations, and apply himself conscientiously to all of his undertakings. In this concentrated effort, there was little room for fantasy, daydreaming, introspection, or social frivolity. (He remarked, "I don't imagine too much anymore, except for in the future, but nothing wild. . . .I haven't remembered an ending of a dream for a long time. I don't know why.") He enjoyed those activities of which he approved, but he was more serious than many of our teenage subjects insofar as he was totally dedicated to his beliefs and aims and kept himself emotionally controlled.

In this context, he welcomed adult encouragement and expectations from his parents, but he saw his efforts and ultimate success as self-determined and independent of these reinforcements. His own views were not essentially different from those of his parents, yet he was convinced that his future could and should be self-determined, and hence he did not want to be deterred or delayed by others in any way.

This stance was reflected also in his polite cooperation in our testing sessions and in the subsequent review of these sessions. Entirely affable and cheerful, Calvin saw his participation in our project as an honor and duty. He was frequently verbose and distinctly proud and self-confident in talking about his academic success and vocational plans, but he was careful to dictate the limits and contents of what he wanted to communicate. He guarded against revealing too personal feelings or sharing any facts that might suggest personal or family weaknesses. Particularly with the female psychologist, he chose to be humble and ingratiating, courteously responding to requests for information or test participation. This he did as though compliant out of habituation, but always with clarity about his own position and with attention to the advantage of aligning himself with adults. He thanked us for our interest in him as a person, but he made it clear that his educational and vocational plans were already so clearly formulated that our test findings (especially about his skills, interests, and personality) could in no way change his decisions. He had definitely decided on a professional career that would allow him to use his realistically superior skills in math, and which incidentally would lead to a secure future.

On the Wechsler Adult Intelligence Scale, Calvin's performance was that of a bright and efficient person, but one who was somewhat concrete and circumscribed in his thinking. His vocabulary was adequate, but not vividly differentiated; grammatical construction was relatively poor for a youth of his high intelligence level. Recognizing his limits in this area, he remarked, "As long as I get my meaning across, I am not too particular." His general information, although good, was limited in range, perhaps reflecting his disinclination to read extensively. He was especially quick and efficient in mathematical computation, but not particularly drawn to attempting to think about theoretical mathematical concepts. He was intellectually capable of understanding casual relationships and abstract and philosophical issues, but by inclination he chose to concentrate on practical and tangible projects, and these he pursued with alert attention to visual details, extraordinary clarity in spatial orientation, and unusual persistence.

His responses to the Rorschach confirmed his high drive for achievement and material success, his limited cathexis for introspection and intellectual pursuits, and his orderly goal-oriented approach to whatever he did. He tended to deny aggressive angry feelings, or when these occasionally came to the fore, he was likely to show mild anxiety or to withdraw until he felt in control of his feelings. He indicated that at times he felt a need to be alone to organize his thinking, to cut down on excessive stimulation, and to relax from the busy, demanding schedule he set for himself. Highly self-absorbed, his interest in people appeared to be shallow and not highly empathic.

Calvin's thematic stories emphasized his strong belief that he could achieve success through his own efforts to get ahead by hard work and total dedication to his aims. For example, he spoke of a young musician who could be successful if he were determined and willing to put out a requisite effort. "It all depends on his will power. If he wants to bad enough, he will do it. If he has the desire to be a violinist." Significantly, he responded to the blank card by projecting a peaceful pastoral scene with no people present. Here, he seemed to be saying that life would be simpler if one were not required to engage in interpersonal relationships, which may involve conflicts, or at least deter one from pursuing his goals.

When we reviewed our battery of tests in relation to his expressed goals and his personal style, Calvin courteously accepted this review, responding in a briskly efficient way. The predominantly cognitive and objective orientation obviously appealed to him, and in this context he was casually and openly proud of his adequate school performance and his job success. He expressed mild disappointment that his language skills did not match his superiority in math. (For instance, he reported that on the American College Test, he had placed at the 88th percentile in math and at the 36th percentile in English. Grades paralleled these test scores, with A's in math and a D in senior English.)

He was pleased that the test results generally confirmed his own choices and plans for a highly ordered and conventional life. After college graduation, he was looking forward to marrying his long time girl friend and to raising a family with values similar to those of his father. He hoped and actively strove for greater economic security. He expected to make his own way even though he was mindful of the emotional support he had received from parental encouragement and from moderately close but fluctuating relationships with his siblings.

Sensible and conscientious, Calvin continued to stress, and presumably will value throughout his life, the importance of economic security and personal stability. Interestingly enough, his wish for monetary reward declined somewhat after he demonstrated that he could be self-supporting. Nonetheless, it is unlikely that he will relax his need to excel or to surpass other members of his family. Nor would this be consistent with his basically conventional approach to life as we saw it throughout his growing years. We can speculate about some of the bases for the stance Calvin took as an adolescent.

The third son born to hard-working, conscientious, strictly religious and loving parents, Calvin was a wanted baby who in his early years enjoyed a special position in his family[2] a situation that provided considerable continuity and predictability of experience, and a high degree of self-respect. A bright, generally healthy, alert, developmentally advanced baby, he seemed to be unusually sensitive to sensory stimulation, especially forceful in expressing his needs, and capable of remarkable differentiation. Yet, he had experienced a difficult birth and postnatally some physical distress, which may have interfered with his capacity and freedom to exploit the natural sensory sensitivity he demonstrated in his early infancy. Even in these very early months, he was distinctly vulnerable to and sometimes immobilized by excessive stimulation in tactile, auditory, visual, kinesthetic, or olfactory modes[3] This suggested some internal blocking and conflict between wanting to experience and wanting to turn away from experience. In addition, his own inclination and capacities were complicated by his relationship with his mother, who was highly empathic to his needs and clearly proud of his developmental progress, but resisted his increasing independence from her. Although capable, loving, and verbally cognizant of his needs to grow at his own pace, his mother was as a function of her own needs, overprotective and constricting, especially in regard to physical expression of aggression, and these prohibitions were reinforced by the father. In meeting these parental standards, Calvin fulfilled their needs but reduced his own spontaneity.

At the same time, his own probably defensively economic inclination to turn away from people or things he disliked or disapproved of had by his third year of life contributed to an adaptational style of sober caution in relating to new people,[4] expressed in both decided integrity and some, at times quite marked, negativistic withdrawal.[5] Then, as throughout his life, Calvin resisted change, was slow to get underway, sized up situations carefully, avoided taking risks of any kind, and interacted in a determined way at his own pace and at his own time. These qualities supported limitations rather than expansion of potential creativity and kept his thinking concrete. It did not destroy his capacity for considerable gaiety or dramatic activity at times, but it did appear to reduce the frequency and range of his enjoyment. Thus, we saw a sensitive baby capable of considerable sensory differentiation, but also one who could be overwhelmed by stimulation. To handle this, Calvin tended to turn away from stimulation and reduced his communication with the outside world, expressed overtly in speech problems[6] in his preschool years. When his symbiotic closeness with his mother was necessarily reduced after the birth of a new baby in Calvin's sixth year, he was for a time phobic of school and preoccupied with the impermanence of human relationships.[7] However, these new developments forced him to turn toward his father and school, where the gratification and rewards of learning appealed to him as a bright individual, and incidentally offered a substitute for human relationships, which he had learned might be undependable. He became a capable and conscientious student, an accomplishment that enabled him to surpass both his father and his siblings. He focused on the concrete and practical subjects (math), rather than those more personal and affectively toned (English). In effect, Calvin erected a barrier first against his own hypersensitivity to sensory stimulation, and second against disappointment by reduced affective closeness with his mother.

The effectiveness with which he did this was later demonstrated during his adolescence when through self-restriction he closed himself off from sensory intake to a remarkable degree. He had reduced the enjoyment of feeling freely, but he had also become immune to vulnerability from his native or potential hypersensitivity.

The stability of his home and the harmony between his parents laid a basis for considerable basic trust, leading to personal integrity. It also made it possible for him to identify so firmly with his parents that rebellion was minimal and parental values were totally introjected. Whatever disappointments he had experienced were by then so forcefully denied that there were no alternative patterns of behavior for him. In his adolescence, he remained determined and self-respecting by deliberately limiting the range of expressed behavior. Consequently, he had little tolerance for deviance in others and could allow himself only limited flexibility. On the other hand, this stance offered considerable gratification because it was predictably and realistically successful, depended on his efforts alone, and was compatible with his apparent cognitive potentialities and temperamental style as they had been modified by his early experiences.

In his adolescence, Calvin presented himself as a studious, conscientious individual who had chosen and assiduously pursued a conventional life style. He was not rebellious toward or in conflict with his parents, but he felt that it was he who would determine his future. By setting limits on his own behavior and censoring what he chose to perceive and integrate, he avoided extreme emotional reactivity and coped with the exigencies of his life as an ideological conservative.

Notes:

[1]Throughout his childhood and junior high school years, Calvin had been very active in sports. He had considered becoming a professional athlete or a coach. However, having met more competition in high school, and recognizing that he was not outstanding in sports, he gave up these aspirations. He also pointed out that he could earn more money and attain greater economic security by choosing another field.

[2]In an earlier summary of an interview with his mother, the interviewer said, "In his family, Calvin seemed to be a very bright little boy; the whole family was thoroughly aware of this and saw him as a sort of wonder child, a little better than the rest of them who had been born into their midst. He was also considered the easiest going of the children. An older brother said that he wished that Calvin was his older brother because then he would learn so much from him and be more advanced. The mother had warned the older boys not to praise Calvin too much in his presence; when Calvin himself tried saying 'aren't I smart?', the mother told him that it is not the kind of thing we say about ourselves. The mother had already attributed some of Calvin's

acceleration to the fact that he had older brothers to model himself upon."

[3]In his infancy, low thresholds in every modality were sources of extremes in both pleasure and displeasure, reflected in very specific and highly differentiated reactions. For example, Calvin frequently rubbed or scratched at smooth or shiny surfaces and appeared to enjoy the tactile sensations of a vigorous rubdown by the father after baths. Changes in facial expression and intensity of movement accompanied even the gentlest touch. Although often highly pleasurable, patting by family members when Calvin was unprepared for it sometimes resulted in facial contortions which looked "as if he had really been whipped." Likewise, he seemed to enjoy gentle sounds like the tinkling of bells sewn on his shoes, a squeeky toy, or the soft voice of the experimenter, but he was likely to be awakened by sharp sounds or overly loud voices. Once severely frightened by the sonorous voice of an elderly neighbor, he remained apprehensive of old people and of loud sounds for several years. On occasion, he cried when his father spoke loudly, but he smiled gayly when he heard his father whistling. Even self-produced sounds sometimes led to changes in activity level. He appeared to differentiate colors at 16 weeks. He was positively responsive to kinesthetic sensations of rocking or moving surfaces and tolerated vigorous play — that is, tossing and rolling — by the parents. Yet, the sudden movements of others or even of his own hands caused blinking. His mother felt that he made distinctly different sounds when he was sleepy, hungry, or in pain. The reader is referred to Bergman and Escalona's article "Unusual Sensitivities in Very Young Children." *(Psychoanalytic Study of the Child, Vol III/IV*, International Universities Press, New York, 1949, pp. 333-352) for discussion of such sensitivities and the adaptive defenses related to them.

[4]When we first saw Calvin at 3½ years of age, he stood stiffly erect, remaining physically close to his mother, and showed no noticeable changes in facial expressions. He seemed to be silently appraising, soberly gazing, staving off any direct contact, whether physical or verbal, with the examiner. With his mother's and, in later sessions, his older brother's help, he was able to string beads or play with puzzles but always at a distance from the strange examiner. Interestingly enough, he was later able to interact quite freely in an energetic and boisterous way. When he felt comfortable, he seemed absolutely confident that he could deal with anything he chose.

[5]Sometimes he seemed completely oblivious to the examiner's suggestions but later followed them. This suggested a quality of negativism and a subtle communication of strong feelings of personal integrity.

[6]Calvin's preschool speech was close to unintelligible, even though he persisted in trying to make himself understood, largely through very effective pantomime. His mother insisted that his poor articulation was "normal" and not unlike her own speech at his age. By the time he entered first grade, Calvin's speech had improved, as his mother had predicted, and did not interfere with very adequate academic achievement. However, it may have contributed to relatively poor performance in language areas throughout his life.

[7]At 6½ years, Calvin expressed his feelings of displacement by a younger sibling by saying, "I'm not the baby no more." He dealt with this by showing how many more things he could do than his baby brother, but he also demanded to be physically close to his mother by refusing to go to school. How deeply disappointed he felt in losing his special position with his mother was clearly reflected in projective tests and in the psychiatric play sessions at that time.

Chapter 6

The Cautious Modifiers

The cautious modifiers are distinct, vivid, usually socially poised individuals with decided interest in and compassion for people and all living things. Introspective and reflective by nature, they are curious about themselves and others, even those who by traditional standards may be considered socially unacceptable. In fact, they often choose to give such individuals special attention, sympathy, and support. In describing her friendship with a boy from "the other side of the tracks," Agnes explained, "I began to realize what his problems were and I helped him a lot and I just seemed to change his whole life, you know....He wasn't even a person. I mean he didn't ever have any ideas about anything. I just molded his whole life."[1] With somewhat less urgency to modify behavior, Flora remarked, "I like friends who are different from me — with different interests and personalities. Then, that way I can have new things, and so does she." In this stance, she reflected the cautious modifiers urgency to broaden their own horizons.

Highly sensitive to and appreciative of human individuality in what others do and believe, the cautious modifiers are cognizant of social inequities and hardships, seek to understand reasons for deviant behavior and protest, and question some traditional values. For instance, Eunice, who had been doing volunteer work with underprivileged minority groups, said, "This feeling of unrest, hippies and all this stuff, I don't agree with, but I think there are things that need to be done. I think we have sat back and said that we are a great country and everything is fine, but you can see now that we aren't, and you can see that there are things to be done. It is going to be up to my generation. It is going to be up to my group to get out there and do it and I think we can. People cut us down because we are critical, but they are just now beginning to see what we are critical of." Not surprisingly, Eunice planned to be a social worker.

The cautious modifiers differ from the censors in their greater openness to a wider variety of experiences, in the subtlety with which they perceive the nuances of things and feelings, and in their empathic, unjudgmental approach to people.[2] Having more freedom to explore and to experience through their own senses, they have a broader range of enjoyment and appear to be more spontaneous than the obedient traditionalists. Being less preoccupied with their personal advancement, they are less concerned about how others might influence them, for good or for bad. Thus, they appear to be more tolerant and less pessimistic than the ideological conservatives.

Still, as realistic young people imbued with a good deal of common sense, and who value parental opinions, they are distinctly aware of outcomes and consequences. Thus, they set up internal checks and balances so that they do not stray too far in their own behavior. In no sense radical, they selectively identify with parental viewpoints, modifying them for themselves without overt rebellion or alienation. They choose to think and experience for themselves within broad self-imposed limits.[3] These characteristics are apparent in their attitudes toward the project staff, in their relationships with peers and family, in their viewpoints on topical issues, and in their self-presentation and self-definition.

Carl expressed the cautious modifiers' generally enthusiastic and warm reception to participation in our research project by saying, "Anything to help anybody else is a real pleasure." Exemplifying these feelings is the fact that our cautious modifiers readily kept appointments, even at times on weekends or evenings when keeping appointments posed some difficulties or inconvenience for them.[4] They were curious about what we proposed to do, how we would use our data, and were very interested in other members of the subject population. Significantly, too, many formed close relationships with our staff, and even after the formal project was terminated chose to come to see us, sometimes to seek references for jobs or scholarships, sometimes to discuss the soundness of proposed marriages or vocational plans, sometimes just to talk or to introduce us to fiances or spouses.[5]

The cautious modifiers extend their thoughtfulness, uncritical tolerance, and warmth to parents and siblings. Although most see their parents as having been strict, they regard strictness as an index of concern for themselves, or as a result of pressures and hardships parents had and continue to face. For example, Amelia, who had gone through a period of feeling inadequate, angry, and unloved during prepuberty, said, "Mother had kind of a bad childhood. I try always to remember that when she doesn't use very much discipline with my brothers and sisters. I think maybe that is part of the reason. She has always tried so hard for us to be happy. I don't think she realizes what she is doing at all, and I try to tell her, but it just hurts her because then she doesn't like to feel that she has failed as a mother. . . .Dad just doesn't know how to act with kids because he was an only child and his parents left him more or less on his own and they weren't affectionate at all. He just didn't learn any affection. . . .I think it is wrong to blame the parents because I think I have real decent parents and they try the only way they know how."

In this comment, we see that the cautious modifiers are, unlike the censors, more able to admit personal or familial weaknesses or limitations and less likely to deny some family frictions. They do so sympathetically, uncritically, and with considerable insight into parental moods and feelings. Sharing the censors' views that parental discipline is not unfair, they often try to avoid arguments. However, they can on occasion disagree openly, but they usually choose to do so only when they feel disagreement will not create serious rifts, or only with the parent who is less likely to be upset. Carl explained, "My dad has quite strong opinions toward things and I disagree. . . .Mom puts it more or less so that I really understand it, but my dad explains kind of hard. . . .If I disagree with my dad, he gets edgy about it."

Byron added that arguments are senseless because restrictions and limits on hours and activities (a usual source of disagreement) reflect love. He said, "God, we haven't had a verbal argument — but sometimes a parting of the mind. . . .I never yell at my parents. I accept them and I don't care to get them mad. It is just easier to accept the curfew. If they are going to set a limit, that means they are concerned and want you in. They don't want you messing around. . . .It is good that you have some discipline because this means there is concern and where there is concern, this means there is involvement."[6]

It is also apparent that the cautious modifiers sometimes use older siblings as intermediaries, as Marilyn remarked. "We talked all the time about everything under the sun and now that she has gone to college, well, we write back and forth and say how miserable we are and everything and she tells Mom." In turn, many of the cautious modifiers in their late teens begin to see themselves as models and supports for their younger brothers and sisters, or at times encourage their parents to hold the line, to set limits and to be consistent in firm handling of their younger siblings. For example, Amelia said, "Well, she is always saying, 'Let me tell you this and what do you think I should do?' [in relation to how to behave with dates]. I think maybe a little bit, I helped her. That is what I would like to do more if I could — help those little kids." Here, we see that they are not angry about the disciplined lives their parents lead and provide for them. Instead, they are appreciative of control for themselves and understanding of reasons why their parents are at times less available or less supportive than the children might wish or need.

Arthur expressed these attitudes when he said. "I think my father expected too much sometimes, but other times I would do something that was pretty stupid and I deserved it. Other times, he would send me after a tool or something and he would call it by some name that I had never heard of. It was just that when I wouldn't know what it was or something, it would make him mad....I don't resent him or anything because I know it just couldn't have been different....He is a smart man. He knows what is coming off." In this commentary, we see some stoical resignation, combined with contained frustration, modulated perhaps by basically warm feelings toward his father.

Realistically, the parents of the cautious modifiers are less control-ling than those of the obedient traditionalists and less demanding than those of the ideological conservatives. These parents give more freedom for independent judgment, as Carl indicated in his comment: "Mom allows us quite a bit of independence to judge what we think is right or wrong. She tells me once or twice what I ought to know and then it is really up to me to decide." Agnes viewed her parents in a similar way, as she said, "My parents have always been very lenient with me....I've made my mistakes, but I have learned by them. I think it is so much better when you can sit down and give your principles instead of your parents' principles." She added, "My parents were never the type that said 'You have to make good grades.' They have always been happy with my grades. Even through high school when they got a little bad, you know, they have always been happy with them because they haven't ever been as bad as my two brothers' grades."

Less demanding parental standards perhaps contribute to less urgency and intensity in the goals the cautious modifiers set for themselves. Hoping to have a comfortable life for themselves and their families and to offer neighborly support to others in their community, they are not particularly interested in high status socially or vocationally. This is suggested by their limited ambition and modest efforts for academic achievement in high school, which they see as pleasant insofar as it affords opportunities to meet and associate with peers from backgrounds different than their own, but not in itself a significant influence on their own growth. Byron commented, "I didn't study at all, not much. I'm not rebellious — you just don't care really as long as you make the final grades. . . .It is called the senior slump." Agnes suggested that her grades varied with her moods, although she had never felt particularly inspired or stimulated by her teachers. "Sometimes I made good grades because I wanted to, and other times I made bad grades because I was stupid enough not to want to do different. . . .I hardly like any of my teachers and I never have really. . . . I want to do my homework and that is it."

Beatrice, with less native ability than Agnes, appreciated teachers who did not rush her and empathized with teachers' problems in adjusting course material to the needs of students with varied abilities, interests, and motivations. Convinced that she would like to teach, Beatrice remarked, "If I take it slow, I think maybe I can make it. . . .I am not very smart. . . .but to teach little kids is great. You can sit and talk to them and they really want to learn. . . .I wouldn't want to teach kids my age 'cause if they don't want to learn, they get kind of smart. . . .I wish I was smart enough to become a psychologist or something like that. . . .I think teaching is something I am more sure of being able to finish. I am more sure I can accomplish teaching, and I think I will get as much out of it and help people, too."

In feeling unpressured for outstanding success, the cautious modifiers are quite able to accept lesser achievements without loss of self-respect or lingering disappointment. Carl, for instance, said, "I guess there is always a little fear in me that something just isn't going to turn out right. . . .I always get over it. . . .If I try hard enough, I might be able to, but if I don't succeed, I can always go back to something else. Say if I wanted to become a doctor, and I don't become a doctor, I can always depend on my knowledge of engines and go to work in a garage."

Although generally less self-aspiring and therefore less demanding of teachers and schools, the cautious modifiers characteristically disapprove of any behavior they feel is discriminatory in their classrooms or in their extracurricular activities. For example, Arthur explained that he had dropped out of sports because the coach was apportioning supplies inequitably. "He would just throw things on the other kid to pick out for himself while he found something special for me. It kind of made me ill. I just didn't go for that at all. After a couple of days I just quit going." Or Estelle, feeling that discipline was sometimes excessive and likely to be determined by personal likes and dislikes rather than the realistic needs of the situation, said, "We had one girl in there that liked to talk a lot and he hated that, and he hit her one day. From then on, I really didn't like him. I couldn't see a teacher hitting a girl, even if she did talk every day. He could have found other ways to punish her."

For the cautious modifiers, any special privileges or status for themselves, whether from teachers or from other students, are likely to make them uncomfortable. Elated with her election as cheerleader, Beatrice commented, "Everybody looked up to you and everything, but rather than to be looked up to, I would rather be in a group of equal people." With firm grounding from parents in democratic principles of equal justice and opportunity for all, reinforced by their own humanistic values and human feelings and belief in the dignity of mankind, these young people are repelled by special treatment, even for themselves.

Consistent with these values is the unpretentious tolerance of the cautious modifiers toward those who behave in ways of which they basically disapprove. For instance, even though they are as opposed to premarital sex for themselves as the censors, they are, unlike the censors, likely to be thoughtful and understanding about how it could happen, have compassion for those who run into difficulty from social rejection, look for mitigating circumstances, and do not automatically reject the offenders. They tend to agree that the behavior rather than the person is bad; that there should be no special punishment for premarital pregnancy; that forced marriage may lead to additional difficulties in immature parents; that adoption is the solution of choice, reserving abortion for special cases of malformation or rape. They are also overwhelmingly agreed that they would not cease to be friendly to such people and would, in fact, seek to comfort and understand them.

In considering whether he might date a girl who had been promiscuous, Carl said: "I had rather take a person for what they are, not

for what they have been. I can't see that they are really bad girls. . . .
I think it is more the boy's fault by wanting the girl to let him." He
added that if pregnancy occurred, "I don't think she should have an
abortion unless it is really detrimental to the girl's life or something
like that. . . .I figure it is taking a life. . . .If the baby were to be
completely malformed, I would say okay then. . . .I believe in birth
control. I think it should be left up to the kids at the time. It is really
our future."

Beatrice, with similar views on premarital pregnancy said, "Everybody makes mistakes. . . .I don't think I would look at her as being
bad. You just feel sorry for her and you wish that maybe you would
have known her, so you could have known why." Like Carl, she
disapproved of abortion in general, but felt that in some cases, such
as rape, abortion should be considered.

In their views about minority groups and civil rights, the cautious
modifers are equally demanding of fairness in education, housing, and
vocational opportunities. They are not adverse to friendships with
blacks, but do on the whole draw the line at interracial dating and
marriage. Allen remarked, "I think race prejudice is stupid. I think
everybody is created equal, but I would not go out with a colored
person, or let my daughter go out with a colored person. I've got quite
a few colored friends, both boys and girls. I wouldn't date a colored
girl; it is against my principles."

In this respect, they resemble the censors, although they grant
that in some circumstances interracial dating and marriage might be
acceptable for some people. (That is, given similar tastes, education,
and values.) They disapprove not so much on moral grounds as on
practical considerations for the tremendous social difficulties the young
couple would have to face. For instance, Beatrice said, "It means a
lot to these people if you just say 'Hi' to them. . . .In grade school,
I would run around with colored kids and you never thought anything
about it. . . .but as for marriage, I think I would just be friends. I think
it presents too many problems. . . .I might dance with a black boy if
he were my friend, or if I worked with him."

The cautious modifiers' feelings about religion again stem primarily from their humanistic concerns for people. Thus, they are
primarily interested in youth groups, usually involving an array of
faiths, and aside from social activities, they are often engaged in
volunteer programs to help the poor, the ill, or the socially disadvantaged. Beatrice remarked, "You have to accept what people think;
you don't destroy it. It is good that people have opinions and it is

good that they go out and do things like for the poor people, the poverty programs, the Indians."

Less concerned about formal religious practices, they may or may not go to church regularly, and are quite free to disagree with some religious tenets. For example, Carl said, "Oh, I go to church on Easter and Christmas. . . .I don't completely believe everything the church says, but I guess I judge for myself what I think is really right and wrong and compare it to what the church says." In a similar vein, Estelle commented, "Well, sometimes I think the things the church thinks are just kind of old fashioned, like some of the things they say are sins — just kissing and stuff. . . .I have had a little bit of trouble getting there lately, but teenagers always do. . . .My sister said she didn't believe in the things the church taught so she didn't go. . . .I sure won't make my kids go 'cause I know myself I sure didn't want to go." Byron, although a more regular attendant and less opposed to formal doctrine, agreed that "The church is losing because it is not up to date. I am all for the changes."

Most cautious modifiers agree with their more traditionalistic peers that they see little room for smoking, drinking, or taking drugs[8]. However, most admit that they have moderately experimented[9] with smoking and drinking, usually out of curiosity or for temporary relaxation. Most have rejected smoking and drinking for themselves, or feel they can control how much they indulge. Carl said of smoking, "Oh, I have tried it. . . .I guess it was kind of like a crutch 'cause I thought in my mind that if I smoked a cigarette, I would feel a lot better, more relaxed. I smoked for a while, but I quit. . . .if someone offered me a cigarette now, I guess I would turn them down." Of drinking, Allen said, "I've been totally drunk once. I don't drink very much, but I drink once in a while. . . .I know when to quit." Byron, in explaining his views about drinking and drugs, said, "It is just an attempt to leave reality. There is no real point to it. . . .whenever you leave your senses behind, you know, and lose control, that is idiotic." Feeling that he could not risk losing control of his own behavior, he had, despite expressed curiosity about marijuana, totally rejected drug use. Like most cautious modifiers, he was not opposed to smoking or moderate drinking on the part of his friends. However, some sought to discourage these habits in close friends.

In dealing with psychological tests, the cautious modifiers are forthright, alert, orderly, and practical. They are very involved in the testing program and are eager to discuss the results of the tests. They vary in the ease with which they communicate, but they are usually quite interested in and willing to contemplate philosophical issues, to engage in fantasy, and to assess themselves introspectively. They usually have definite opinions on most topics, yet they can consider a variety of options and explore mitigating circumstances. Generally quite comfortable and satisfied with themselves as people, they rarely appear to be motorically awkward or tense, even though they may verbalize some anxieties and self-doubts. Hence, they tend to interact with modulation, with distinct consideration of the examiner's needs, and rarely criticize procedures in any way.

On the Wechsler Adult Intelligence Scale, they are frequently superior in evaluating social situations and in assessing human needs and motivations. They tend to use a highly differentiated vocabulary, which although not always grammatically correct, reflects individuality in thinking and self-expression.

On the Rorschach, they are likely to be alert to aspects of shading, suggesting their sensitivity to the world around them. They are likely to be responsive to feelings as indicated by their awareness of color, but they do so for the most part unimpulsively and without loss of intellectual control. Eager to take in a broad range of experience, they are likely to be quite productive and to make use of all the potentialities of the experience by using perspective in space and by giving equal attention to whole and small and large details.

The cautious modifiers, as curious, humanistic, and tolerant, yet somewhat cautious youth, are generally comfortable[10] with themselves. Carl said, "I am pretty sure of myself. . . .I guess I am open to things. . . .and I am willing to change my thoughts about it. . . .but not to take every suggestion that somebody might have." Willing to look at and explore most topics, values, and behaviors, they set their own limits, choosing their standards as appropriate for them. Respecting and admiring parents, they identify selectively, questioning some values and some behavioral standards. Thus, they are freer to experience than the obedient traditionalists and less concerned about personal advancement than the ideological conservatives. Solid, thoughtful individuals with deep concerns for people, and particularly abhorring anything they see as unfair or inequitable, they frequently choose to support or help less fortunate or more impulsive peers, but they do not often engage in nontraditional behavior.

Probably contributing to this stance is their own moderation, apparent in their drives from the time they were infants, and the moderate demands placed on them by parents who are almost invariably involved but not highly controlling or pressuring. With considerable freedom and capacity to experience for themselves and to express their feelings, they can be in individual ways quite realistically self-aware and at the same time especially considerate of others. In these ways, they are an integral part of traditional society as they experience it, but at the same time, they can modify traditional viewpoints on many issues according to their own keen perceptiveness and thoughtful evaluation. Perhaps an important contributing factor in this generalized tolerance and selective identification with their environment is the fact that well over a majority of these youths, as will be documented in Chapter 7, have themselves weathered or learned to compensate for serious personal handicaps or family hardships.

Notes:

[1] The cautious modifiers differ from the censors in this respect; they are not only less critical of others, but feel a responsibility for helping others, of improving their status, or in some ways altering their behavior.

[2] In their lack of punitiveness or condemnation of others, they are distinctly different from the censors who are inclined to isolate themselves from persons whose behavior they consider "bad."

[3] They are neither as hamstrung about what others might think as the obedient traditionalists, nor as concerned lest others influence them adversely as the ideological conservatives.

[4] In the nearly 20 years of longitudinal studies, a number of families moved out of the city. We were greatly gratified that most of these youths at our request or sometimes on their own initiative arranged to come to Topeka, usually in conjunction with a visit to grandparents.

[5] In reaching out to us and using us as sounding boards, the cautious modifiers along with the passionate renewers were distinctly different from the censors, who maintained a much more impersonal relationship, were less likely to take advantage of our offer to discuss test findings with them, and rarely sought our help or advice.

[6] On the whole, cautious modifiers have a relatively close relationship with both parents. Fathers, although as busy as those of the censors, tend to be more directly involved in child rearing.

[7] Here again, we see how they differ from the ideological conservatives, who make every effort to align themselves with adults who may be able to forward their personal advancement.

[8] In the 1960s, drug usage had not emerged as a serious issue in the Topeka community. Hence, few of our subjects were exposed to this temptation. Only one of the cautious modifiers had tried marijuana and he commented, "I haven't had any real urge to do it again. It wasn't really that much fun for me. I was a little worried about the news leaking out that I had. . . .and my parents finding out."

[9] Most cautious modifiers began smoking in their junior high school years; by their senior high school year, most have discontinued the habit. Drinking, usually beginning

in the sophomore year of high school, is for most boys almost a puberty rite, but few continue to drink, or if they do, do so moderately. Girls are similar in smoking habits, but usually choose not to drink, at least on dates, partly to avoid relaxation of their standards against premarital sex.

[10]This does not mean that they are without pressures or self-doubts at times, although in their own moderation in all things, they probably are exposed to less pressure than the ambitious ideological conservatives or the less personally controlled passionate renewers.

Chapter 7

Victor, Faith, and Floyd: Cautious Modifiers[1]

VICTOR

At 17, Victor, a sturdy, good-looking youth, made it clear that he was tired of school and determined to enlist in the army after graduating from high school. He knew that his parents disapproved, but he felt that this decision was his right and something he had to do to broaden his horizons, to see something of the world, and to give him time to consider what he meant to do with his future. He explained, "I have to get away and see what it is like....My parents want me to go on to college, but they aren't going to make any decision like that for me. They couldn't — they know they couldn't....maybe when I get out of the army, I will still want to go, but right now, 4 years of hitting the books just doesn't interest me."

He based his decision to enlist on the realistic facts that his high school grades were probably not good enough to satisfy requirements for college admission, and that his vocational aims were in flux. Having struggled throughout his childhood with some difficulties and frustrations in learning as a result of some sensory deficits, he felt he needed an interim period to recoup his energies and to think things through. Later, when he had chosen a definite career, he was confident that his persistence, self-control, and willingness to work hard would give him a comfortable, satisfying life. He said, "I have never thought that I wasn't going to get what I wanted. I don't know what I want to really do, but I have these feelers so I am going to go out and try them....I have no doubt that I will make the decision when the time comes, and it will be the right one." He thought, too, that if he still felt unready to cope with college after returning from the army, then he could use his skills and knowledge in mechanical fields to find a suitable and rewarding occupation.

His urgency to enlist did not mean that he approved of the United States participation in Vietnam. Rather, he felt that "We were extremely dumb for getting mixed up in it without the UN....Here we are over there dying for nothing — well, not really for nothing 'cause we have to keep them [the communists] from spreading — but not everything we do over there is perfect, and I feel that we have to stop the fighting pretty quick. I don't mind going and dying for my country but we are just fighting for that line....I want to get there. I figure I have to see what it is like....I want to get out and see what is going on in the world." This need to find out for himself colored many of his attitudes and values about school, his family, sex and marriage, personal habits, religion, politics and social viewpoints, and so on. For instance, he said, "I definitely am more interested in my social life right now than I am in scholastic life. I feel right now it is more important. I know I will have to get back to the books sooner or later....It is hard for me to sit down and study, but I do if I am interested in it, and if I understand what I am doing." He added that he liked teachers who make learning vivid, and who help students probe for deeper meanings in what they are learning. He said of one teacher whom he had admired, "She always comes up with some little deal that interests me....We can read a book and she can really get the true meaning out of it."

In the same way, he objected to forms of discipline that interfere with growing up, becoming more independent, or learning for one's self through one's own efforts and experiences. Referring to some relatives, he said, "I don't approve of the way they brought up my cousin....This is just keeping the apron strings tied down longer....I have looked for the *why* myself."[3]

Speaking of his parents, Victor indicated that discipline was no real problem because the relationship involved mutual respect and he had been given a good deal of independence. He admired and felt close to both of his parents and used them selectively for support and help. For some help with everyday problems, he turned to his mother; but when serious decisions needed to be made, he felt more comfortable with his father. He said, "I don't get homesick. When

I am away, I think of them, but I don't wish I was back at home....They have brought me up pretty good....I wish we had a little more time together but our relationship is pretty close. We see eye to eye with each other. We can have an argument[4] and it is not the end of the world. We can have a real loud argument with each other, but we respect each other. I am not a little kid that doesn't know anything, and they aren't just old people that are too dumb to understand what is going on....When things bother me, I will go to Mom, but when things are really important, I go talk to my Dad....because he is a man probably. I went to my Mother about my grades because I was probably ashamed to go to my Dad....My parents aren't too bad. Ever since I was younger they have made me get all of my studies and stuff and they cared enough that they would ask where my homework was and where my books were. Now they aren't pushing me too hard and I am not working too hard. They sort of realized it is time to pull off a little."

Victor went on to say that whereas he probably would raise his own children much as he had been raised, his way of handling specific aspects of child rearing would necessarily be dependent on the individual needs and qualities of his children. "That depends on how my kids are. You can't take one household and put it into another. It doesn't work." For himself, he demanded freedom of personal choice, and he meant to give this to his children. "I don't like to be blocked....I definitely do want to get away for awhile. I have to breathe out a little more....I don't dislike my parents. I don't want to run away from them, but I am walking away."

Victor was equally forthright and genuine in explaining his ideas about sex and marriage. Having dated several girls more or less steadily, Victor decided that he was not yet ready to be tied down. "Going steady never has appealed to me....I think we have more fun with each other now that we know we don't have to be with each other....That is not for me right now. I like to enjoy myself." He could see that for some teenagers marriage is appropriate. "I don't care. I think if somebody out of high school wants to get married, he should go ahead. He is going to have a heck of a time getting on in the world because he is really going to be tied down....I don't care who you are — you are going to be dependent on your parents until you are 21....You just can't do anything until you are 21....I wouldn't want any kids until I was 25. I don't know if I will have that much control over it or not, but it would be nice just to enjoy each other for a couple of years and sort of get on our feet....I want to know the girl....and just want to enjoy her."

Victor felt that premarital sex was morally wrong, but he could understand how easily it could happen, perhaps even to him since he enjoyed kissing girls and thought all boys at least consider having sex relations with attractive girls. In the event of pregnancy, he thought both the boy and the girl should be held responsible, but that marriage should not be forced. He pointed out that a double standard of sexual morality was perhaps unfair, but "that is the way it is....You know as well as I do that the boys will go to the prostitutes rather than to the one they will marry....There is the double standard, and there is the standard where you should never have sex relations unless you really are in love and engaged to be married....and there is the standard of any time, any place — free love....I figure that if the boy is the man he should be, he should be able to seduce her if he wants, but I think that he shouldn't....I think it is bad for the boy to get off scott free, but they shouldn't be forced to marry....nine times out of ten, or more so, it's not going to work. I don't think she should be punished. I think an abortion would be the best way out....If somebody tells me he has had sexual relations, I don't think any worse of him, but if someone tells me Mary has had sexual relations, my opinion is a bit different than my opinion of Jack. I can't help it; that is the way it is."

Victor was equally thoughtful in offering carefully discriminated judgments about such social habits as smoking, drinking, and using drugs. He pointed out that many of his friends did smoke and that he had tried smoking in his junior high school years but later rejected the habit as a waste of time and money and as unpleasant to the taste. "Most of us do smoke....I can't see smoking. It is a waste of money and there is nothing to it. I don't think it tastes good. In the ninth grade, I was doing a little bit, but I don't have the habit. I cut it out for wrestling for 2 years, and once you have gotten away from it — well, as a senior in high school, you aren't big and bad by smoking. It is just accepted....one thing that I think helped, too, is that my parents wouldn't care if I smoked."

Victor had begun drinking moderately in the eleventh grade and even on occasion had enjoyed the sensation of feeling high. However, he felt that he could control himself and set limits as to when and under what circumstances he would drink — that is, not with girls and not when he was driving. "I'm always conscious of the fact that

I am pretty intoxicated and I am careful. We won't get plastered and go out and drive....sometimes we drive up to a cabin and get absolutely intoxicated and it won't hurt anybody. We will be out in the woods and won't be driving or anything....It would just be us boys. My dad isn't going to tell me not to go out and drink either, 'cause he knows I am going to do it, but he says not to get carried away, and if I get caught, I deserve everything I get." He added that his crowd was careful to arrange that at least one boy was sober, to protect and help the others, and to avoid damage to the car. "The driver doesn't want to crack up his car....It can be a hunk of junk and it is his pride and joy, plus the kids don't want to get hurt either, so it is pretty logical. Whoever is driving can stay away from it. We don't get plastered and go out and drive."

Of taking drugs, he said, "There definitely are kids but I don't know them . . . that is up to them. If they want to do it, go ahead ....I know the dangers involved, and it doesn't enthuse me at all. I can get my kicks taking some girl out."

Victor had some questions about formal religion[5] "I believe, but I have always doubted. . . . You are not supposed to question Him. I can't figure out why you can't. . . . I ask why too much. I can't accept the rules without asking why."

About racial matters[6] Victor honestly admitted that he had some prejudices, but again he was in the process of formulating opinions, ready to reserve judgment and to respond to minority people on an individual basis. "I am prejudiced definitely, but there is a lot of them that I respect. I try to keep an open mind....They shouldn't have to be demanding their rights because they should already have them. As a human being in the United States, they shouldn't have to demand this." Thus, in all of his views, Victor chose to discriminate, to tolerate different viewpoints, but to set his own standards. He wanted to find out for himself, not to be told or to be bound by others — even by parents he deeply respected.

Many of Victor's feelings and his typical style of coping were apparent in our test sessions with him. Considering our project scientifically worthwhile, he was usually cooperative and involved, but at the same time he was entirely capable of protesting against procedures he experienced as overly long or difficult. He also reported that at times, he came to the sessions feeling tense, nervous, and depleted because of a series of problems in the extended families of both parents. Then he was less open and less direct because he was preoccupied with and empathically shared parental concerns for the welfare of his grandparents? It was significant, too, that he was at these times highly sympathetic toward and supportive of his parents, particularly his mother.

On the Wechsler Adult Intelligence Scale, Victor demonstrated good general information — but indicated that he believed facts were less important than understanding — applying good common sense and coming up with sound judgments on the basis of facts. Showing a good deal of sensitive insightfulness into both himself and others, he chose to adopt tolerant viewpoints toward others and to reserve for himself the right to go along or to be different.

Very persistent and disliking to be deterred from goals he established, he felt he could, despite some distinct learning disabilities, achieve these goals. In this stance, he was aided by his capacity to pace himself, to accept alternative goals, and to defer judgment. Thus, he preferred not to be hurried or forced into a routine for which he was not ready. In this respect, he regarded his "slacking off" in his senior year as a logical adaptation to a realistic situation.

He agreed that his vocabulary was "not as good as I would like it to be," but at the same time he tried to find "the right words at the right time, other than the common words." These efforts sometimes resulted in unique and even poetic formulations.

Quite observant when he chose to be, he was particularly aware of the quality of things and remarkably alert to details. This was especially true of all motor performances, which he handled with considerable gracefulness and care.

On the projective tests, his urgency to experience broadly was suggested by high productivity and attention to nuances of the Rorschach cards. For instance, he described "a couple of colored kids, staring at each other. I say colored because of the shadows, the big lips, the way their heads are turned and their hands are out." He was able to use most of the scoring determinants flexibly and frequently described his percepts in considerable detail. At the same time, he consciously tried to control impulsivity and to avoid becoming overwhelmed or discouraged by difficulty. With a very positive sense of self-worth, he was willing to accept responsibility based on carefully thought out decisions. Basically outgoing, friendly, and sensitive, he made it clear that he enjoyed life with a great deal of zest.

On the Thematic Apperception Test these characteristics were equally clear. Here we saw a boy who respected and loved his family, but who felt he must move away to become independent. Although sorry for any discomfort or unhappiness this might impose on his parents, he was definite about the necessity to leave. "The daughter feels kind of bad that she is leaving, but she wants to go, and she *is* leaving. . . .Time has a way of taking care of all those things. . . .It is pretty well wrapped up. . . .People recover from separations and even some deaths and in the long run they are all going to make it."

Victor's urgency to see for himself, and to make up his own mind on the basis of his own experiences, had been characteristic of him from our earliest contacts with him. At 4 weeks of age, he was considered a very active and developmentally advanced baby with strong preferences and distinct urgencies to explore his environment. Apparently always curious, he had been insistent in being held so that he could look around, a fact that pleased his parents because they felt it signaled the development of his independence. At the same time, his mother had remarked, "But of course, nobody could get away with holding him in any other way than as he liked."

At 3½ years, these qualities were still marked and his mother then described him as strong willed and determined, as "A child for whom fences and cupboards and high shelves seem only a challenge." Never one to be satisfied with superficial reasons for prohibitions, he had on several occasions left the family yard, later telling his mother, "I just got to go." Respecting his curiosity to explore and his high activity level, his mother did not see him as a naughty or disobedient child, but rather one whose zest to experience sometimes led him into difficulties with other children or occasionally into property destruction.

Beginning in his second year, Victor experienced a good deal of stress from repeated illnesses and a series of accidents, resulting in temporary hearing loss, a variety of visual problems, some difficulties with balance and coordination, and markedly poor articulation. Then his urgency to explore was restricted by these handicaps, which later also interfered with learning in the early grades. However, from parents, grandparents, and some outstanding teachers who continued to support his individuality, he was encouraged to learn to pace himself, to appreciate quietly the beauties of nature, and to develop his natively positive reactions to people. Thus, his secure self-worth remained undimmed and he never felt entirely defeated. In retrospect, he remarked, "My older sister was an exceptional child as far as maturity was concerned, and I was one of the biggest brats. I was always getting in trouble. I have compensated for it pretty good. I like the way I am turning out."

In the interim years, Victor's social assets and his positive attitudes toward people, reinforced by his loving, consistent parents, helped him weather many frustrations and difficulties and to adopt a realistic outlook for his own future. At that time, he had explained, upon realizing that he was surpassed academically by many of his peers, "I feel bad when I first do it [fail in school tasks], but then I get over it. I just do my best." In these years, he saw his mother as quite demanding, sometimes more protective than he would have wished, but also loving and supportive. He easily identified with paternal warmth, with some difficulties in vocational adjustment and in hardships in the extended family. Consciously trying to be, like his father, persistent and careful, he was at times very discouraged and frustrated and then was briefly irritable and careless.

Always eager and spontaneous, he enjoyed many social and recreational outlets and automatically expected to be respected and treated fairly. In turn, he granted these rights to everyone with whom he came into contact. Keenly aware of his shortcomings and handicaps, he was never one to be stopped by difficulties. Basically confident of the goodness of life, he never considered that he could fail completely, even though his goals might be delayed or deferred. Improving in both speech and motor areas as his general health improved, he was able to maximize his resources and compensate for most of his weaknesses. The sensory defects which had in his childhood led to frustrations and conflicts between his urgency to find out for himself and his ability to do so were by then considerably reduced. Altogether, he had mobilized a good deal of strength and resourcefulness in coping with some major learning disabilities.

In his adolescence, Victor continued to press for and to enjoy a good deal of autonomy. His quest to experience and be independent had been fostered, too, by healthy, stable, compatible parents who loved him for what he was and encouraged his individuality. Having received almost continuous reinforcement of a secure sense of self-worth, Victor was always able to ask for needed help. Hence, he never felt defeated. His self-confidence varied from time to time, but he never entirely doubted that he could achieve what he wished. He had always been one who could raise questions, protest against what he did not like, and ultimately reach decisions on the basis of his own experiences and considered judgment. He enjoyed people and things, and he sought and was deeply sensitive to a wide variety of experiences. He wanted and was able to experience life richly and was outstandingly sympathetic in his warm understanding and assessment of people. The limits he set were reality based and self-imposed restrictions on his own behavior. Thus, he deferred some decisions (as, for instance, in regard to vocational choice and child rearing standards) and was entirely confident that he could make these appropriately when necessary. A hallmark of his coping style was his insistence on openness to his own senses and his own experiences, a characteristic equally impressive in Faith, our second cautious modifier.

FAITH

Tall, slender, poised, and confident, 17-year-old Faith presented herself as one who "keeps wanting somebody to tell me to do it or don't do it, and nobody will. I am glad that they don't. I know I must learn to make up my own mind....I believe teenagers have to find out for themselves. They have to experience for themselves." Later, more directly and confidently, she added, "I'm growing up and I realize that I am going to face my world, my generation, and I have to learn to be me. I can't live on what other people tell me. I can't live by my parents' standard. I have to live by my standards."

With these views, she was a happy girl who was enjoying her life immensely. In quite remarkable ways, she had grown from a shy, restrictive, and often miserable child to a vigorous, spontaneous teenager with an active social life. Having come from a deeply religious family with strict fundamentalist viewpoints, she, in her ninth-grade year, sought God's help in prayer for the specific purpose of reducing her inferiority complex and increasing her capacity to approach people. She attributed her increasing social success, personal confidence, and joy in living almost entirely to God, whom she sincerely believed enabled her to understand her parents better, to resolve some major conflicts with a younger sister, to help guide her sister toward religion, to meet peers more graciously and openly, and finally to feel comfortable with and enjoy relationships with boys. Her relationship to God was deeply personal, much like talking to a close friend who is also a wise and supportive counselor in helping her deal with problems in everyday living. Then, once she knew how to make friends, she believed they helped her, as she in turn helped them, to maximize her intelligence and creativity, and to become a richer individual.

In her senior high school year, Faith was looking forward to college where she planned to study art or home economics to prepare herself to teach. She had chosen this field for a number of carefully thought out reasons.[8] First, she felt she had some skills and knowledge in these areas. She pointed out that she designed and made her own clothes, that she had tutored a number of students, participated in and took leadership roles in a variety of clubs (such as the Future Teachers' Club), was active in a church-sponsored youth group, and played the piano for Sunday school. She questioned only whether she had adequate patience to teach children who might not be as highly motivated as she, and whether she had enough artistic talent. On the latter issue, she had been reassured by her art teacher who had told her that general knowledge and familiarity with techniques are more important than exceptional talent.

To her, a far more important reason for choosing to teach was her liking for people and her intense desire to help them, as she felt she had helped her peers throughout her high school years.

Above all, she felt a need to tell others how she had gained strength from her very personal religion. "In the ninth grade, I began to realize that I didn't have any friends and I always thought that everybody hated me and I began to realize that wasn't the way it was. I just didn't know how to let them know that I wanted to be friends....I was still quite indrawn and scared to death....I had no social life except I would go to church, but it wasn't satisfactory. I couldn't fully enjoy it....I was so caught up in myself I didn't really understand or observe what was going on....My only friends were adults at church and they couldn't understand me because they were adults and I was a child....I knew something wasn't right. I knew I was miserable. I got home half the time crying from school. . . .I didn't know what was the matter. I just knew I was unhappy. I started asking God, 'I don't know what's the matter but something has got to change because I can't live like this. I can't stand for it.' So He just began to make me realize that I wasn't mature enough."

In this process over a 3-year span, she chose to discuss[9] her problems with her parents, with whom she quite openly disagreed at times, first about her choice of friends and secondly about standards of personal behavior. "Mother fought me on having this friend for about 2 years and she finally gave up. I think now she realizes that I am not going to let other people sway me. She was afraid she was going to ruin my reputation. . . .that she was going to ruin me as far as God's voice was concerned. . . .I told mother that I was not going to leave her. She needs me because she hasn't learned to find herself. . . .She needs my friendship[10]. . . .and this last year, I have rebelled against my parents' standards, not against their religion at all, but against the standards we were forced to feel were vital and our relationship that we desire with God. I don't believe that they are vital, and I have rebelled against them. My parents don't know what to do with me."

Specifically, she took a stand by objecting to parental disapproval of wearing slacks, swim suits, short skirts, jewelry, makeup, and of going to movies and dances. Yet she did this openly with admiration for her parents' persistence in maintaining their own standards. "I told them I am going away to college next year. I am going into the world by myself. I want to be prepared for this world and I want to prepare now and I want you to help me. I want to go to movies and I want to go to dances....If I find out that they are wrong, I want to have somebody to come running back to. I want you to be here and help me because next year when I go away, I won't have anybody to come running back to. I also asked them if they would please help me grow up....I don't understand them at all. I guess it is just that their feelings are so strong they just can't understand me. I know they don't understand me and I can't exactly blame them. They went ahead then and said that I could go. They don't want me to go; they think it is terrible that I do, but they won't forbid it....It bothers me to know that they don't approve of it. I don't want to go against what they say. I don't want to disobey them....or do things behind their back, but I am going to do these things sooner or later, and so if I know they aren't going to approve, I just may not tell them."

Faith attributed her strength in striving for independence partly to parental trust and the openness of her communication with her parents, partly to support from friends, but predominantly to her very special relationship with God. She explained, "I have always been very good and my parents know that they can trust me....My friends kept telling me, 'You have got to stand up. You can't be tied to your parents' apron strings all the time.'...Oh, I think God talks to me through my own conscience....He helped me a lot and I told Him I was scared at the high school, and if He would help me I could make it and I did all right. So I accepted it as a challenge. Now this is a place where there is new people with a whole new world opening up to me. With God's help, I am going to go into that world and be a success, or better, find happiness in that world."

Thus, Faith changed many of her viewpoints but she continued to disapprove strongly of some kinds of peer behavior though she tried to be tolerant and understanding. This was true of her views in regard to drinking, smoking, use of drugs, and sex. She said, "Some of my friends disappointed me very much. . . .One of the guys I have grown up together with. . . .has gone out and done a lot of things that I still feel are very, very wrong. I feel they are unholy and harmful to the body which I think is God's temple. And I wonder — well, if I start letting down in these areas, I might start down in those areas, too. I talked to one of my girl friends the other night and she said these other things (smoking and drinking) are becoming a temptation to her and she knows it. . . .But the thing of it is that I used to feel these things were so wrong and now I have changed my mind." Interestingly enough, with these modified views, Faith felt comfortable in joining peers in public places where beer is served, knowing that she could refuse to drink without losing the respect of some friends who do drink.

Faith's views about sex and marriage, although still relatively traditional, were also colored by her new tolerance. She said:

> I think God has given me a great capacity to love, but He wants me to learn how to use it for Him because if I only let it be natural, then I am going to hurt myself and that is all. . . .Mother hasn't explained much about the male, but she explained very much about the female, and we understand it pretty well. I was a little shocked. . . .sometimes I would just sit and think about sexy things when I first knew about it, when I was very young — oh, I think in grade school. It embarrassed me very much but I liked to draw pictures of nude people. . . .I think most kids would have trouble with it when they were older, but I have gone through it, and it doesn't bother me anymore. When I think about it, it is horrible. I hate to admit I ever had such feelings. . . .I think premarital sex is wrong because God has made it for marriage. . . .It scares me to death 'cause I know how easy it can be. . . .Because of my rearing, I am prone to condemn a girl like that, but I don't want to because I know that she is human. . . .She will need more help than ever. . . .I think she has had her punishment. Her guilt is going to be so great.

Faith did not believe in forced marriages because she felt they would probably be unhappy. She felt babies conceived out of wedlock should be kept by the mothers, even if they were unmarried, if they were able to care for them. Otherwise, she would recommend adoption.

In her new-found tolerance, she was able to maintain some friendships with people who behaved in ways totally at odds from her principles, without in any way relaxing the standards she set for herself. In fact, she welcomed friends she saw as different from her. This she did partly because she hoped she might by showing her concerns and offering support, in some way modify the behavior of which she disapproved. Most of all, she sincerely believed that she could improve the status and outlook of peers by introducing them to her very useful, practical, and functional use of her religious faith. To do this, she meant to proceed cautiously, slowly, and patiently.

Faith's stand on race was less clear cut. On the one hand, she had some black friends, but she drew the line at intermarriage and at interracial dating which could lead to intermarriage, an outcome posing social problems for the couple and their children. She would not date a black boy because "I think there is too much possibility of intermarriage, and it causes unnecessary gossip. Intermarriage — I don't approve of it. If somebody else wants to, it is okay, but I think it would be awfully hard on a child. I think a person who does this is extremely thoughtless of their children because they are not accepted by any group." She pointed out in this regard that blacks would not be accepted in her church, largely because of fears of intermarriage. Since she felt she could maintain a friendship with a black boy without eventually marrying him, she regarded refusal of church participation or membership as an unfair deprivation of the peace and strength religion can offer. Yet, she admitted that her elders were probably right since some young people might be more impulsively drawn into an unacceptable heterosexual relationship. Here again, we saw her differentiating between the behavior and opinions which she could tolerate in others and what she felt was appropriate behavior for her.

She tended to see racial struggles and protests as communist inspired. "I think that it is communistically based, I think that there are some communists that have come in and gone to the lower class Negroes who they know don't have much education, don't understand, and get them all shook up. I think they have gone to them and gotten a few leaders. I think the leaders are probably communist. I don't know whether they are or not, and I think they have gotten them riled up to try to get us more conscious of things that are going on at home so we will forget about them and they can carry on their activities a little better."

Her views on Vietnam were not entirely formulated. She wanted to avoid thinking too much about it. "It is hard for me to even think about that or face it. I can't understand or imagine war because I have never been in a place where it was, but the stories I read and the things I hear are so horrible and yet it doesn't seem a reality. It just seems like a horrible nightmare that isn't real, but I know that it is. You think of somebody going over there and fighting in the war and coming home, but that's not the way it always is." Her feelings here were largely determined by her knowledge that her boyfriend, who, incidentally, was from a background considerably different from her own, might enlist, and her expectation that enlistment would probably break up their relationship.

Faith hoped to marry, preferably someone who shared her religious viewpoints, and ideally a man training for the ministry. She fantasied at some length about the pleasure she would have in being a pastor's wife and in fact was of the opinion that God may have ordained this position for her. However, she realistically remarked that as a pastor's wife she could not expect to have the material comforts she wanted, a nice home and clothes. "I don't expect I will be wealthy, but I hope comfortable, and I will be able to make the best of what I have. I expect that I won't have all the nice things I want to have. I just love nice clothes. I want to have a very well-dressed family. I don't expect that I will have all that I want, and I don't think I will have too much of it because. . . .I believe very strongly that God has called me to be a pastor's wife." If this happens, she felt sure she could adjust to the economic deprivation because she would regard the outcome as God's choice.

Faith also hoped to have children, whom she planned to raise within the church, as her parents had done. However, she specified that she would introduce her family to a less restrictive religion and to a life more culturally oriented than her own had been. She commented, "I want to raise my children with a fear and love for God. . . .I sometimes pray that God will help me to be the mother I should be, so my children will see that a relationship with Him is something real and great, and that it is the greatest thing that can happen to anybody. I want them to experience this first. I will probably as a parent impart to them my standards, and I think pretty much that I probably will raise them the same, but there are things I think I will do different. I will teach them when they are younger to make their own choices instead of having them made for them. I will have more good literature in the home. . . .classical music and things like this, and they will be able to recognize a few paintings — be able to recognize paintings by their style and things like this. . . .I want it to be natural to them."

Her feelings here reflected considerable closeness with her mother in her growing years and in her adolescence greater appreciation for her father. She felt that her mother had been too restrictive in following and promoting her religious beliefs and saw herself and her father as more tolerant and more hopeful for the future of the world.

Thus, in her adolescence, we saw a girl who largely through her own efforts or, as she saw it, through the help she received through prayer had achieved a new self-concept and new social skills. In this process, she modified many of her viewpoints and became a much more tolerant, understanding person. She had chosen to substitute supportive humanistic religious beliefs for a restrictive religion. Then she was able to form closer personal relationships with friends of both sexes and to experience the world more richly. She said, for example, "I love the outdoors. I almost have an obsession for the clear blue sky and green trees, green grass, green meadows, green forests, and a clear blue sky. . . .I want to see outside because these things, more than anything else, seem to personalize, impersonate you know, and it seems that He knows that these things mean a lot to me. . . .He has given me a clear blue sky and He knew that I needed it to keep me in good spirits."

Our psychological tests largely confirmed what we learned about Faith in the interviews she had with both authors. On the Wechsler Adult Intelligence Scale, for example, she appeared to be somewhat naive insofar as her general information was concerned. She knew relatively little about geography, science, or history, possibly because she had been restricted in her reading, not allowed to go to movies or to watch TV extensively. However, she was not defensive about her lack of information (as she had been when she was younger) and was at times able to make logical yet not always correct guesses. She was also able to recognize that her general knowledge was somewhat limited. She believed that her schooling had perhaps not been as rigorous in this respect as she desired, but more importantly, she felt that the public schools had done little to help her think for herself or to integrate the facts they presented.

In the humanities, where she had a great deal of curiosity, her understanding and appreciation were superior. She was equally good in solving practical problems, especially when human relationships were concerned. Typically, she attributed her success in these areas to help she obtained from God through prayer. She also made it very clear that whereas she could question some traditional standards, she would not oppose parental wishes without their knowledge.

Throughout our tests, Faith demonstrated a vivid and rich vocabulary. She indicated that clarity and self-expression were important to her.

On motor tasks, Faith worked in a concentrated but unpressured way, using her hands delicately and gracefully. She was outstanding in her appreciation of spatial relationships, perhaps resulting from long training in art. Altogether, it was clear that she was a person of superior intelligence, although one whose creativity was sometimes inhibited by her preoccupation with establishing her independence within the limits she set on her behavior.

On the projective tests, Faith was quite productive and clearly achievement oriented. She showed appropriate consideration of reality and was not impulsive, even though at times she was distinctly individualistic in her perception. She had unusual appreciation for beauty and for human feelings.

While broadening her interest and knowledge, she always kept herself within the bounds of good judgment, logical thinking, and caution lest she stray too far from traditional thinking.

Comparing the tests given to her in her adolescence with those administered in her prepuberty years, we were impressed with her tremendously increased capacity to understand people and to observe the world about her. Also notable was her much greater optimism and her zest for enjoyment of living, reflected in warm interpersonal relationships. Having chosen to identify selectively with parental standards, she had more personal sparkle and was thoroughly enjoying experiencing for herself. In this respect, she was using fully her considerable warmth and sensitivity for people.

Faith's stance in her adolescence was to some extent foreshadowed in our observations of her coping maneuvers as a child, and in other respects it was understandable in the light of childhood experiences.

As an 8-week-old infant, she was vigorous and sturdy, despite a number of early illnesses. She was also particularly sensitive to people and to sensory stimulation, which she was equally able to show an interest in or turn away from if she disliked.[12]

At 2½ years, she suffered from a serious undiagnosed illness, followed by a tonsillectomy. Perhaps because of these setbacks, and because a sibling was born about this time, she spoke unclearly and was somewhat passive, shy, and physically awkward.

Sibling rivalry continued to be marked throughout her childhood, but in her adolescence, Faith adopted the view that her sister needed her help to mend her somewhat mischievous ways and to acquaint her with the real support she found in her personalized religion.

In the middle years, her parents considered and rejected the possibility of psychiatric help to alleviate a variety of fears, excessive criticalness, constant bickering with the younger sister, and a generally unhappy approach to living. On our tests and in our observations at that time, Faith maintained a stiff posture, constantly looked worried, was obsessively neat, and seemed emotionally inhibited. Her play was routine and showed marked shifts in energy levels. She was quite curious and attracted to learning, but she had some distinct difficulties in learning to read. Nonetheless, she showed moments of zestful enjoyment and was able to express her displeasure quite openly, even though she moderated her protests by unusual concern for doing things as she thought her mother, and we, expected.

In her prepuberty years, Faith was exceedingly unhappy and overconscientious and later told us that she had frequently thought of suicide. She was as critical of herself as she was of others. Again, the possibility of psychiatric help was considered and rejected by the parents, largely because they feared such treatment might interfere with the strict religious practices the family followed. However, the mother, who was herself hypercritical of others and not socially adept, then began to relax some of her standards, particularly in regard to the kinds of clothes and jewelry her daughters might wear. It was also at this time that Faith took her problems to God and emerged with a less restrictive, more humanistic religion.

In some ways a vulnerable child as a result of her restrictive background and her early illnesses, Faith emerged as a sturdy teenager, capable of considerable self-determination. She did this within family standards, openly defying some parental injunctions, thus maximizing her good native intelligence and sensitivity without alienating her parents. In these ways, she was a good example of a cautious modifier, but one whose strong reliance on her religious beliefs was idiosyncratic.

To illustrate further the individual range of behavior with the typical coping styles of those we call cautious modifiers, we shall next describe Floyd, a youth who, despite considerable variability in his functioning and at times considerable personal disorganization, was intent on experiencing for himself.

FLOYD

As a high school senior, 17-year-old Floyd, slightly obese and physically sluggish, dressed in well-worn clothes, and at times noncommittal, remarked soberly that he had recently become "dead serious" about wanting a college education. He regretted that in his failure to recognize this need earlier, he had not taken full advantage of high school. Despite acknowledged superior intelligence, he had not sought to be outstanding academically, nor had he participated extensively in extracurricular activities. He was proud to have been nearly totally economically independent from his parents since his seventh grade year and even at times to have contributed some of his earnings to his large family. He bought all of his own clothing, maintained one car in running condition, enjoyed tinkering with several others, and kept himself in spending money by repairing and rebuilding engines. He liked his family, particularly respecting parental togetherness in the face of severe adversity. He expected his life to be similar to that of his parents, yet hopefully more economically secure. At the same time, he was convinced that it was important to be a part of his own peer culture, to set some goals to provide challenge, and to modify his life as he saw fit.

Having been pessimistic and not very happy in his prepuberty years when his family had been particularly hard pressed by illness, discouragement, and economic limitations, his mood had taken an upward turn, and he was able to be more hopeful about his future. He said, "Well, it's all in the past and I would rather go on into the future. . . .I don't think it will be any easier but probably more fun. You wouldn't be doing all of the proper things all the time; you would probably be messing off all the time. . . .I can look forward to it, and I want to try to make it as happy as I can. . . .You have to set goals on something, something to reach for. . . .You anticipate the worst and hope for the best. . . .That way, it comes out pretty good. . . .If you lose sight of hope, you don't get anywhere. . . .It is just that you don't want to give up." In a series of sessions with him, we experienced both his hopes and frustrations, his positive and negative feelings about himself.

In the first session with the female psychologist, there was a poignant appeal about his appearance and manner, an alternate moving toward and away from interpersonal advances. Honoring many previous contacts with the examiner, he was friendly and cooperative, but not altogether spontaneous. He rarely looked directly at the examiner and often giggled in a somewhat inappropriate and silly fashion, as though embarrassed with sobriety and inactivity. His neat, clean clothing, which was too light weight for the cold day and which he had obviously outgrown, barely covered his heavy body, a fact of which he was self-consciously aware as he repeatedly pulled at his shirt as though to make it more adequate. His hands, scarred and badly discolored with oily stains, looked disproportionately large and seemed to be attached rag doll fashion to arms grown too long for his skimpy sleeves. His hair was long, uncombed, and not entirely clean. He slumped in his chair as though totally lacking in energy. One empathically felt a sense of defeat in him, the more impressive in remembering the vigorous, lively child he had been.

Floyd's discomfort was registered in his mumbled husky speech, which frequently made it necessary to ask him to repeat himself. On these occasions, Floyd replied as briefly as possible, seeming to be unwilling to commit himself beyond the necessity to preserve social amenities. Nevertheless, his grammar and vocabulary were adequate to good, and there were occasional glimpses of vivid appreciation of beauty, of visual alertness, and of carefully discriminated thinking. He was not indifferent to the interview, but he rarely took initiative in communication, and he spoke with an indolence matched by his physical torpidity. He had no problem in understanding, but he was not enthusiastic in verbal interchange. On a few occasions, gaiety, broad humor, and graphic fantasies made his mildly depressed mood the more striking.

In telling about his large family, Floyd spoke warmly, but he kept his comments factual and relatively brief. Giggling, he admitted, "It's kind of hard to keep track of them all." He reported that his oldest sister was away at school, but he did not know what she was studying or how she was progressing. Of the younger siblings, he said simply that all were in school. He said almost nothing about his mother and spoke of his father primarily in connection with shared interests in auto mechanics. Nevertheless, it became clear that he greatly admired his father's skills. He did not feel very close to either of his parents but admired their honesty and fairness, seeing himself as differing from them primarily in being more tolerant of others, less bound by fundamentalist religious viewpoints, and more willing to consider new ideas. He felt he conformed when he wanted to and quietly went his own way without overt conflict when he disagreed with parental standards. He expressed disappointment that his parents could not take him "as seriously as I would like for them to." Then, he added stoically, "That's the way parents are."

Generally unenthusiastic about school experiences, he felt positive only about auto mechanics and industrial arts because these subjects kept him active, and because he had in the shop been given a leadership role that allowed him to help others learn about things in which he was interested and outstandingly competent. He disliked struggling with the details of English grammar, but he liked literature and enjoyed reading the daily newspapers, specifically mentioning editorials, current events, and sports. He dismissed his poor academic record by saying that he had rarely studied, preferring instead to listen carefully in class and to take good notes. If he were given an opportunity to repeat high school, he would spend less time "goofing off." He described his teachers, with the exception of one biology teacher, as adequate but not interested in stimulating students to develop their own interests, nor sufficiently concerned about their students as individuals. He had been interested in sports in junior high school, but he did not participate in his high school years and had taken no active part in social or extracurricular school events. This was partly a function of lack of time since he worked throughout high school. Perhaps more immediately relevant was his lack of money for the equipment needed; in fact, he repeatedly mentioned the limited funds in his family, not with great resentment but with resigned acceptance.

In our standard test battery, Floyd did not push himself for excellence. On the whole, his general information was good but somewhat spotty. He seemed rather provincial at times. It was clear that when his interests were aroused, he took pains to learn a lot about a subject, but if he was not interested he did not put forth much effort. For instance, even though math appealed to him, he did not carefully think through problems, rarely checked answers for accuracy, and was often content with approximations. His memory, like his information, was excellent in those areas he considered important, but he easily lost track of associations and did not press himself to pursue something he could not recall immediately and without effort. He wrote slowly and laboriously and with little attention to neatness or legibility. He was outstandingly well coordinated, logical, and efficient in all motor tasks, which apparently roused him from his initial lethargy. Thus, the quality of his performance varied considerably, alternating between indifferent compliance and spurts of interest and concentration. His test behavior clearly suggested a depressed mood and disinterest or apathy about using his intellectual superiority fully, possibly because he felt — as he had for many years — conflicted feelings about doing better than his passive, hard-working, and poorly educated father, who had barely managed to make ends meet.

In the projective tests, we learned little more about Floyd, partly because he spoke so softly that the usual taped interview was largely inaudible, and partly because he chose to be brief and left untapped the rich sensory experiencing[13] we had seen in him in earlier years. He responded in a global fashion with little attention to detail or differentiation and failed to respond to color or texture. He repeatedly referred to animals who were weak or gentle creatures, or in some way inadequate or restrained. His Thematic stories were very brief, almost entirely factual, had little indication of feeling or story development, and often had indefinite or undetermined outcomes. There was a pervasive sense of environmental pressure in which the hero was more often overcome by disaster than able to deal with it constructively. The bleakness came out repeatedly in unadorned stories of human misery; parents were harsh and lacking in understanding; parents argued, were ill, or died; somebody was ill or beaten. Only on the blank card in which his story was entirely determined by his own imagination was he able to come up with a happier scene. "Well, I see a picture of trees and hills, and it is autumn and the leaves are brown. There is a small stream running through here and a squirrel jumping. And here's a boy out hunting squirrels. . . .He feels like he is free; he is having a lot of fun. He is all excited. . . .[The examiner interposed a question about the outcome.] Bad for the squirrel and good for the boy."

Thus, we saw in this session a youth who apparently felt squashed by an environment he often perceived as harsh and unrewarding, and which had in some respects diminished his ambition and his pleasure in intellectual pursuit. Yet he found pleasure in nature, and he showed parallel capacities to experience quite vividly at times and to express his percepts in a differentiated fashion when he chose to do so.

About his aspirations Floyd was somewhat vague, saying that he would, of course, finish high school and he might join the navy if he were drafted. Unlike many of these youths, Floyd was not opposed to the war in Vietnam. He believed war is necessary. "If you have to go, you have to go. Somebody has to go, you know." He did not believe that his recent decision to go to college was determined by a wish to avoid the draft. However, his face brightened as he remarked that possibly he could go to college to seek a degree in engineering. Still, he doubted that he had enough capacity to persist to reach such an idealistic goal, and realistically he was aware of the difficulties he would meet in financing such a plan.

On the other hand, when at a later date test findings were shown and objectively explained to him, he became increasingly involved, direct, and alert. He listened with increasing interest to alternate suggestions made to him about scholarships and educational and work opportunities he might pursue. Defeat and disinterest dropped away. He looked distinctly more alive; he sat erect; he spoke more forcefully. He readily admitted his own part in his poor grades. He made it clear that college was for him an improbable accomplishment but one that distinctly appealed to him. He recognized that his wishes to do creative work and to be challenged were inconsistent with the vocational choice in unskilled or skilled trades. His self-esteem seemed visibly to improve as test results, comparing him to other teenagers, proved to him his practical mindedness and decisiveness, his capacity to form and stick with convictions, his potentially high intelligence, his diversified interests and skills. On the other hand, he was not unaware of his tendency to become discouraged and depressed, of his poor study habits and slow reading, of his occasional unsystematic and unorganized approach to disliked or unrewarding tasks, and of his need to have his ambition stimulated and encouraged by continuing recognition and reassurance from important others who respect him. In fact, he regarded his girl friend, of whom he seemed to be sincerely fond, as filling this role. He said, "It helps to have somebody believe in me." Yet the prospect of leaving her if he were to join the Navy was matter-of-factly dismissed with the remark, "Well, that's her problem." Floyd's depressiveness was considerably less pervasive when he was seen 6 months later by the male psychiatrist. In retrospect, he saw his early life as "fairly happy, I guess — as happy as any childhood....I don't think it's all smooth for anybody." He went on to say that he thought he felt most unhappy "Right along the age when you first become a teenager, because you don't know what is going on." In contrast, he believed the happiest time of his life was when he acquired his first car. "It is just that it is yours and nobody can tell you what to do with it." In these remarks, we saw a fairly realistic appraisal in which bad was balanced by good, along with some selective forgetting. We also saw an appreciation of independence that was perhaps in inself an index of maturing in Floyd, who had struggled so long with intense sibling rivalry and with conflicts between wanting to grow up and wanting to remain dependent. Furthermore, it seemed a positive indication of growth that he was then able to take some personal responsibility for his life and to recognize the support he had received from his family. "Well, definitely my parents helped me, but basically, it's got to be in you to want to, 'cause if you don't want to, you can't."

Reminded of his earlier pessimism and depressive outlook, Floyd said he did not remember, although he thought things in general were better now. This included his grades and the fact that he felt more sure that his parents loved and trusted him. He explained that he had felt unloved and misunderstood, but that these feelings were now in the past. "It is a bunch of bunk. . . .You just get tired of not getting along with your parents all the time, so you decide you are going to get along with them and you do. . . .You can see their point, and how they want you to *do something*, and *be somebody*, and *come out right*." He went on to say that he really enjoyed his large family and many siblings: "I used to think they were a bunch of brats. They are okay now. . . .I wouldn't want it any other way really 'cause it was more fun to be there." Hence, he no longer wanted to stay out late and was less secretive about his activities. He also voluntarily cut his long shaggy hair because "they [parents] complained about it. . . .It was always getting in your way. . . .It was hard to keep combed and clean. . . .It was basically rebellion, I guess, against the older people, but I was curious about how long it would grow. . . .I went and looked in the mirror one day and decided I didn't like the way I looked, so I cut my hair." Aware both of parental objection and of his probable reasons for wearing his hair long, he decided to cut it primarily because he found long hair unattractive for him [but not necessarily for others] and inconvenient to care for. He also hinted that since it was time to be more responsible and manly, he needed to rid himself as much as possible of his curly hair, which he regarded as effeminate.

By his late adolescence, Floyd had learned to appreciate some things about his father, but he also resented some aspects of both parents' behavior. For instance, he found his mother's standards inflexible and often inwardly seethed over what he considered excessive nagging. He enjoyed working with his father on cars and saw him as skillful, and patiently teaching Floyd techniques of automotive repair. Floyd made it clear that no compulsion was involved: "I didn't have to help him." But as always, he was realistic in reporting that the relationship was not always everything he wanted. He thought his parents were unwilling to see his side of things and were incapable of learning new ways of doing things. He explained that he avoided open expression of anger by driving into the country where he could be alone. "You can sit there and be talking about a way to do something, and they don't listen to you even if it is an easier way. They go ahead and do it the hard way, so it makes you mad and you just get up and leave."

Floyd indicated, too, that he preferred his father to his mother. He said, "I think it is 'cause I know him better. I just get along with him better than I do my mom. . . .Oh, she is griping all the time. . . .Aren't all women angry all the time?. . . .Always nagging about something. . . .She is critical of everybody. . . .Most women are critical of their husbands. . . .Well, when I was small, I guess I thought she was pushing him around too much. . . .There is nothing he can do about it really. . . .Oh, he could of, but that [hitting or verbally castigating her] would have made a bad impression on all of the kids. . . .I always thought he did pretty well considering. . . .'Cause most women are nagging about everything. That is just the way women are." Thus, he tended to see his father as long suffering, yet he saw no other way; it is not suitable for husbands to hit or yell at their wives; it would not be good for children. In the long run, Floyd seemed to think it is better to hold one's temper, to avoid arguments and fights, and to accept stoically what cannot be changed.

Floyd's perception of his parents' relationship as sometimes stormy but on the whole comfortable and supportive led him to feel that marriage and a family are desirable. He reasoned that, "It is just inevitable that you will probably get married. . . .You don't have to, but really you kind of want to 'cause who wants to spend all their life with just themself. You want to have somebody to have fun with and to share things with." However, he no longer intended to compete with his father by having 15 children, as he had expansively told us he wanted when he was a child. Now, 4 would be enough.

He felt he would raise his children much the same way he had been raised. "I think my parents have done a pretty good job. . . .In some areas, I would be more strict, like — I don't know. I think right now they probably give my younger brothers and sisters too much freedom. In other areas, I would be a little more loose than they were. . . .like they used to make me dress the way they wanted me to, and I think they should be able to dress like they want to. . . .Baggy pants and stuff like that. . . .I think it is important to conform with your group because if you dress different, everybody is going to think you are an outcast or something....Between what everybody else is wearing now you have a pretty wide choice. You are influenced by the style they are wearing now, of course. You try to pick something in that range that you like." In other words, Floyd thought his parents might have compromised about dress, but he believed consistent firm discipline was appropriate. Interestingly enough, he objected to what he saw as greater leniency with his younger siblings, perhaps also implying that his parents had been too strict, or at least more strict, with him![4]

Floyd liked girls as people to go out with and sometimes to "kiss every once in a while....make out, but we don't do it all the time." He set definite limits as to how far he thought heterosexual relationships should go. He explained, "I don't believe in premarital sex; I think it should be after marriage....I think it is pretty much their own business, but I don't think it is right." Characteristically, he set limits for himself, but he did not reject others because of their sexual behavior, nor did he feel that girls who become pregnant before marriage should be punished. He felt abortion might be acceptable in cases of rape, "But if you just had abortions whenever you wanted them, that would encourage prostitution and that wouldn't be right." He believed further that marriage should not be forced because of pregnancy; the choice should be determined by mutual consent of the couple, not by parents, and only if the boy were financially able to support a family.

Floyd had learned about sex from friends, but he believed children should be given sex information in their junior high school years, possibly by a gym instructor, or earlier by the parents if they wished. On the other hand, he believed sex information would probably be best received and most accurately conveyed to groups of boys or girls in school. "It is basically in the person himself. If he is going to go out and have sexual intercourse and all this, then he is going to do it whether you tell him or not....It seems like when they [the parents] tell them, they try to talk over their heads, you know what I mean, and they don't come right down and tell them it is wrong and all this. They try to show them why it is wrong and what the aftereffects are, but they should just come right out and be frank with them....They should approach them more as adults and not as inferior kids....They talk down to them and not on their level." Floyd valued honesty, frankness, and a realistic approach in giving sex information, at a level understandable to children, and without the needless apprehension that knowledge in itself might encourage premarital sexual behavior.

Floyd had definite opinions about smoking and drinking. For instance, he chose not to smoke after discovering that several members of his family had cancer. "I just don't like the odds of smoking 'cause cancer tends to run in our family. . . .Everybody has tried it, I think, but I just didn't like it. I couldn't see any sense in it. . . .Most of the guys I run around with — they don't care either way. If you do, that's your business. If you don't, that's your business. . . .My girl friend used to smoke. . . .She just wanted to try it, I think." He went on to say that his girl friend quit smoking with his encouragement. In this instance, he set his own standards, tolerated different standards of others, but expressed concern and made some effort to modify behavior in someone he cared for.

In regard to drinking, he said, "Oh, I don't drink that much. I just do it every once in a while. . . .I don't like beer; it is nasty. . . .It tastes good, some of it. What doesn't taste good, I don't drink. . . .cherry vodka or something that tastes good. Lime vodka — it tastes pretty good. . . .I am just not that much interested in drinking. Lots of kids are, but they just do it 'cause everybody else is doing it. . . .I just sit around and watch everybody get drunk. . . .I usually wind off dragging everybody to the car and take them home. I'll get some coffee and sober them up. . . .If they are old enough to want it, they are old enough to know how to get it. . . .They say the only reason they are drinking is because it is forbidden. . . .If my parents knew, there would be some hell raised." Here, too, we saw Floyd making his own decisions without depending on his parents' viewpoint. He tolerated and helped those who differed from him.

About his religious viewpoints, Floyd was somewhat less definite. On the one hand, he still regularly went to church, although he was no longer forced to. He believed, too, that religious viewpoints sometimes deterred him from doing things, such as stealing. He admitted that he had taken tires from gas stations when he was younger, but he had stopped, despite never having been apprehended or punished, because this behavior "stung" his conscience. "I just decided not to do it anymore and I don't do it." He thought he drank less than some teenagers because of religious prohibitions. He explained, "Well, first the idea was forced upon me. I didn't like it too much, but after a while it gets to making sense. It is for your own good." He expected to send his children to church, at least until they were old enough to make their own decisions.

On the other hand, he had mild doubts about the meaningfulness of religion, more serious doubts about the absolute truth of some articles of faith, and he totally rejected some restrictive aspects of his family's religious beliefs. He doubted the existence of God, tentatively proposing that evolutionary theories of creation "make more sense than the Bible story does — well, I don't know. . . .I can't make up my mind what to believe — half of it is true and half of it isn't. . . .Some of this science is hogwash. . . .Like atoms. You know, things made up of atoms — that is kind of hard to believe because if everything is made up of atoms, and they can't see them, how do they know they are there? You still can't prove it because you can't see it. . . .There is no real proof for anything." In a similar way, he questioned the existence of a devil, of life after death, of the resurrection, and of the virgin birth. Still, he advanced the notion that "This Jesus might have come from an advanced race or something," and the Virgin Mary might have been "some kind of space woman." He felt that he still had to make up his own mind. "You got to take it all in and then get your own opinion."

He was clearer about his feelings in regard to racial matters and civil rights. He pointed out that he had grown up in an integrated neighborhood, and said, "I can't see that they are any different from anybody else." He had some Negro friends whom he felt were fully accepted in his peer group. He felt everyone should have equal opportunities and did not object to living near minority families, but he drew the line at intermarriage. "That [intermarriage] gets to me. . . .I can't see all of this race and religion stuff. They are people, and it is their own belief and that is what they are, and you can't change it, and so you might as well try to get along with them. All this racial strife and religious strife, it is for the birds. People got to get along together. It is not helping anything. . . .It is just my own opinion. All of these riots and things — people are just bound to get sick of it after a while. . . .A lot of people just go out there to see what a riot is, and they get involved in it 'cause they want to see what is going on. Myself, I would like to see one. . . .I did once. . . .I didn't participate. I just watched." Again, we saw an example of a self-made and selective decision; Floyd was tolerant and approved of racial equality in education, jobs, and housing, but not of intermarriage or of rioting. As in many situations, he cautiously watched the riot; he did not get personally involved.

Looking into his background and early experiences, we found

some facts consistent with his coping style as an adolescent, as well as some other facts that might explain the variability we saw in him.

As a 12-week-old infant, Floyd's sensory thresholds were considered to be unusually low; hence, he was subjected to both extremely pleasurable and displeasurable experiences. An avid feeder and usually a sound sleeper, he was totally absorbed in whatever he was doing. Hence, he was sometimes disturbed, when eating or sleeping, by sounds and changes in illumination, even those which at other times were apparently experienced as pleasant. In the same way, he was sometimes seen to be startled by his father's footsteps or voice if he had been unprepared for them. The infancy observers felt that his usually alert vigilance was at these times relaxed, and that therefore he was particularly disturbed when taken unaware.

A healthy, contented baby with few illnesses, he had usually stable autonomic functioning and smooth vegetative functioning. Highly responsive to people, he elicited a good deal of attention and positive recognition. However, he was sometimes quite inattentive to objects unless he was interested in bright colors or attractive sounds. Thus, he was both highly sensitive and remarkably stable in bodily functions.

An active, alert baby, he had advanced motor development and varied patterns of vocalization. He was able to comfort himself by sucking when tired or frustrated, and at the same time able to reject foods or objects which he disliked. With a helping mother who was unusually relaxed, soothing, shielding, and protective, he appeared to be developing comfortably at an advanced rate.

In his preschool years, Floyd was a vigorous, sturdy child who easily made contacts with strangers. Motorically agile, he moved with considerable grace and economy of effort. Although he verbalized a good deal of aggressiveness, he was unusually gentle in manipulating objects. He seemed totally delighted with fantasy and enjoyed embellishing reality. Very bright and quick to understand, he dealt with structured tests in a uniformly superior way, but he nearly always surveyed a situation carefully before acting. He was a much loved and admired child and seemed totally confident, yet he had developed a touch of stoicism in appreciating that material possessions were hard to come by in his poor family.

In the latency years, he was comfortably compliant at most times and still quite free to interrupt or modify situations. Despite his generally excellent motor skills, Floyd's writing was markedly sloppy and he sometimes struggled with such ordinary tasks as unlocking a door.

Sometimes his hands, which were even then quite large for the rest of his body, appeared to be ineffective for ordinary manipulations.

For a child of his ability, his reading skill was poor, even though he liked to read and was interested in current events and world affairs and discussed some scientific developments eagerly with amazing accuracy for a boy of his age. On the other hand, he did not push himself to perform if he was disinterested. His ambition definitely lagged behind his capacity, and there were signs that he felt pressed by decreasing maternal time and attention as the family increased each year.

When we saw him again in his prepuberty years, he was still obviously alert and intelligent, but more restrained in verbal communication and less ebullient. He often made superficial efforts on our tests and was less inclined to press himself for clarity about our demands or in his own presentations. He was also distinctly less interested in fantasy and inclined to avoid feelings or contacts with women. He was absolutely certain of only one thing — that harsh punishment follows too free expression of impulses. He then saw both parents as almost always angry or irritated. One sensed that he felt himself in a bind insofar as he had isolated himself from closeness with his mother in reaction to her diminished time with him, and he was not yet able to identify with a father he regarded as too passive and in some ways, at least as a provider, inadequate. Floyd appeared to be moody, discouraged, and unable to use his good intellectual resources efficiently.

Over the years, then, we saw a sensitive youngster who was especially reactive to changes in his environment and highly dependent on recognition and reassurance. As the family grew and parental attention was by necessity divided among many children, he soured on the world to a considerable degree. However, his consistent tendency to evaluate a situation — to watch from the sidelines, getting involved only when he wished — contributed to a functional coping style, to modest achievements and to some informal leadership roles with peers.

As he matured during his adolescence, Floyd became more independent of his parents; he looked for and found support in a variety of peer relationships that gave him some reassurance that he was loved, even by his parents.

He was then able to form opinions about many subjects, and his standards, although often quite similar to those of his parents, were adopted after considerable thought. His decisions were based on the facts as he saw them, but he was cautious in becoming involved in controversial issues. Often he chose to watch tolerantly but with reservations about how much he wished to participate actively. He was not opposed to change, but he did not change his views simply for the sake of change. He accepted peers as they were, seeing their behavior as their own business. He was realistic, sometimes stoical, but he was at times quite capable of enjoying through his senses or of turning to fantasy. He enjoyed a fairly full life, was perceptually alert and thoughtful in decision making, and had a wide variety of interests spanning athletic, artistic, scientific, and mechanical areas. For these reasons, we saw him as a cautious modifier.

Notes:

[1] In this chapter, we have given three examples of the coping style of the cautious modifier, partly because approximately half of our subjects chose this stance, and partly because we wanted to illustrate the range of behavior demonstrated by this group.

[2] In his childhood, repeated ear infections, myopia, structural anomalies in one eye, and the possibility of some mild aphasic problems were distinctly handicapping.

[3] The reader will notice that this quality of seeing for one's self was expressed to some degree by all cautious modifiers. In this, they differed from the obedient traditionalists who relied totally on parental viewpoints, and from the ideological conservatives who pushed themselves to conform to or surpass parental models. At the same time, the cautious modifiers differed from the passionate renewers in being less immersed in personal perception and in setting definite limits as to how far they proposed to act upon their new insights. They were more aware of risks and less willing than the passionate renewers to take chances that could interfere with traditional security and stability. They were like their parents in adopting values of hard work and responsibility. Hence, they questioned established institutions, but they were generally not inclined to be personally involved in changing or modifying what they saw as inappropriate, unfair, or wrong in our culture.

[4] The cautious modifiers felt free to talk with their parents, to discuss and sometimes to argue with them about ideas and issues. They then used parents' perceptions selectively to make up their own minds. The passionate renewers tended to avoid open discussion with parents, yet they were distinctly aware of parental viewpoints. They experienced more vividly, they expressed themselves with more intensity, and insisted on being their own masters. Thus, they avoided open conflict and coolly moved behaviorally farther from parental standards.

[5] This is another example of the coping style of the cautious modifiers. Whereas ideological conservatives did not question religious training or practices and continued to participate in formal religious activities, the cautious modifiers raised some questions, but often continued to attend church and to practice the religious habits they had been taught. In contrast, the passionate renewers questioned more seriously and had either already given up participating in formal religion or proposed to do so once they left home. They also believed they would not raise their children in the church, in contrast to all of the censors, who planned to follow parental example in relation to religious

practices, and to the cautious modifiers who despite some questions planned to provide religious instruction for their children.

⁶Victor's parents, particularly his father, were very outspoken and definite in their disapproval of integration and protest. Victor chose to make decisions about minority groups on an individual basis. He recognized his prejudices and was beginning to question their validity.

⁷Having moved away from Topeka, these pressures were maximized when we saw him in his high school years. His empathic warmth toward others was characteristic of all the cautious modifiers and differentiated them from the obedient traditionalists and the ideological conservatives who were less humanistic. It also differentiated them from the passionate renewers, who although concerned about the welfare of mankind, were more self-absorbed and less interested in permanent or long-term commitment to others.

⁸The reader will note the quality of difference between Harriet's and Faith's stated reasons for going into teaching. Whereas Harriet lacked personal commitment to a chosen profession and was vague about why she wanted to be a teacher, Faith clearly saw her chosen profession as an opportunity to help people.

⁹Like Victor and the other cautious modifiers, she discussed her problems and questions with her parents. Faith did this in highly idiosyncratic ways, incorporating the religious values of her parents as she modified them in personal and creative ways.

¹⁰The militancy with which she stated her position on religious issues was perhaps more characteristic of the ideological conservatives, but unlike these youths, Faith hoped personally to modify peer behavior, even of those not generally acceptable to the more class-conscious traditionalists.

¹¹Faith developed considerably more tolerance for divergent viewpoints after she found new social outlets in her prepuberty years. She differed from the ideological conservatives who are absolutely sure of the total rightness of their own viewpoints for all people. Faith was sure of the correctness of the views for herself and of their probable support to others, but she did not totally condemn others as inferior because of their differing viewpoints. She was more aware of social and temperamental determinants of behavior, over which she realized individuals had little personal control.

¹²Unlike Calvin, she was not overwhelmed by stimulation and always showed good capacity to regulate the intensity of her responsiveness. If she felt overstimulated, she was quite able to turn away and to comfort herself by nonnutritive sucking.

¹³As a preschooler, Floyd had impressed and charmed all of our staff by his vividly told, tongue-in-cheek tall tales. An accurate observer, he frequently exaggerated visual and auditory stimulation, simulating horror, and then laughing mischievously.

¹⁴In an earlier interview his mother had agreed with his assessment. Having been an active, alert baby, a negativistic, stubborn preschooler, and a somewhat elusive and underhanded latency-age child with mild delinquent tendencies, he had been punished more than his siblings. Empathically, his mother excused this behavior on the basis that his curious mind led him to try new and not always appropriate or socially approved ways of doing things.

Chapter 8

The Passionate Renewers

With marked perceptiveness and a strong urgency to explore the nuances and subtleties of every phase of their environment, the passionate renewers live dramatically and intensely, with relatively little concern for personal risks or social acceptability. They seek and savor sensory experience of all kinds, enjoying the rewards of richness of perceptual detail, originality in self-expression, and wide-ranging areas of interest. Curious to the point of insistence, these youths probe new ideas with considerable depth of feeling in their search for clarity and intellectual honesty. Hence, they are at times passionately enthusiastic and determined in pursuing an immediate topic of interest, quite willing to give free rein to their imagination, act boldly upon their intuitions, and question established tradition irreverently. With these behavioral patterns, they can at times be quite confident of themselves. At the same time, the intensity with which they experience is demanding, sometimes frustrating and conflict-laden, and frequently disappointing – especially if peers and parents do not share their perceptual style. Then their confidence can fade and a high degree of self-doubt appear.

Perhaps for their own protection from the vulnerabilities their sensitivity imposes, these youths are also observed to prefer a light touch, sometimes avoiding seriousness, prolonging childish pleasures, and delaying total commitment to things and people. Thus, they appear to be enormously tolerant of and deeply humanistically concerned for others, but not always close or desirous of long-term relationships. As Clinton succinctly said when considering the difficulties of interpersonal relationships, "Since you can't cope with it, you kind of walk softly across it."

Passionate renewers need and value personal privacy; demand opportunity for change; and stoutly defend their right to rise to or sluff off challenge, to be mature or immature. Most of all, they insist on freedom to make their own choices, set their own goals, lay out their own timetables. In their eyes, independence, individuality, and personal dignity are prerequisites for growth for themselves and should, according to our best democratic traditions, be granted to all people.

In this stance, the passionate renewers although in no sense alienated from their parents or irresponsible in satisfying parental demands, seek to formulate their own value systems and standards of behavior. To do this, they often avoid direct confrontation, particularly on topics that might lead to prohibitions. For instance, Otto, a bright youngster who was planning to do graduate work in a field similar to that of his father, persuaded his parents to allow him to live apart from the family in his own apartment. He remarked, "I just didn't like being dependent. I was financially independent anyway [from a part-time job], but I wanted to do things for myself and make my own judgments. I didn't want to have parents around to direct me and tell me that it was now 12 o'clock, so I should turn out the lights and go to bed."

More ambivalently and with considerable sadness but no less determination, Viola also moved away from home. She did this to ease long-standing conflicts between herself and her father, whom she experienced as unduly punitive and restrictive. "Here I am a 17-year-old little girl popping out of the house. . . .There will be nobody to look after me but me. . . .My mother said that I was always the type that wanted to be independent. I always did think for myself, and they knew I could always do it. . . .I never was the type that wanted people telling me what to do." Significantly, both she[1] and Otto set their own restrictions as to hours and activities they permitted in their apartments, and both regularly communicated with their parents.

Others, although not physically separating themselves from their families, achieved the independence they wanted by confiding selectively only what they thought their parents could or would tolerate. Shirley, who efficiently raised animals and participated in a variety of service activities in the community, enjoyed discussing political and social issues with her father but stayed clear of more personal topics. She said, "I couldn't hold anybody in the world in higher esteem or in higher respect than my dad. . . .We will sit there and yell sometimes, but my dad is a person and I can't really talk to him about everything. . . .I told him to admit that he just didn't want me to believe any different than he does, and he said that was right. . . .I guess I have become a little bit more liberal than he, but we agree on politics and pretty much on religion. . . .I don't want to be just my father's daughter. I just want to be me. I want to do things on my own." Elaine, a girl who had resiliently dealt with some major family stresses and had become a supportive figure to her mother, more openly confided in her parents about dates and personal behavior. However, she, too, valued and demanded a right to think for herself. She remarked critically of some of her peers, "They really didn't have a mind of their own, and I think I did more than a lot of them. . . .I suppose I had learned through my family, or through thinking, to think a lot." Valuing her father's fairness, his practical assessment of situations, and his fun-loving nature, she believed he had taught her to make her own judgments by asking her to assess the reasons for her behavior.

As Elaine suggested, the passionate renewers' urgency for individuality comes out clearly in peer relationships insofar as they seek a wide variety of associations but become deeply involved[2] only to the extent and for the time they wish. It is important to them to tolerate but not necessarily to emulate the behavior of others. In them one senses always a certain reserve, arising partly from a need to avoid the rebuffs they had already experienced in the past. For example, Clinton, after being rejected by a girl friend, said, "I was afraid to get emotionally involved because I didn't want to stick my neck out and get it chopped off again. . . .My involvements with girls were more likely to be good friends with them." He pointed out, too, that some distance from male associates is desirable because a customary realistic understanding of both faults and assets sets limits to closeness. "He and I know each other forwards and backwards. If you ever wanted to get into a personal argument, you would really be set because you know each other's idiosyncrasies — how much you like and don't like, and how much you can take of what. . . .We don't cross each other. . . .We are so close in some things that when we differ it's more noticeable to us. . . .When you get to know them that well, you have the feeling that you can reveal yourself only so much." Possibly because the relationships they develop are so deeply personal and so free of pretense of any kind, they have few close friends and even with these they are protective of their privacy. Furthermore, they are clear that their values and personal philosophies are in a state of flux; hence, they resist being pigeonholed or labeled. In this regard, Edith said, "I always change. My thoughts are always changing and what I am expressing to you about my feelings on anything right now are just me now."

With these feelings, the passionate renewers prefer to delay commitment. Thus, they infrequently join clubs, put off dating or going steady at least until the senior year of high school, and seldom anticipate marriage until their late 20s.

Generally enjoying and effectively managing their lives, yet at times disappointed in people and in the ineffectiveness of some adult institutions, the passionate renewers are quite able to engage in and relish childish behavior. For example, Clinton described his pleasure in a summer job in which he did not "have to be productive" or well dressed. He remarked, "I don't look so terrible, but I sort of enjoy being able to." For Dora, this meant being free to climb trees or to ride her horse into a pond. For Irving, it meant occasionally "goofing-off" on a dull job or playing tricks on associates; "It was so dull there. It was more fun to do something wrong. I think that's one of the main reasons why people do things that are wrong — just for the excitement of it. We didn't do anything malicious, like stealing — just kid pranks."

These viewpoints are reflected in their feelings about school, which they generally accept as a part of their preparation for adulthood but do not regard as particularly meaningful or exciting or as contributing to their value systems. For example, Clinton was attracted to a profession in the behavioral sciences, but he had not decided on a college major and did not strive for excellent grades. For now, he preferred to "goof around. I don't know that I can do *A* work either. . . .The sort of things I had in high school just weren't the sort of things that touched my imagination. I have a few courses that inspire me, but there are so many where the teachers just dish out the course and that's it. The grades weren't that important for me." Matthew, who excelled in math, agreed: "There are some classes I just sit in and couldn't care less. When I get bad grades, it is usually because I don't like the class. I hate those teachers who just tell you stuff. I kind of like the discussion more." Shirley, an equally capable student and one with many interests, made similar comments, "I never get inspired in a classroom. . . .There are so many things to explore — and I feel like the last 6 years have been pretty much of a waste. . . .I memorized what we had to know for the tests, and then it was forgotten. . . .It's really weird, because I feel I'm getting dumber rather than smarter. . . .I prefer teachers who really make you think, and really make you work. . . .But as it is, I really don't care if I make my grades. I'm just having a good time." In all of these comments from thoughtful, able youth, we see a thread of disappointment, resulting in diminished efforts to do well academically. Quite clearly, these youths who so urgently demand freedom to "do their own thing" are equally demanding of guidance and excellent instruction from adults.

In the passionate renewers' feelings about religion, we find further documentation of their directness and honesty, along with their pleas for consistency, flexibility, and meaningful application of values. Whereas beliefs vary from frank atheism to minor criticisms of religious practices, all decry pretentiousness, lack of openness, and the lack of relevance to their immediate lives. Clinton explained, "I am very much against demoninations of churches. . . .I believe in God, yes, but that's about where it ends. . . .I finally told my parents that I couldn't hack it anymore, that I had gone through going to church and Sunday school every Sunday all these years. I wanted to be free because I was old enough to join the church, but I wasn't old enough not to join the church. . . .The more open churches get, the more I can approve of them. It's the pettiness that I can't go for. . . .I can accept anybody's religion. That's their right. . . .I believe in God and I have my own values; consequently, that's really all I need. I try to get all the advantages of religion without the disadvantages, and I can do that without a church."

Dora went further in questioning both the existence of God and the value of religion to her. She said, "Sometimes, I just kind of doubt it. I just don't really know what to think about it. I belong to the church, but I just don't feel that it helps me much. . . .How do people know there is a God?. . . .I just don't understand it sometimes, because it just doesn't make that much sense. . . .I am usually forced to go. . . .I kind of doubt that I will go after I leave home."

Lester particularly resented inconsistencies and rigidity in his religious training. "All the stories of saints and all the stuff was wrong, and a lot of us kids then didn't know what to believe. . . .I think I was a little bit skeptical because some of that stuff they teach is outlandish." He professed to believe in God and continued to go to church because his parents urged him to do so, but he felt organized religion had little personal meaning for him. He thought many of his peers shared his doubts. "I don't believe in organized religion because I don't think organized religion has that much to offer to a person....Through all the years of Catholic teaching, I guess you would call it brainwashing, they've taught you that if you ever quit the Catholic church you can never go to heaven because that was the only way to salvation and all that kind of stuff. They taught us that heaven was a place and hell was a place....It's kind of sickening really all this stuff that they taught that really isn't true....I don't see any good in it because I think the only way a person is going to get rid of his sins is to be sorry himself, and I don't think any priest can forgive them for you. I have just about come to the conclusion that I don't believe that Christ was actually God. I think he was probably one of the greatest men that ever lived, but I'm not quite sure I actually believe that he was God....I think heaven isn't really a place but the state of being. I think it is the fulfillment of yourself and the attainment of all of your values....The first thing I started questioning was the Bible because everything in the Bible was said to be true. I couldn't see it because when I was about in the sixth grade we had science and things like this, and they taught that the world had evolved over billions of years, and so I applied this to the Bible and I couldn't quite believe it."

Elaine, who described herself as fairly religious and as one who had found her religion supportive at times of stress, believed that her strengths were not "so much in the church as in myself....Our church wasn't terribly stable, so this kind of shook me on the church a bit and made me wonder if there is really a need for churches so long as you got religion anyway....But you need something firm under you and religion helps."

The tolerance and quest for individuality in these youths are illustrated by their views and practices in regard to smoking, drinking, and the use of drugs. Clinton might have been a spokesman for the group as he said of drinking, "I don't disapprove of drinking....The only reason I don't is because I don't feel a need for it, but I don't have any moral reason for it....I refuse to yield to social pressure....I try to judge for myself." He applied the same reasoning to smoking and the use of drugs.

Elaine added that her moderate drinking habits were a part of her standards of being a lady. For others, "It's their business, if they are old enough, if they are not just doing it to show off."

Celeste quit drinking because "I decided it wasn't worth it. I didn't need it. I decided that beer and liquor were too messy: they make you feel bad and you can't walk straight and stuff. I thought marijuana was a lot better. Then I decided I didn't need it either."

Edith, who told us, "I want to try everything once. . . .To do everything and see everything and be everything," tried smoking and gave it up; tried drinking and quit; tried pot and continued to use it moderately as a relaxing and enjoyable perceptual experience. She set limits on using other drugs because she did not "want to become a slave to anything."[3]

None of these youths rejected others who engaged in these habits, seeing them as individual choices and no basis for endorsing or rejecting a friendship. Shirley remarked, "There are very few people who don't drink. I don't think drinking is wrong, but getting drunk is degrading to a human being because it makes you less of a person. . . .I don't smoke, but I don't mind if anybody else does. . . .I feel that marijuana used wisely is an experience. . . .I have friends from all different groups — some from the intellect group and some from the far-out group. . . .What is important is to be completely honest. . . .You need to know all aspects of their lives, from how they feel about red tennis shoes to whether or not they believe in God."

They view premarital sex tolerantly, as behavior that is normal but perhaps unwise, at least in the high school years; as behavior that is wrong only if it is not a part of a close relationship. Matthew's views were similar to those of most of the passionate renewers: "I don't think it is really too wise, but. . . .I wouldn't look down on them because everybody thinks about it, and some of them do it. They can still be good kids." Clinton made the additional point that most teenagers can be more open about sex than their parents, and consequently they are less hung up about it. "I think in general that kids are all for premarital sex and it doesn't matter one way or the other. They are not strictly for it, but they aren't fundamentalists that think it is terrible and that a person will never see heaven and all that stuff. I think in general there is mild attitude toward it. Kids are either mildly for it, or mildly against it." Shirley expressed a similar viewpoint in saying, "I don't condemn them. I know some of my friends who have and I don't tell them they are terrible and a sinner. Norms have changed, and it isn't as important anymore."

In the event of premarital pregnancy, the passionate renewers are predictably tolerant, seeing no reason for punishment. They are united in urging that each case merits individual consideration, depending on how the two people feel about each other and the welfare of the unborn child. They strongly reject forced marriages and tend to prefer adoption. Some approve of abortion.

The passionate renewers are interested in people, quite often express a desire to help the poor, deprived, or disadvantaged, and extend similar solicitude toward anyone in trouble. They seek intellectual understanding of why people behave and feel as they do, and consequently they refrain from condemning those whose behavior runs counter to accepted social standards. One girl, for example, without the knowledge of her parents who she believed would have disapproved, contributed money from her allowance to help a friend obtain an abortion. Another volunteered in a drop-in center for Indian students and helped set up a recreational center for blacks in a nearby city.

Realizing that human beings make mistakes, they value tolerance, but at the same time they are able to criticize both themselves and others. In fact, they are so aware of human imperfections that they tend to devalue romantic ties on the realistic basis that people do not always live up to expectations, or that they may change.

Seeing their parents as generally open and perhaps more liberal in their views on civil rights than the community at large, they are aware that parents are not entirely free of prejudice. They claim that they are less prejudiced than their parents, but they admit with typical analytic honesty that they, too, although they espouse democratic principles of equal opportunity for minority groups, ordinarily draw the line at interracial dating and marriage, at least for themselves. Attempting to understand their own feelings, they explained that prejudice is deeply rooted in human behavior, that it is based partly on fear of those who are different, and that in the end racial problems are to be solved only by cooperative efforts and some compromises on the part of both races. To do this, one must learn to know individuals, not just accept a generalized group stereotype. In this vein, Shirley said, "I have to admit that I am getting a little bit prejudiced against Negroes as a race. . . .Violence is no way to get anything. . . .This feeling of you owe us everything — I don't agree with. . . .You don't want to be prejudiced but I am scared of them in a group. . . .I have several Negro friends. . . .but we don't really mix that much. . . .At social affairs, the Negroes are dancing over there and the whites are dancing over here. There is not discrimination; it's just by our own choice. Whites date white and blacks date black. . . .At our school, a Negro boy is dating a real nice white girl and this is a big gossip thing. This kind of thing doesn't bother me. I feel that it is her life. When you look at them as two people, which is how you should look at any person, they are very well matched. They have very much the same beliefs, same ideals, same interests. . . .They might get married. It's up to her. It's nobody else's business but hers."

Here, as in all of their views, the passionate renewers try to look honestly at the facts as they are aware of them. By preference, they are tolerant and choose to assess each person individually.

Looking ahead in their own lives, they, like Edith, plan to savor as much of life as possible. They hope to travel, to meet different people, to explore a wide range of interests, to experience broadly. Many appear to be attracted to danger, such as parachute jumping, scuba diving, motorcycle riding, drug experimentation. They love the beauties of nature, creative arts, or unusual facts and characteristics of almost any subject from mushroom hunting to atomic physics. Whatever they choose to explore, they follow with zest and infinite capacity for detail, but not necessarily with great orderliness. Not surprisingly, their grades are less important to them than the learning — if it is stimulating.

Compared with their peers, they have less urgency than the obedient traditionalists for social status, less urgency for academic and vocational advancement or material rewards than the ideological conservatives, and are less cautious about outcomes of their behavior or thinking than the cautious modifiers. In this sense, they are freer to explore for themselves and to act on their own insights. They are more willing to defer judgments and to leave plans for the future somewhat indefinite. Temperamentally inclined toward contemplation and introspection, they enjoy an intellectual depth of thinking and feeling. At the same time, the range of experiences to which they expose themselves also creates problems and conflicts, with associated fluctuations in emotional functioning, especially in levels of self-confidence.

In the psychological tests, the passionate renewers are likely to be verbally articulate, obviously enjoying play with words, ideas, and feelings. They demonstrate a broad range of general knowledge in the arts and sciences and are attracted to abstract thinking. Although they can often recall many details of their early lives, they are relatively poor in rote memory tasks. They perform adequately on motor tasks but are generally less outstanding here than in verbal areas, partly because they tend to resist or be indifferent to time limits.

In projective tests, they are usually quite productive and analytical and seek to integrate the many details to which they respond in well-integrated whole answers. Quite often, they use intuitions and hunches, particularly if these lead to unusual or dramatic outcomes. Self-reliant and independent, they set idealistically high goals but often defer their pursuit to explore tangential interests. They are capable of self-organization to achieve a goal but do not value routines or schedules highly. They freely reverse figure and ground, suggesting a capacity for critical appraisal and discontent with conforming for the sake of conforming. Generally open in experiencing and reporting a wide range of feelings, they are likely to be enthusiastic and confident at times, pessimistic and insecure at other times. Highly individualistic, they seek and respect individuality in others. They are realistically aware of strengths and weaknesses in others, so they are tolerant and friendly but are disinclined to expect or desire long-term commitments.

Contributing to the passionate renewers' coping style are natively high sensory sensitivity and high drive to explore and find out about people, things, and ideas. Their curiosity cuts across "typical" masculine or feminine interest areas;[4] girls are as interested in politics, social issues, and sports as boys, and boys are as interested in the arts and homemaking as the girls. Both sexes prefer a family living style in which both parents share child rearing.

It is also important to point out that the parents of these youths provided highly individualistic models, being themselves relatively open to experience in granting their children considerable freedom of choice. Fathers, although often deeply engrossed in their vocations and a variety of other interests, were generally available and very involved in child rearing. Mothers were generally skillful homemakers, even though they, too, were often involved in community or personal activities outside the home.

At the same time, most of these youths experienced some maternal deprivation as a result of illness, divorce, or death, perhaps contributing to a sense of impermanence and unsatiated dependency in the early years. These realistic losses — whether temporary or permanent — apparently contributed both to the independence these children developed and to some pessimism, reserve, and emotional distance. That they were able to emerge as vivid, dramatic individuals with a good deal of zest for living was an index of their own resilience[5] and firm parental support.

Notes:

[1]Interestingly, too, Viola's grades improved after she moved away from home. Supporting herself with a part-time job, she managed to finish high school, take some special courses preparing her for office work, and later married.

[2]The passionate renewers differ from the censors insofar as they want to know people thoroughly, but they tend to resist enduring relationships or overt symbols (engagements, rings, etc.), which suggest force or pressure, that is, having to behave in a certain way. Charismatically, they expect and demand to set the conditions and limits of any contract, formal or informal, in which they become involved. It is as though they demand to know others thoroughly, but enjoy presenting themselves with a veil of mystery. A part of them must always be private and unique, therefore incapable of being reached by others. And, to the extent that this is true, they are never entirely satisfied in their interpersonal relationships. Their demands are always insatiable.

[3]After completing college and beginning a professional career, Edith kept these views. By then, she had explored a number of ways of altering consciousness, had immersed herself in a variety of creative and artistic pursuits, and was enthusiastically planning new and original ways to follow her chosen career. She had no intention of marrying or having children. Interestingly, too, despite her enormous zest for living, she described herself as "lazy," by which she apparently meant that she had no urgency to become rich, famous or outstanding. For her, it was enough to enjoy, without having to sell others on her originality and excellence.

[4]From their earliest years, girls in this group were observed to be physically active and curious; a number were described as "tomboys." Boys in this group, although interested in sports, were not outstanding athletes. Observers, families, and the youth themselves often suggested that as youngsters they had shared the warmth, mischievousness, and intrusive explorativeness of the cartoon character, Dennis, the Menace.

[5]As a group, the passionate renewers had been able to see positive and negative aspects of any experience even from their preschool years. For example, one 3-year-old pointed out the beauty of the rainbow after the rain. In their sensitivity, they did experience both "good" and "bad" and thus expected to find both throughout their lives. These issues are discussed in detail in Murphy and Moriarty: *Development, Vulnerability and Resilience* (Yale University Press, New Haven, Conn., 1976).

Chapter 9

Evelyn: A Passionate Renewer

In speaking about her parents, Evelyn, at 18 years of age, saw no point in arguing with them because "I'm never going to make them see what I believe in. I might be able to tell them, but they are never going to understand. They have their ways and they feel that their ways are the right ways and if I don't agree with these ways, I'm just going to upset them. I know it is going to come some time because I don't agree with everything they think." She explained that she had, despite parental objections, begun going steady in the seventh grade, an activity she was able to engage in without guilt and with full personal responsibility. "If I had gotten into any kind of trouble, then I couldn't have blamed it on my parents. It would have been my fault." In the same way, she later in her high school years ignored parental advice against drinking and smoking and concealed these habits from her parents because she knew they would have been hurt had they known. Besides, she wanted to be personally responsible for any dangers to herself. By her senior year of high school, she continued to smoke, but she had voluntarily given up drinking as a waste of time and too expensive, She preferred to avoid being dependent on any sources of strength outside of herself. "It's not good to have to depend on something else, like taking drugs or taking liquor....If I am such a weak person that I must depend on liquor or drugs, or actually anything for enjoyment to live life, then I'm not a person at all. I'm just sort of a shell that runs around, and I would have to be dependent on other people. . . .In that way, it is wrong. Why should I have to cause trouble for society when they have trouble enough?"

Evelyn meant to experience life and set her own standards, freely and flexibly shifting goals or setting her own limits as she deemed it appropriate in relation to time and place. She demanded the right to enjoy experiences, to be an individual on her own terms, and even though this stance reduced closeness to her parents, she did not lose respect for them or lack understanding of their viewpoints. "My parents have taught me more than they realized. In other words, I have a sense of fair play. Sure I may lie to my parents, but I don't lie to other people. I have a sense of justice, of things that are right and wrong to me. . . .I feel that I can be happier if I make the goals for my life now and on my way to those goals just do the things that make me happy and make other people happy. I think it is a better attitude for life rather than saying, 'Why did God create this whole mess in the first place?' Try to make the mess better, and do what you can for yourself and for the people around you. Don't be so cut up with abstract things because it really doesn't help. You will go round and round in a circle all of your life. If you look at the good things around you, you'll be much happier, and why shouldn't you be happy?"

In these respects, and in others we shall illustrate, Evelyn is a good example of the passionate renewers: she questioned traditional values; felt concerns and respect for people; sought "now" experiences; spontaneously shifted values and felt free to express a wide range of feelings from positive to negative; and was accepting and tolerant of viewpoints both more conservative and more liberal than her own. During adolescence, she led a richly creative life that was foreshadowed throughout her growing years, a product of her considerable strength in dealing with her environment, and of the predominantly stable continuity of her family background and rearing. Yet growing up was not always easy for her, nor was she without pressure and conflicts or periods of depression, discouragement, doubts, and insecurity.

Characteristically, Evelyn who had by then moved out of town, had written just before her 16th birthday to ask when we might want to see her again. Her brief letter was casual, but she made it clear that she would welcome an opportunity to talk about some current difficulties, and she questioned whether she needed professional psychiatric help. In response to this request, we made her a special appointment with a woman psychiatrist who found Evelyn to be eager to talk and obviously intent on making the most of the situation to seek some solutions and direction.

Attractive, alert, personable, and appealing, Evelyn tried to involve the doctor in an intimate relationship, which was intense but gracious. Complaining that she could not discuss her problems with her peers from whom she felt isolated in certain respects, or with parents who felt her concerns were excessive, she focused on three areas: intellectual ambitions, sexual life, and religious duties. In each area, she raised serious questions, thoroughly delineating the sources of her confusion, and astutely pointing out inconsistencies in adult thinking. As always, her capacity to synthesize and evaluate was impressive.

Feeling different from her peers in her urgency to find answers to these questions, she experienced feelings both of superiority and inferiority. On the one hand, she felt contemptuous of less reflective teenagers, but on the other hand, she felt guilty about her depression and demandingness in the face of the stability and love she had received, and which she saw as greater than that available to many teenagers. Empathic toward others, she reproved herself for her dissatisfaction, and she also feared the dislike of peers who might resent her superiority. Hence, she consciously tried to avoid being too outstanding. This was apparent as she discussed her attraction to a professional career in which she would use her intelligence, but which she recognized might further isolate her from her peers, decrease her chances of becoming a wife and a mother, and set her apart from her parents, who she thought failed to understand her yearning for intellectual pursuits. To be true to herself she must achieve, yet in so doing she felt she might bypass others and arouse more jealousy and resentment. Furthermore, she saw housework and homemaking as drudgery that had robbed her mother of self-fulfillment. Combining home and career seemed impossible; that she knew professional women who had done both offered a glimmer of hope but gave her no firm confidence that she could do so.

In the same way, she argued with herself about how she could handle her sexual urges. If she pursued a career, she felt that she "should not" engage in premarital sex, but as a receptionist she had already been tempted to respond to propositions that could be advantageous and pleasant. Then again, on the negative side, she resented the degradation of "being used as a sex object." She wondered whether her concerns were unusual and sought reassurance that other teenagers shared her concerns.

Contributing to her depression and confusion were her observations of contradictions, inconsistencies, and weaknesses in parents, teachers, and ministers, who she thought failed to live up to the moral and ethical standards inherent in their religious background. She was very critical of her parents who in her eyes were unable or unwilling to look at sham and hypocrisy; for this reason, her father was totally unapproachable and her mother prone to dismiss Evelyn's questions with cliches. Especially abhorrent was her mother's avoidance of "hot issues" by suggesting that Evelyn's worries were unwarranted and could be solved by taking them to the Lord. From her fundamentalist background, Evelyn had perceived God as a stern and not particularly indulgent figure; hence, practical solutions to her problems could not be obtained through religion. These she must seek for herself as a concerned individual. In addition, she was critical of the church as a social institution, which she saw as falling short in practice of the high principles for which it stood. Human frailty in general and her own weakness, including her vanity, weighed heavily on her. She regretted the inflexibility of the small town in which she lived, but at the same time she reproached herself for the critical stance she assumed.

It was clear that Evelyn experienced intense confusion and a sense of floundering, yet in her ambitious search for clarity and truth she showed considerable psychic strength. She asked whether she was more dissatisfied and confused than most teenagers, and whether she could meet, without psychiatric help, the pressures she felt to be increasing. At that time, her good judgment and resourcefulness appeared to be assets which the psychiatrist encouraged her to use in making her own decisions and in helping her to master the conflicts she faced. This Evelyn fervently wanted and honestly tried to do.

Evelyn was next seen for our regular series of interviews and psychological tests (with the psychologist) during her senior year in high school when she was 17½ years old. She was a tall, slender girl, physically attractive in a rugged, healthy way, socially charming, verbally articulate, and in response to these challenges and demands as self-assured as she had always appeared to be. She was clearly aware of her cognitive and perceptual strengths and used them constructively to increase enjoyable experiencing and for vivid self-expression. To be an individual in all respects was a major goal; this was apparent in everything she did and said. For example, she enhanced her natural beauty by her unique choice of color and design in her clothing. She disapproved of rigid protocol by adults in relation to dress, but she also rejected the unkemptness of some of her peers. At times, she facetiously and consciously overstated her point, as when she said in describing her future home, "I don't want a house that looks like every other house on the block. . . .I might paint it orange with maroon polka dots." More often, she made considered statements out of careful introspection and a wish to be exact. She spoke dramatically for the most part, but she was not bound by formal rules of grammar. She used a vivid vocabulary, including many current slang and colloquial expressions. Dramatic, almost theatrical in the vocal range and the intense quality of her varied facial expressions, postures, and gestures, she expressed an equal range of moods and feelings, sometimes bitter and discouraged, sometimes enthusiastic and gay, but always contemplative and predominantly positive and hopeful. Her sound judgment continued to be a prominent feature of her thinking; in addition, she had clarified some of her values and apparently felt comfortable with her flexible hang-loose attitude toward others. She was able to tolerate and appreciate standards of behavior that differed from her own, demanding only that similar tolerance be granted to her.

Looking back over her earlier life, as the fourth of six children, Evelyn described her early childhood as neither entirely happy or grossly unhappy; she would not want to change it or relive it. Philosophically, she remarked that there was nothing to do but to go on since her childhood was behind her. She was glad, too, to have weathered a period of "morbidity in my junior high school years when there was no purpose for life." She added that she had kept these depressive thoughts under control by keeping herself busy with concrete activities. Then, also, time itself reduced the intensity of her anxieties, although she admitted that "finances, sex, and education" still worried her. However, at this point, these concerns seemed more realistic and less overwhelming than they had just a few years before.

She felt that her increased maturity had in large measure been fostered by solid warm relationships with her two older sisters (especially the elder) who had served as confidantes and feminine models. As maternal supplements with more softness and understanding than her somewhat old-fashioned and less emotionally available mother, her sisters helped her to appreciate more fully the strengths of her mother's affection and encouragement. In the same way, she could better appreciate the steadiness and basic warmth of her father, even though she saw him as an unbending member of an older generation. Her prepuberty concern about "the troubled adolescent" was reduced, perhaps because her older brother had by then resolved his conflicts with his parents by leaving home. In a way, her conflicts with her parents had been vicariously played out through these siblings, so that she experienced less direct or overt conflict. She avoided confrontation about differences in values by keeping her own counsel and by refraining from discussing ideas or feelings she felt would upset her parents. She quietly made her own choices without making an issue of them or drawing them to the parents' attention. Seeing this stance as somewhat dishonest, she felt guilty, but her guilt was partially relieved through the support of her sisters.

As a high school senior, Evelyn was academically and socially successful and participated in a number of group activities and some rewarding solitary experiences. For instance, she belonged to several language clubs, social service and dramatic groups, played the piano for a church group, and liked to attend high school spectator sports. She tremendously enjoyed reading, relishing the sound and meaning of words in historical novels and biographies; she described books as "overflowing" her room. She liked modern art because it was "different and doesn't follow a pattern." She set high academic standards for herself, having earned good grades and won some awards for achievement.

By choice, she preferred teachers who maintained a disciplined but flexible classroom structure that stimulated the students' curiosity and developed their capacity to think for themselves. She considered these traits marks of intelligence and valued them in herself. "I have always enjoyed my independent thinking. I don't have to rely on anybody else for an answer." Definitely planning a teaching career in the social sciences or foreign languages, she had already enrolled in a teachers' college. She was enormously pleased[2] that her responses on the Strong Vocational Interest Test validated her special interest in teaching, a profession compatible with her social service orientation and high intelligence. Yet she worried that her somewhat unorthodox convictions might conflict with the rigidity and conservatism of some school systems. By holding responsible jobs in high school, she had proved to herself that she could earn her own way through college. She chose to do this to attain a life she expected to be more personally rewarding than that her parents had achieved with more limited education. It was important to her to engage in something that would be useful to society and give her economic independence to pursue these aims.

In the structured tests, she was logical, productive, cognitively organized, and exact but always looking for new meanings. She constantly demonstrated an outstanding capacity for introspection and repeatedly explored and stressed the importance of why things are so. She felt a need to conceptualize rather than to memorize, remarking that she liked to understand globally, although she could concentrate extensively on details provided they seemed relevant to her.

In the projective tests, Evelyn's reality testing was excellent, but she was also much attracted to fantasy. She lingered over details of color, size, and shape, speaking in softly caressing tones and frequently associating many nuances of feelings with structural details.[3] Often, she gave several alternate interpretations to the Rorschach cards and easily moved backward and forward in time and space. Her sense of drama was apparent in her thematic stories as she played several different roles with vocal differentiation or sought new adventures and experiences through foreign travel or association with unusual "far out" or "weirdo" friends.[4]

All this she savored and found very satisfying but occasionally depressing and anxiety producing. She was sometimes detached and self-centered in her efforts to sort out her goals and to search for her role and her place in society; nevertheless, she could on occasion seek and enjoy intimacy. At the same time, she was deeply concerned about human welfare and desirous of assuming a responsible role in improving society about which she was critical but also remarkably tolerant.

Several months later, when she was 18 and close to the end of her senior year in high school, Evelyn was seen by the psychiatric author (PWT). Then, much that we had learned about Evelyn from our observations and tests came into focus, making us more keenly aware of how much she pressed to be actively and personally involved in the changing world in which she lived.

Evelyn had enjoyed being "a guinea pig" for our study. She remarked that her association with the staff "had an influence on me and broadened my outlook. The questions you have asked me made me think when I might have been idle. It has also been a pleasure to know people like you." This she demonstrated by her seriousness and honesty in probing her feelings and beliefs with reflective evaluative incisiveness, which was often intensely dramatic but totally free of deceit of any kind.

Evelyn was forthright and direct, never particularly modest or unassuming. Clearly aware of her intellectual skills and of the breadth and depth of her thinking and feeling, she felt she had achieved a good deal of maturity. She was less clear about whether she was well adjusted because she still struggled with doubts and anxieties, although she relished being able to think for herself and to look critically at the world and at herself.

Evelyn welcomed increasing social independence and political responsibility. Having long been interested in politics[5], she believed that she and other 18-year olds were capable of intelligent voting. She based this opinion on her feelings that youth could become enthusiastically involved in goals because they were freer to take risks without being hampered by family responsibilities or bound by tradition. With this freedom, youth could be more open to new knowledge and more concerned with human welfare. "I've always been interested in politics. I've been paying income tax for two years now. . . .I think you probably could get more votes out of younger people because if you ever got them enthusiastic about something — well, they don't have the responsibility to a family, and they will take more risks and be more involved in it. . . .An older person with a family won't always do that, sometimes even if he really believes in something. He can't always do what he would like to do."

Stressing her right to make choices based on her own convictions, Evelyn advised her younger sisters to do what they thought right even if their parents objected or did not understand. "I told them that when our parents told me I couldn't do something I thought I should, I went ahead and did it anyway. Maybe the first two or three times I felt bad about it, but after that, it didn't make any difference because I could get away with it. . . .If it had been rebellion, I would have told my parents that I was going to do it anyway, but I didn't." It is important to note that she did not regard her behavior as rebellious or disrespectful.

In this way, she justified smoking, going steady, and dressing as she wished, but she disapproved of drug usage and of premarital sex on a purely sensual basis or as a form of rebellion. She remarked that many teenagers become sexually involved because they are seeking love, without fully understanding the real meaning of love. "Most teenagers who do have premarital sex are either the kids who have never had any love at home and are looking for it, or think that they are in love with this person, and then find out later that it was really sort of a sensual thing instead of love. . . .Real love is like my love for my boyfriend. I feel that I can make him a good partner. We are compatible. I respect him and admire him. I think he is honest and has a sense of justice. We care about the same things. We like to discuss those things. We are both about the same intelligence. We love music and like about the same songs. I think more than anything, being able to grow into the kind of love that my parents have. It's an old and mature love."

She stressed that when there are mutual respect and shared interests, sex is a natural part of love, not a sordid or temporary sensation. "Before my sophomore year, I hadn't even kissed a boy. I found it wasn't so bad, that it was really quite nice. Having children isn't that horrible. . . .I like the idea of sex and I like the idea of sexual intercourse, of getting married and of having children. . . .Personally, I think it's wrong to have sexual intercourse when you're so young. I feel that it is all right as long as you're sure you can handle it, that you are old enough. . . .It's your life and if you have the drive and you must satisfy it, satisfy it. But a teenager has so much of his life ahead of him and the pill doesn't always work anyway."

She described how she had several years earlier dealt with a proposition from an older man by saying that she did not need to go to bed to be a woman, nor was she yet a woman, preferring to be what she was. "All I am is a damn 16-year-old kid and I'm going to stay a 16-year-old kid until I am 17, and then I'm going to be a 17-year-old kid. I like being a kid and I don't want to be a woman yet. . . .Lots of kids don't realize you can have fun with the rules, that being a kid is just all right and they should enjoy it. . . .You will remember how much fun you had when you were a kid. . . .It's the silly things you did, like playing down in the creek, or picnics and things like that."

She added that premarital pregnancies should not be condemned; girls who become pregnant should not be forced to marry or to destroy the life of the unborn child. She could see that young marriages could be hazardous, perhaps a deterrent to further emotional adjustment, and injurious to children who need the stability of a family based on mutual heterosexual love and concern. If these conditions are not present, then unwed mothers should place the child for adoption. "I know how I feel about sex and if I got pregnant I wouldn't want people to condemn me. I would probably be condemning myself. I think it's wrong to punish them like criminals. They are not criminals for satisfying their own sex drive. Forcing a boy to marry a girl is, I think, ridiculous. If he doesn't love her, what kind of family are they going to have? . . .Of course, it would affect the children. If a child is coming, beginning to grow, I don't think that the life should be taken. I think it should be given a chance. I think the best thing would be for the girl to go away and give the child up for adoption."

Evelyn expressed similar humanistic opinions about civil rights, but she felt they were, unlike her views on sex, not new or unique with her since they reflected what she had heard from her parents. "I have the feeling that education is one of the most important things. . . .If we can educate this generation and future generations in the problems of the Negro, we can show that there have been a lot of patriotic Negroes and that Negroes are human beings. . . .You can't classify a person because of his color or the way his hair curls or the thickness of his lips. . . .If we give them a chance, I'm sure they would be more industrious than they are. . . .Well, my parents aren't prejudiced. You see we've never had any real contact with Negroes. . . .I think my mom and dad are pretty smart people, they really are. . . .I think they are more liberal than I thought they were about such things as politics and civil rights."

Evelyn felt she had probably moved farthest from her family in her views about religion, especially in the ways religious beliefs affected her behavior. We have already described her resentment against and refusal to be bound by restrictions in relation to dress and smoking, as well as her liberalized views about sex. Her views about drinking and the use of drugs also demonstrated these changes. Explaining how she felt about drinking, under what circumstances she drank, and the limits she set, she said, "My parents don't know I smoke, and I drink too, and they don't know I drink. . . .I never did have a complete drink until about a year and a half ago. . . .I don't like liquor so much any more. Last fall, maybe it was the year before, a girl friend and I would go out and get drunk every Friday and Saturday. I got to the place that I didn't have any money for anything. . . .Older people can't understand where these kids get their beer or the liquor, but it is really easy. We made wine in chemistry and a bunch of us kids got together." She explained that her drinking usually took place out in the country in a group party or sometimes in the company of a single girl, never on dates.

> I don't like to drink when I'm going to be on a date or something like that. Now a beer, I don't mind that, but to go out and just plan to get drunk with a boy, I don't think that's a good idea. A lot of times there will be keg parties. . . .Everybody brings their cups and goes out to the slab and stands around a fire. It is usually

pretty much fun until the cops come. . . .Well, they've never come when I was out there. . . .We didn't have any trouble getting into bars or anything like that. It was pretty simple really. For about the last 6 or 7 months I have been buying my beer. When I want a beer, I just go in and buy one. . . .A lot of times, it is not easy for you to find somebody to buy hard liquor for you. If nothing else, you can get some old man some place to go and buy you a pint. You can give him a dollar or two and he is happy. I don't like to buy hard liquor. It costs too much and you have to drink all you buy before you go home because you don't have any place to put it. Then you are really polluted. . . .Most people who see you in a bar. . . .don't think anything of it, whereas if my dad was there and he saw me coming in, he might raise a little cane. . . .My dad would probably stand by while my mother gave me a lecture, and then my dad would give me a lecture. Probably all that it would amount to is lectures. . . .Well, what can they do? If they say that I have to stay home for the next six months and make straight As, how are they going to enforce it? If I want to go out, all I have to do is walk out the front door and say that I am leaving, and there is nothing they can do. Of course, it is going to hurt me worse than it will hurt my parents. It might hurt their feelings, but overall, it will hurt me worse. I've never been caught yet. . . .One night we bought a pint of sloe gin. We sat there and literally chugged that whole pint. Of course we had mixed it with cokes and didn't feel a thing. We were so mad about that. But, see, we never get too much that we both can't drink it and one of us still drive. When I come home at 12 o'clock, I just walk on in, and say that I'm home and go on to bed and that's it. . . .I get thick tongued and sometimes I stagger, but I think a lot of it is psychological really. When I come in the house, I can talk a lot better, and I could walk a straight line even in the dark. . . .I don't really do anything wrong when I'm drunk. I just sort of waste my time getting drunk, and my money too. I haven't been drunk for a long time anyway.

Thus, she had apparently enjoyed drinking with friends and was interested in its effects on her. She had successfully concealed it from her parents, and in the end reduced the amount of drinking by her own choice.

She had been tempted to try marijuana on an experimental basis, but this habit had never really meant a great deal to her. "I have smoked marijuana before, a joint, just a cigarette. . . .It sort of made me dizzy, but it didn't really do too much. That's the only experience I've ever had with it. It's the only experience I'm going to have with it. . . .If I tried it again, I would probably want to try it again after that, and I would be wasting my money, time, and potential." Here we saw her awareness of her insatiability and her efforts to control it.

In addition to her rejection of the behavioral restrictions her fundamentalist religious upbringing imposed, Evelyn had many doubts about the meaning and truth of religious doctrines. "My parents would feel that if I had been living close to Christ, I wouldn't have problems like that. [Conflicts about behavioral changes.] But even if this were true, what would you do? Here you are, you have given a whole life to this Christ, and what would happen if you were to die and end up in a world just like you are living in now. Or what happens if you die and it is a deep sleep? What happens if you die and everybody is in hell and there is no heaven? Or what if you just wander around in space? What happens if when you die all the things you believed in were nothing but fairy tales?"

She had not found satisfying or complete answers to these questions, but ordinarily she could put them aside by keeping herself busy with other things, many of which she found rewarding experiences in themselves. In lengthy soliloquies she raised her questions and looked for models on which to base her answers. "Well, every once in a while, I will get depressed thinking about things like this. I don't mind it so much for a night maybe, for a few hours. The next morning I get up and try to get busy on something. . . .just to enjoy life and the things around you. Well, how can you enjoy the things around you, if you just sit and brood? There is no way that you can enjoy things. I think what I did more than anything else was to observe other people. What do other people do? Look at the happiest people — what are they doing? The happiest people are the busiest people. I felt like this is what I should be doing too."

She had chosen to adopt some parts of Christian ethics, to emphasize the support of humanistic values in religion, and to live for today. "Actually, I think your religion should be incorporated with other feelings like your feelings about civil rights, about the government. Not so much that the government has to be a Christian government, but that it should have some ethics that correlate with Christian justice, which I think is good justice. . . .It's not the doctrine that counts, it's the belief in Christ and the love that you have for each other. . . .Doctrine is too shallow. This is something that I sort of picked up from the hippy movement. Everybody says that the hippy movement is horrible; well it is, but I have picked up one good thing out of it. And that's that this world should have a little more love in it. Not so much bickering and red tape and doctrine, doctrine, doctrine. . . .They need a little more concern for people. . . .I live now for what I can do today."

Thus, in adolescence, we saw Evelyn as a girl of considerable strength, as one who was able to question some parental standards without rejecting those parts of their value system she could see as desirable and relevant. She was thankful that her parents had allowed her freedom of choice, and this she chose to pursue in a spontaneous, unfettered way with full enjoyment of all that she could experience through her senses and evaluate through her evolving thinking. She was well aware that her behavior was at times inconsiderate of or stressful to her parents, yet to preserve her integrity she must make her own choices. She wanted to be an active participant in the new generation, to live in the present unbound by tradition. In this process, she suffered doubts and anxieties, and even at times considerable emotional instability, but she followed a pattern of independent thinking that had been handed down to her by her family.

Throughout her life, Evelyn was a complex and intriguing individual, and her coping style was a logical extension of much that we observed in her as a young child. Even in infancy, she was well able to express her needs and to behave in distinctly personal ways. She did this by pushing aside disliked toys or foods, by refusing to be hurried, by loudly demanding wanted attention, or by irritably protesting to be left alone when she was tired. In her early childhood, she had an undaunted sense of her competence, an attraction to learning and intense experiencing, predominantly through her visual alertness, secondarily through responsiveness to tactile, kinesthetic, and auditory cues. At 3 years, she had been attracted to textural differences and nuances in tones and intensities of colors. She had liked to stroke soft surfaces and clearly had enjoyed the rhythmic sound of her voice as she carried on lengthy self-directed soliloquies while playing.

Equally impressive was the range of feeling, thinking, and behaving she showed throughout her life. She experienced intensely[6] and richly, was ordinarily realistic in her thinking, and expressed herself vividly both verbally and nonverbally. Yet she could by choice at times seek quiet relief in a self-absorbed way. As one observer had said of her,

"She could easily step into activity when it pleased her, and as easily step out of it when it no longer held her interest." As a preschool and latency-aged child, she regularly sought refuge and support in play with imaginary companions. In her adolescence, the fluidity of her thinking and the lability of her feelings sometimes blurred the boundaries between reality and fantasy, but these always remained within the confines of the regression of the ego.

Although an obedient model child in her preschool years, always an excellent student, and never a behavioral problem in school, she increasingly questioned teaching methods and resented impersonal and authoritarian teachers. In her adolescence, she made it clear that she wanted to develop and organize her own ideas, to have some choice of academic content, and to participate actively in the learning process. She totally rejected rote learning of material for which she could see no relevance.

In all of our sessions, she was cooperative and usually eagerly involved in everything we asked of her, but she was task oriented and did not form lasting relationships with any of the staff members over time. She remembered the place and the activities in which she had engaged, but she did not recall staff members' names.

A very bright, creative individual, capable of fine discrimination, good judgment, and with a high integrative capacity, she had great urgency to evaluate and reflect. She was drawn toward trying everything, experiencing everything, but at the same time she was pressed by conflict and at times close to becoming overwhelmed by the intensity with which she experienced. Never satisfied by a conventional stance, she developed a volatile expressiveness, emerging in her garrulousness, especially in her prepuberty years and continuing with only slight modulation in her adolescent years. She always sought meanings and implications; thus, by inclination and capacity, she was open to experience and to change.

Furthermore, her natural inclinations were supported and encouraged by the progressive orientation of her parents who pushed for and were effective in working toward higher standards of living. Although fundamentalist in background, Evelyn's parents were less restricted by their religion than some of the other parents in our study. Hence, they relaxed their early prohibitions against movies, dancing, and the like by Evelyn's prepuberty years. In addition, Evelyn's parents encouraged independence in thinking and autonomy in behavior and were more tolerant than many of the other parents in regard to racial matters. Probably also contributing to Evelyn's integrity was the unity and the support of the sibling group, which had been particularly fostered by the father throughout Evelyn's life, especially in her pre-school and latency years. Thus, the groundwork for individuality was laid in the attitudes of Evelyn's parents who permitted and promoted her inborn capacities for experiencing richly.

At the same time, other factors in Evelyn's family life contributed to some disequilibrium in this natively modulated baby. Most important was her mother's early and intermittent insecurity and depressiveness, which was manifest in postpartum depressions after each of her 6 pregnancies and reported to be most intense after Evelyn's birth. These depressions had temporarily subjected Evelyn to recurrent periods of deprivation of maximal maternal loving care, differing from the devo-tion, appreciation, and admiration in the interim periods. They had also given Evelyn a sense of instability and rejection, delayed and confused her achievement of a feminine identification, and in her prepuberty years contributed to some conflicts about and diffusion in her own identity. Later, in Evelyn's senior year of high school, as her mother became more confident, Evelyn was more able to appreciate her mother. However, she was never able to become very close to her mother or to other female adults.

Clearly, Evelyn surpassed our more traditional subjects in her capacity to savor life through all of her senses. She lived more passion-ately and intensely than our cautious modifiers and demanded more distinct individuality by pursuing and responding to experience of all kinds. She was, like the latter, intellectually aware of the risks to which she might expose herself, but she differed from them in being more ready to express irreverence for tradition and to act upon her own judgments. Her commitment to flexibility and renewal, as well as her marked emotional lability, brought her both great pleasure in ex-periencing and some displeasure, perhaps most notable in her isolation at times. In these respects, she had moved further along our continuum of perceptual openness than the majority of her peers and fully exem-plified those teenagers we called passionate renewers.

Notes:

[1]Characteristically, the passionate renewers had broad reading interests. Literally, they seemed to taste and live vicariously the realistic or fanciful chronicles they read. They could with imaginative intensity float down the Mississippi with Tom Sawyer, become a Gandhi or a Schweitzer, struggle with the problems of *The Ugly American,*

or suffer with Maria in *West Side Story.* In the range of their choices and in the avidness with which they devoured what they read, they differed considerably from their more traditionalistic peers.

[2]Like all the passionate renewers, Evelyn was eager to learn whatever the staff could tell her about herself. This was another example of how they differed from other youths, particularly the obedient traditionalists, who although politely interested, saw less purpose in reflective self-analysis.

[3]Here again we saw how she sought and relished sensory experiences. This was characteristic of all the passionate renewers.

[4]The reader will be aware of the degree to which this choice differed from Harriet's preference for more conventional companions.

[5]The passionate renewers were distinctly aware of what was going on in the world and could at times be passionately devoted to causes. How actively involved they became depended on whether they became discouraged with the hazards and difficulties associated with seeking and promoting change, and on the emergence of new interests. In marked contrast, their more traditionalistic peers focused on their own advancement and were relatively indifferent to causes and effects of social and political events.

[6]The intensity with which Evelyn experienced everything, her capacity to throw herself into anything which appealed to her, and her skills in behaving very idiosyncratically while simultaneously enhancing adult approval are well illustrated in her religious conversion at age 6. Having already been much admired for her capacity to learn Bible verses, to sing hymns, and to sit quietly through long church services, Evelyn reacted with her usual individuality and intensity to her pastor's call for "witnesses for Christ." Pressing her mother to accompany her to the altar, Evelyn was told she could go by herself if she felt old enough to be a Christian. On a second occasion, however, her mother went to the altar with her. Then, with impressive zeal, she witnessed for Christ 30 times in one week. Later, as she recalled these experiences, she said that her conversion had been one of the happiest times in her life. In her words, "You know how you feel after you have had a bath and you're nice and warm and all cuddled up. . . .You feel like now I'm really on the road upward. . . .People were happy for me, and they showed their affection by coming down and shaking hands and talking to me." These comments taken from the prepuberty psychiatric interviews were reported along with a full discussion of Evelyn's religious feelings and beliefs in Charles W. Stewart's book, *Adolescent Religion,* Abingdon Press, 1967, pp. 186–209.

Chapter 10

A Quiet Renewal

> The conversion of a single individual from one
> way of life to another is seldom without the most
> profound continuities of soul.
>
> For what the past had to teach judgment is not
> how to continue making judgments on the
> grounds of the past but how to make fresh
> judgments on whatever unanticipated grounds. It
> is judgment that must be free if freedom is to
> occur at all, if novelty is to emerge at all, if
> creativity is to occur.
>
> Michael Novak[1]

In our study of midwestern adolescents, one of the most striking findings
is that well over a majority of the youths we saw had developed values
and views differing from those prevailing in the community in which
they were raised. Futhermore, as we looked closer at the values they
had developed, these values appeared to be almost identical to the
values being flaunted in a militant way by many young people elsewhere
at the time. Living and working in the conservative Topeka environment, we had no idea that so many young people in our own backyard
were developing views and values that were in tune with trends on
the two coasts. The reason we did not anticipate this is that these
young people, as we have already stressed, did not develop their views
out of rebelliousness, and they were not mad at anyone. Since these
young people alerted us to the "quiet revolution" in the midwest which
parallelled the more exhibitionistic and militant "youth revolt" else-

where, we have seen evidence of it all around us. Quite naturally, we have asked ourselves why so many of these youths chose to leave the traditional field. The answers we have are admittedly speculative, but they do fit experiences we have had in our own lives and with many other contemporary young people here in the Middle West. Therefore, we have decided to include our thoughts here.

First of all, we believe it is impossible for any people who have held on to their senses not to perceive somehow that the world and mankind as a whole are in a major transition. Our subjects would have denied conscious awareness of this fact, but like Keniston[2] we see their actions as conveying an underlying awareness of historical traditions. McLuhan,[3] Brzezinski,[4] Bell,[5] and Mead,[6] among others, have claimed in the last decade that we are about to leave the Industrial Era and enter an entirely new era in which many traditional life styles, values, and goals may no longer be adaptive or even applicable. Sensitive young people quite naturally would perceive this and begin searching for new answers, for new ways to adapt to new situations.

During the 1960s, the news media gave wide and often sensational coverage to what they saw as a passionate rejection of the "establishment" by young people. They often referred to the widening "generation gap," "alienation," or "disaffiliation" of the "counterculture." The underlying assumption was that we were dealing with a youthful rebellion — or even a quest for revolution. Professional studies (especially the outstanding ones by Keniston)[2,7,8,] remained much more sober but still sought as their subjects primarily those young rebels of middle class origin who were working actively for political and other changes in the way the nation conducted its affairs. Even in these studies, then, it was possible to come away with the impression that the dramatic events involving youth in the 1960s — for example, the hippie movement, the drug scene, the college riots and other protests against the Vietnam War — were exclusively associated with revolutionary or counterrevolutionary goals. (See Keniston[2] for a lucid discussion of the topic.) In addition, particularly now that the universities appear calmer in the 1970s, the conviction is expressed by many adults that the "youth revolt" of the 1960s was nothing but a passing fad, on par with the goldfish swallowing or crowding into phone booths or Volkswagens of earlier young generations. Keniston[2] in retrospect sees the events of the 1960s as the impotent protest of young people who had become obsolete.

Alternatively, we are proposing here that however foolish or violent youth behavior elsewhere may have seemed, these young people were trying somehow to cope with the new situation which they consciously perceived only vaguely or not at all. A sociological study done by Simmons and Winograd[9] before the quest and optimism of the hippie movement[10] were politicized into militant and pessimistic violence, identified a quest for a new ethic which they called the "hangloose ethic." We became interested in this study because the views our sensers developed were strikingly similar to those incorporated in the "hang-loose ethic." Simmons and Winograd described the following five criteria for this new ethic: (1) irreverence, i.e., questioning or totally ignoring conventional values and views; (2) diffuse and pervasive humanism, stressing the values of human feelings and the dignity of human life; (3) pursuit of direct experience as a goal in itself and as a means of learning and growing; (4) spontaneity, i.e., the ability to respond to whatever is happening at the moment; and (5) an untutored and unpretentious tolerance, allowing people to do anything they want as long as it does not hurt others. Each person was assumed to be basically different from all others; therefore, being different was a basic quality of being human.

When we heard these same views stated by our sensers, we did not yet know about Simmons and Winograd's study. We had no inkling that we were observing, while it was occuring, the spread of this struggle for a new ethic throughout the nation, and, as we see it, throughout the world. The lack of rebelliousness and anger in our nontraditional subjects was indeed based largely on tolerance, which resulted in warm respect and compassion for and acceptance of their parents and their community. Their tolerance of differences made it unnecessary to rebel against parents or other adults or to convert them. As far as possible, our nontraditional subjects wanted to avoid hurting their parents while pursuing and forming their own lives with intense determination. These young people differed from Simmons and Winograd's "swingers" by their low interest in drugs when we saw them. However, the drug scene in Topeka had not really started at that time and was to become important only in the years after our subjects had already left high school.

Our subjects differed fundamentally from those young people whom Keniston[7] called the "uncommitted." At the outset, our sample included a broader socio-economic range than Keniston's since our sample included children of blue collar workers as well as of some owners of small businesses and a few professional fathers. Our nontraditional young men and women lacked the "alienated outlook," which Keniston characterized by four criteria. These were: (1) a distrust of commitments, with a repudiation of intimacy in group activities, a rejection of American culture and hesitation to act; (2) a pessimistic existentialism — pessimism about the world and its future, the essential aloneness of man, and the impossibility of creating lasting values; (3) anger, scorn, and contempt, which includes self-contempt, and a belief in the basic egocentricity of man; and (4) an aesthetic quest — living for the moment, "being," "feeling," expressing oneself creatively but without gaining companionship or success.

As we have shown, our sensers did not distrust commitments. They did not reject or see themselves as outside the traditional American culture and experienced no conflict in acting on the convictions they were developing. They were not pessimists and thought that new, lasting values could be, and needed to be evolved from the old values. They valued themselves, and as we pointed out before, they were not angry at anyone or anything. They were staying with their own senses, but not in the totally self-centered sense of Keniston's "uncommitted" youths. They clearly sought companionship and with only a few exceptions were planning eventually to marry and to have children.

Keniston's[8] "radicals" were deeply absorbed by "the movement" in which they participated while working in "Vietnam Summer," an anti-war group. They found satisfaction in the fact that they were "with it" and saw themselves as a part of a groundswell. In striking contrast, our sensers did not seem to want or need a "movement" or any other national cause. They welcomed relationships with peers who held similar views, primarily because they enjoyed the interaction with the other persons, not because they had a common cause. As a matter of fact, they associated with and were closest to peers who were being excluded by the social elite because of their clothes, looks, race, or other factors, rather than because they expressed non-traditional views.

In our sample, there were practically no conscientious objectors. Only one boy said he intended to go to Canada if he were drafted. Our censors viewed going to Vietnam as fulfilling one's duty to one's country. Our sensers instead saw it as a commitment required of them. They believed they would enhance their own individuality by making that commitment. Going to Vietnam for them offered an opportunity to cope with overwhelming difficulties and experiences. This in turn, they felt, would contribute to their further growth. They anticipated with interest the companionship and exchange of thoughts and feelings with others they might meet in the service. The possible need to kill, a thought full of horror, was nevertheless viewed with a fair amount of curiosity.

Keniston's subjects and young people like them elsewhere totally dominated the news in the last half of the 1960s. This left the impression that youth was moving into an "uncommitted" direction. For this reason we consider it so important to report our findings. Although our sample is small, we have independently, through our separate experiences in the Midwest (e.g., AM working with youths in a walk-in clinic, and PT with freshmen medical students recruited from small Oklahoma towns where they have lived all their lives), observed time and again the same nonrebellious, nonmilitant development of nontraditional views, which then are lived out with intensity. We do not believe that the changes that can now be observed nationally in the life styles, life goals, views, and political behavior of many Americans can be fully understood without recognizing the tremendous quiet renewal that is taking place and stands out clearly in the heartlands of this nation.

The militant revolutionary or exhibitionistic youth counterculture on the two coasts, which was primarily a sensationalistic product of the news media, appears to us to have concealed those profound changes that were being made by their peers in the rest of the country. At the same time, the more militant youths elsewhere and our sensers have much in common. Like Keniston's "radicals,"[8] our sensers stressed the importance of "growing up" and of self-respect. Both groups left their futures wide open and rejected living conventional lives. This vagueness about the future did not affect the self-confidence of any of these young men and women. Keniston's and our subjects shared a strong sense of continuity with the basic values of their families. The parents of many of Keniston's subjects had developed more "radical" views and generally supported and cheered their radical offspring. This explains the feelings of continuity in those youngsters. It is harder to understand the same feelings in our subjects, many of whose parents were deeply tied to tradition, strongly disapproved of their children's changed views, and vigorously attempted to undercut and stop their sons' and daughters' quests. The parents of the passionate renewers in our sample tended to have more liberal views, but none of them could be characterized as politically radical. Although one of the fathers in this group was an avowed atheist, even he could not be called a radical insofar as most of his other viewpoints and his behavior fitted well with traditional community values.

None of our subjects was able to resolve this paradox. Nor can we do so, beyond emphasizing our strong feelings that the "new" views of contemporary youth in many ways may be a modern version of the values dominating the pioneer era in this country particularly in the heartlands.[11] The frontier days and rural living necessitated questioning established values because the situation often was so very different from the situation for which the values had been established. Human beings were respected because every extra pair of hands helped. It was necessary to cultivate realistic perception for the sake of survival amidst all kinds of lurking and sudden danger. For the same reasons, the ability to respond spontaneously and flexibly were valued highly out of practical necessity for survival. These are the same characteristics Simmons and Winograd's "swingers"[9] and our sensers were seeking to cultivate in themselves. There many be deep meaning in the fact that nontraditional youth in this country during the 1960s tended to revive the styles of dress from the frontier days. The feeling of continuity in our sensers may very well stem from their being in touch with the strong undercurrent in rural Kansas (and in their urban homes) surviving from the pioneer days.

For this reason, we have believed it to be imperative to include as much information about our censors as about our sensers. We see our total sample as representing a continuous spectrum, with polarities rather than opposites.[12] Deeply influenced by what we learned from these young people, we see changes as continuous rather than discontinuous. Thus, change cannot be understood by studying only one extreme or the other but has to include the many shades between these two polarities. The four substations we have defined within the spectrum should be viewed in that spirit. We are are not describing conservatives or liberals, but young people who at a certain point in history have chosen different ways of coping with the task before them at that particular time. We firmly believe that the choices they have made have significance not only for understanding their lives, but also for understanding all of our lives today. For we, too are constantly choosing ways to cope with what is in ourselves and in the world which is changing so unpredictably and at such dizzying speed.

Notes:

[1]Novak Michael: *The Rise of the Unmeltable Ethnics.* New York, The Macmillan Company, 1971, p 192.

[2]Keniston Kenneth: *Youth and Dissent: The Rise of a New Opposition.* New York Harcourt Brace Jovanovich, 1971.

[3]McLuhan Marshall: *Understanding Media.* New York, New American Library, 1964.

[4]Brzezinski Zbigniev: Technetronic Society. *Encounter.* 30 (1):1–19, 1969.

[5]Bell Daniel: The postindustrial society, in Ginzberg, Eli (ed): *Technology and Social Change.* New York, Columbia University Press, 1969.

[6]Mead Margaret: *Culture and Commitment: A Study of the Generation Gap.* Garden City, New York, Doubleday & Company, 1970.

[7]Keniston Kenneth: *The Uncommitted.* New York, Dell Publishing Co, 1960.

[8]Keniston Kenneth: *Young Radicals.* New York, Harcourt Brace Jovanovich 1968.

[9]Simmons JL, Winograd Barry: *It's Happening.* Santa Barbara, California, Marc-Laird Publications, 1966.

[10]Keniston (footnote 2) called these young people the "cultural wing" as opposed to the political wing, of the counterculture, He apparently does not accept that the hippies themselves staged a funeral and declared the hippie movement dead at the end of the Haight-Ashbury Flower Power Summer in San Francisco.

[11]In *Youth and Dissent* (footnote 2 above), Keniston also proposes a developmental viewpoint in looking at the behavior of youth in the 1960s.

[12]For an incisive discussion of the difference between opposites and polarities, see Harris Sydney J. *The Authentic Person: Dealing With Dilemma.* Niles, Illinois, Argus Communications, 1972.

Chapter 11

Adolescence in a Time of Transition

> Identity and time perspectives are both derived
> from the social systems in which we exist. Our
> identity is a figure which we fix against the
> ground of the time perspective we acquire.
>
> Benjamin D. Singer[1]

Over 10 years ago Henry Maier[2] suggested that the use of the term
"adolescenthood" would "define adolescence as a distinct entity rather
than as a period of transition and change during which a person moves
from childhood to adulthood." He went on to suggest that "peer
associations and peer groups, with their relevant group norms
serve as the major avenue for ego development and ego repair in
adolescence."

The chapters describing the spectrum of choices our subjects made
in adolescence support Maier's contention that adolescence is much
more than a period of transition from childhood to adulthood. Those
same chapters do not back up Maier's suggestion that the peer group
is the main matrix for adolescent development. Our subjects by and
large felt part of — and associated with — peer groups, but their
development appeared to be independent of those groups. The study
by Nesselroade and Baltes,[3] which we referred to in Chapter 1, strongly
suggests that another major influence on adolescent development at
this time[4] is the historical period in which that development takes place.
Their cohort[5] of 1970 was different from the cohort of 1971, which
in turn was different from the cohort of 1972. They could explain
these differences only on the basis of historical change.

In the previous chapter we attempted to summarize our under-standing of the historical era in which our subjects lived through their "adolescenthood." It is interesting to us that during that same time as preeminent an authority on adolescence as Erikson felt compelled to change his formulation of adolescent development drastically. Previously, Erikson had discussed the main task of adolescence as being the crystallization of a firm ego identity. If the individual failed in this task, "ego diffusion" resulted. In his reformulation based on his observations of dissenting youth in the late 1960s, Erikson[6] still sees the task of adolescence as the acquisition and accomplishment of "ego identity," but he now sees the adolescent as having to go through a crucial phase of "ego diffusion" to accomplish this goal. During "ego diffusion," the adolescent expands the boundaries of the self to "include a wider identity, with compensatory gains in emotional tones, cognitive certainty, and ideological conviction." This diffusion occurs in "states of love, sexual union, friendship, of discipleship and follower-ship, and of creative inspiration."

Erikson[7] stressed that adolescents must emerge from the ego diffusion with a potent new vision of life as well as of themselves[8]. This is the identity they are working toward. If the adolescents' efforts misfire and they remain unable to develop a clear formulation of life and of their places and roles in it, they end up in ego confusion, which Erikson defined as a state in which the person has the delusion of acting meaningfully, although he really is not doing so.

To us this definition of ego confusion has come to mean an ego identity that is not related to, or is not adaptive, in the historical era in which the adolescent develops. For in the society in which adolescents today grow into adulthood, little is given or structured. There is no fixed, existing society to fit into, as society continues to change at a rapid pace and in totally fluid, unpredictable ways. For example, some young people with Ph.D.'s from top universities cannot find jobs and must train in fields other than their chosen ones. Male and female roles, as well as the goals of marriage and parenthood, are being rethought[9] by many young people in the face of world overpopulation and world food shortages. Little wonder, then, that Erikson perceives that the new identity has to include a "vision of life" — which could be seen as an effort to create some *gestalt* out of the chaos around us.

If this is correct, and we believe it to be, adolescents today can be seen as updating adolescent development to fit the historical era in which they live. They do this automatically and undramatically (as demonstrated by our subjects and those of Offer[10] and Nesselroade and Baltes[3]) because they have not known anything else. Yet, the change in their adolescent quest requires the adult world to re-examine its own preoccupations and expectations, as we are trying to do in this book, and face the real world of today.

Erikson's first formulation[6] of the quest for identity fitted the time when the concept of "adjustment" was important — one had to "fit in" in a society which was given. In preparing for life in a constantly changing world, the adolescent now has to place more emphasis on himself, and the task becomes one of coping. Hence our interest in the adolescent coping styles of our subjects. The emphasis we have placed on distinguishing between censors and sensers is crucial as adaptation to an ever-changing and, therefore, partially unfamiliar environment in part requires more emphasis on the senses, on awareness, and on reality testing.

Coping involves emphasis on internal balance and lacks the aspects of concession implied by the term "adjustment." Furthermore, coping implies realistic perception and awareness with a minimum of ideological interpretation and hence, distortion. Depending on the limitations inner realities place on persons, their coping efforts allow them to deal appropriately with reality without making concessions. This comes about because reality is no longer seen as an enemy, but as a given, a part of the total picture, the border pieces of the picture puzzle. Perceiving the overall picture depends more on realistic awareness than on intelligence. No wonder, then, that intelligence was not a factor setting apart our censors and sensers. What distinguishes them is the realistic awareness they allow themselves. The censors derive much or most of their awareness from tradition and from various ideological sources, and they feel little need to explore the world with their senses. The sensers are not altogether free from tradition or ideologies but seek to revise their life views more on the basis of their perceptions and awareness, rather than on the basis of what was handed down to them in their culture and in their upbringing and schooling.

In our censors we may observe the result of not having achieved a full identity in Erikson's new sense.[7] He observes that individuals who do not emerge completely from ego diffusion tend to "retrogress" to earlier psychosexual stages. According to Erikson, retrogression to the latency phase of psychosexual development results in what he calls a "post moral" position and "preethical pragmatism." Here "what works is good, and it is man's fate to be in motion and to set things in motion in league with a divine engineering power." This is a slightly more explicit, and possibly more extreme, version of the censors in our sample. The lack of emphasis on fully using their own senses may be seen as having impeded them from coming to a total "vision of life" and thus having necessitated a mild retrogression. The aspect of "strictly playing by the rules," so prominent in latency age children becomes the basis for the compromise these adolescents work out for themselves as a way of coping with a world they for one reason or another can or will not allow themselves to perceive fully.

We do not want to imply here that the similarity of the censors' coping style to Erikson's description of retrogression represents a value judgment. Past human experiences, in the form they have been given, no longer directly relate to the world of today, but they still contain many hard-fought conclusions and treasures of wisdom. Thus, Margaret Mead[11] was only partially right when she in a recent book, *Culture and Commitment,* called the adults of today "immigrants from another era." Since we emerged from the nightmare of the "melting pot" ideology, we have discovered that many of the "old world" traditions have much to teach us. This is also evident in the renewed interest in history among young people today, as compared to the pride young people took in the 1960s in being called the "ahistorical generation." A total break with the past as many militant young rebels in the 1960s advocated is obviously not realistic, possible, or even desirable. The presence of censors in our society will ensure continuity while the sensers work out new coping methods in a vastly changed world. Much of what the censors preserve can then be applied in a new way in a new world. On their side, the sensers seem to agree with Fromm as he wrote: "man is stronger the more fully he is in touch with reality....The more he can grasp reality on his own and not only as a datum with which society provides him, the more secure he feels because the less completely dependent he is on consensus and hence the less threatened by social change....Awareness means doing away with illusions and, to the degree that this is accomplished, it is a process of liberation."[12] The sensers indeed were on a constant quest, via their senses, to reach full awareness of reality around them. In the process they discarded a number of traditional beliefs and in the end felt freer.

Nevertheless, being more aware of the world and its problems of living does not mean that one necessarily has the answers to those problems. The sensers did not feel they had the answers, experiencing what they were doing more as a search and a process of becoming. They were intensely invested in reaching an overall view of life but anticipated that reaching that view would take a long time.

As we observe their adolescent development, as well as that of the censors, we should note that both groups had experienced the rebellious feelings and excessive mood swings, so often associated with all of adolescence, only during their junior high school years. By the ninth grade they had by and large put all this behind them. This corresponds to Offer's[13] finding that his subjects had tended to be rebellious at ages 12 – 13 and subsequently showed no "volcanic eruptions" or participation in protest movements. Instead, they were open and responsive, with accurate reality assessment and self-observation. They had a quality of impressive "ego-resiliency."

Thus, by the tenth grade both Offer's and our subjects showed so much overlapping of the two phases Blos[14] called "adolescence proper" and "late adolescence" that these phases seemed to occur simultaneously. Some of our subjects even showed features Blos ascribes to "post adolescence." Since our data are vulnerable to memory distortions in our subjects, we cannot be completely sure of this. There were enough suggestive data, however, to present this observation as a strong possibility. Some of the more articulate young people described the simultaneous development of: (1) more objective, analytical, reality-oriented cognition (Blos' criteria for adolescence proper), (2) crystallization of strong, unselfish concerns too important to allow for postponement or compromise (Blos' criteria for late adolescence); and (3) strong efforts to come to terms with parental ego interests and attitudes (Blos' criteria for postadolescence).

We noted that this type of condensed or telescoped adolescent development was particularly apt to occur in the sensers, and to a lesser degree in the censors, probably because of the former's investment in reality-oriented cognition. However both groups showed a great deal of concern about working out any differences they might have with their parents along dimensions that would place them in Blos' postadolescence.

Therefore, the existing descriptions of adolescent development need to be updated. This is evident also if one compares our findings with those of Douvan and Adelson,[15] who did their research in the early 1960s. They found that parent-adolescent conflicts were less severe than was generally thought, but they also found significant differences in the types of identity boys and girls achieved. Boys tended to avoid fantasy through concentration on reality or by reorganization of fantasy in terms of realistic plans. The girls showed more discontinuity between fantasy and reality planning: for example, their sex roles might be in conflict with work. They also were found to have more diffuse sexual impulses and to depend more on external control, whereas autonomous morality, the urge to be free, to be one's master, was almost entirely a masculine stirring. Interpersonal relationships were more important to girls. Douvan and Adelson listed the key terms in understanding adolescent boys as: "erotic, autonomy (assertiveness, independence, achievement), and identity." In girls, they listed: "erotic, interpersonal, and identity."

There were some sex differences in our sample; more censor girls were classified as obedient traditionalists than ideological conservatives. More senser girls were termed cautious modifers than passionate renewers. These differences were not pronounced, however. As is evident from the preceding case study chapters, the girls did not differ very much from the boys in their respective groups in the type of identity they were seeking. To be sure, our subgroups are too small to allow generalizations. Nevertheless, the unmistakable changes taking place in this country, manifested mostly in the vastly increased assertiveness of women, lend an important perspective to the trend in our sample toward less difference between the sexes. And the trend toward activity in boys and passivity in girls observed by Douvan and Adelson in the early 1960s cannot be found in our sample, with the exception of the obedient traditionalist girls.

What we have seen in our sample, then, is a tendency toward earlier puberty, followed by a brief rebellious period, which is usually over by the age of 15. Subsequently, a much more emotionally serene period begins, marked by the adolescent's turning toward the world and avoiding alienation from the parents. Thus, there are no clues in our sample to the tremendous national problem of young runaways. Good statistics on the runaway problem are not available, but some have suggested that runaways may number close to a million a year. In most instances there is major conflict between the young runaways and their parents, which even professional mediators cannot solve. Consequently, many of the runaways remain permanently separated from their homes. The only guess we have about this is that either the young runaways' parents are less invested in their children than the parents in our sample tended to be, or that the youngsters failed to achieve a workable ego identity and retrogressed to earlier psycho-sexual stages, in the way described by Erikson.

Periods of ego diffusion were described by our sensers, especially the passionate renewers. However, these periods were not close enough together to be termed a phase, as Erikson suggested. Therefore, instead of ego diffusion, these periods may exemplify episodic "regression in the service of the ego," a mental mechanism that Kris[16] considered essential in creativity and artistic creation. Having the ability to regress in this manner, the artist can grasp larger contexts and integrate them. Our sensers may likewise have used the periods of diffusion of the self as a means of developing a clearer, more integrated picture of a confusing, kaleidoscopically changing world. It is interesting to note in this context that both McLuhan[17] and Fromm[12] have seen art as being far ahead of science because of its ability to grasp new entities and "wholes." Bruner's[18] emphasis on training in intuition and his advocacy of more use of poetry in the teaching of mathematics point in the same direction.

We need to emphasize that the openness to perceptions involved in the cognitive style of our sensers does not in itself necessarily lead to the crystallization of a firm ego identity or necessarily to a type of inner organization often referred to as "mental health."[18] However, we must also realize that the usefulness of the concept of mental health is itself open to question today.[19] The criteria defining mental health may also be outdated. Simmons and Winograd,[20] students of the early hippie movement in Southern California, hinted at this as they wrote: "Far too many of the scientific forays into the nature of psychedelics and tripping measure the voyages only by their preestablished standards of what is normal, or what is stability and self-control, of what reality and a reality-oriented person is supposed to look like." The fact that we found "mentally healthy" and "less mentally healthy" subjects in both censors and sensers may be an artifact of our preestablished standards, which focused on "coping" rather than "mental health."

Having data on our subjects from infancy, we naturally became curious about what links we could find between infancy data and the coping style our subjects had chosen by the end of high school — and of the main part of their teenage years. Several of our subjects were alert and sensitive as babies, yet ended up as censors. Other similar babies grew up to be sensers. In studying the reasons for the final choice, we came up with a number of closely interrelated factors.

First, the degree of adequacy of genetic disposition and of congenital neurological and physical intactness determined, especially during our subjects' early years, the freedom they had to exploit fully great or substantial innate sensitivities. For example, after one of the sensitive male babies had been included in our sample, we discovered that he had mild, nonspecific organic brain dysfunction. The neurological difficulty was just great enough that the child had to learn to limit incoming stimuli in order to remain organized. To do this, he slowed himself down, worked more compulsively, and curbed his capacity for rich cognition. As a result, this young man at graduation from high school was a cautious modifier rather than the passionate renewer he might have become.

One of our girl subjects had a pulmonary embolism at the age of 6 months. Although she originally appeared to be a fairly curious and sensitive infant, this early illness (as well as increased maternal solicitude and control caused by this illness) somehow seemed to decrease her vigor and her ability to hold on to her own cognition. By graduation from high school, she was an obedient traditionalist who had identified almost completely with her mother. Another subject went through a severe illness in the preschool years and was disabled for years afterward. As a small child she had shown great potential for sensitivity. Her struggle to regain full functioning after her illness caused her to curb her awareness of sensory experiences. When seen during the prepuberty phase she was more restricted in cognition than when she was seen again before graduation from high school. Even then, she was just barely a cautious modifier. Another of our subjects was hypersensitive as an infant. His current militantly conservative stance may represent the solution he devised to being flooded with stimuli.

Second, the degree to which individuals have achieved what Erikson[21] calls "basic trust" influences, and sometimes limits, the freedom youngsters have to use their innate cognitive potential fully. Neurological and physical difficulties during the first year of life may make it difficult for children to achieve basic trust. However, the quantity and especially the quality of maternal care during the first year also influences whether or not a given child can achieve basic trust to a reasonable degree. Several mothers of censors in our sample vigorously raised their children to rely more on the mothers' cognition than on their own innate senses. Raising the children this way appeared to meet the mothers' needs. These mothers were controlling and overprotective; and the children remained overly tied to their mothers and were kept immature. All of the more perceptive and active infants of these mothers by the end of their high school careers had become militant conservatives and not obedient traditionalists. This may have been due to a strong identification with mothers who vigorously had set and defended limits all their lives.

Equally significant in this respect is the fact that all of the subjects who, when last seen, were passionate renewers, without exception had been described as "lively, curious, self-assertive" as preschoolers. Observers of these preschool children described them as vigorous and self-confident children who showed a high degree of autonomy and "could always do the impossible." Such assertiveness and autonomy rest on a solid feeling of basic trust.

Everyone of our cautious modifiers had received excellent care and had had a positive experience in infancy, laying the groundwork for a good measure of basic trust. However, in quite a few of these young men and women, there was a history of traumatic intrafamily pressures during childhood and adolescence, particularly in the mother-child relationship, but sometimes in the relationships with their fathers. One might say that the favorable early experience allowed these subjects to develop enough basic trust to experiment, but the insecurity surrounding them in later years struck a balance and allowed only for cautious experimentation.

Erikson[22] has clarified that basic trust has to be counterbalanced by a certain amount of mistrust that will warn of danger and teach the child to anticipate discomfort. An optimal ratio of basic trust and mistrust must be achieved. The cautious modifiers differ from the passionate renewers by having less trust in a positive basic trust/basic mistrust balance. This may explain why they do not question established values as vigorously and persistently as the passionate renewers.

A third factor, which is intimately related to and interdependent with the two factors already mentioned, is related to the source from which persons seek their ego integrity, that is, the capacity of the ego to retain integration under changing circumstances. Obviously, a person who does not have reliable physical and neurological endowment and who does not develop a reasonable amount of basic trust will have more difficulty in achieving and maintaining adequate ego organization on the basis of his own inner resources. In contrast, the passionate renewers appear to us to have a maximum capacity for basing their ego integrity on inner resources. This is manifested, for example, by their aforementioned ability to use regression in the service of the ego. The inner strength on which the ego in these individuals is based is positive and not defensive. Therefore, they can at all times allow themselves free rein in using their sensitivity and cognition in a constant search for a more encompassing understanding and formulation of reality, without fear that they will be overwhelmed by whatever their curiosity leads them to explore.

Censors require varying degrees of environmental support to maintain their ego integrity. They are also accustomed to seeking and using the kind of outside support that will set limits for, rather than give free rein to, their cognition. The cautious modifiers, while relying much more on inner than outer resources, have difficulty maintaining ego integrity when circumstances become extreme. At that time they seek some environmental support or remove themselves from the threatening perceptions by withdrawing physically or mentally.

We hope that we have illustrated that the coping styles around which our adolescents built their identities are on a true continuum, along which individuals can move back and forward. As we have stated before, life circumstances or psychological events may cause these young men and women to choose a different coping style — even though that appears unlikely at the present time.

We are now also ready to describe further the adolescent development after the rebellious period has ended at around age 14. Beyond that point, the adolescent appears to exert a great effort to further refine the coping style he acquired much earlier in life and to adapt that coping style to the demands and increased responsibility of adult living. All this is played out in a peer setting. The availability of peers provides encouragement and support, but the seeds for the coping styles chosen were sown long ago and do not come from the peer group. Furthermore, somehow it is in the air that times and the world have changed radically. This may come from watching TV, reading magazines, communicating with peers, or other sources. Our subjects could not pinpoint this for us. What is important, however, is the essential choice they make to build their budding adult identity on a censor or senser framework.

If the censor framework is chosen, the adolescent carefully studies all the rules of adult living and begins to adopt them in his or her daily living, thinking, and feeling. This involves gradually distancing oneself even more from one's direct sensory experiences, so that sensations do not come to awareness any longer without an attached label — stating whether what is perceived is acceptable and can be pursued further or is unacceptable and should be avoided or ignored.

The censors in our sample found little or no nourishment for their new identities in their schools, even though these schools prided themselves on representing the best of the culture's traditions. The censors were no more impressed with or influenced by their teachers than our sensers, an ironic sidelight on how badly contemporary schools are out of touch with practically their entire student bodies. Why schools fail to reach their censor students may be related to the neutral position they have to maintain in these days of concern regarding the civil rights of all subgroups and all students. This forces censor students to seek reinforcement primarily at home — in our sample mostly from their mothers. Some reinforcement also came from some adults in the censors' churches, but not as much as we had anticipated once we had arrived at our spectrum. Again, perhaps the churches, like the schools, are more affected by the times we live in than is apparent on the surface and than was comfortable for our censors.

Censors monitor every aspect of their development — managing internal drives, impulses, feelings, and fantasies, and carefully controlling incoming sensations, choice of companions, adult models, activities, and experiences. If there is any ego diffusion in Erikson's sense, it lies in the adolescent censor's deep immersion in devising inner and outer controls that will function effectively and automatically. The achievement of such automatic controls may cause censors to refer with so much conviction to what is for or against the laws of nature.

As we indicated already above, the censors show an element of latency preoccupation with "the rules of the game," "fairness," and "unfairness." Whether or not this represents retrogression to the latency phase, as might be suggested by Erikson's[7] recent reformulation, it should be stressed that our censors emerge with a very strong identity, whether they be obedient traditionalists or ideological conservatives. They show no trace of ego confusion, unless they are placed in an unfamiliar setting and have to deal with topics for which they do not as yet have labels. This occurred in our interviews with the censors and caused them to react with some discomfort or even indignation. In every instance they soon found a way of coping with the disturbance and could return to their usual selves.

The sensers' development after the age of 14 is less smooth and less predictable. The young adolescents become more and more bold in exploiting the high sensitivity with which nature endows them during and just after puberty. As they look at the world around them, they find that things are not what they seem or are said to be. Wider and wider inconsistencies, contradictions, and even falsities are identified, thoroughly examined, and then judged on the basis of whether they are real or "phony." In each instance the resolution is applied to the sensers themselves, in terms of how they decide to change their behavior to fit the situation as they see it.

Many hours are spent in figuring out what life, people, and the world are all about. Discussions, particularly with peers who also are asking questions, are considered very helpful. However, our sensers did not indicate that they had gotten their answers from these discussions. They arrived at the answers in a highly personal fashion. Subsequently, there was some testing of the new answers, which then might be modified depending on what evolved from the experiments. All of this required a great deal of sharpening of the senses. Very early our sensers appeared to become aware of how their senses might be derailed by various ideological thoughts and attitudes, and they worked at freeing their senses from such prejudgments. For this reason they received little satisfaction from their schools, where everything presented had been carefully precooked and packaged in specific ways.

The sensers, particularly the passionate renewers, did not want or seek outside reinforcement. They were engaged in an internal quest, one so personal that they could not borrow or rely on the sensory system of anyone else. Again, we did not find a sustained period of ego diffusion here, merely an episodic intense inner preoccupation with particular questions. As a group, the sensers were curious about the world around them, and since that world was so fluid, it seemed that they did not want to work out too fixed an identity for themselves. Instead, they seemed to strive for an identity that would allow them to become aware of any and all changes in themselves, others, and the world at large, and yet to maintain some kind of overview, to see some overall *gestalt*. This may approach the "view of life" which Erikson included in the definition of the new adult ego identity, although a more accurate term would be an "approach to life."

With this approach went a great, sometimes insatiable appetite for and interest in everything in the world, but mostly its people. Many of the sensers showed a strong wish to work with and to help people. The payoff for them would be a larger and deeper view of what was going on around them, or, as the young people used to say during the 1960s, what's happening.

To sum up, then, the psychological task of adolescence is no longer the achievement of an identity primarily directed toward fitting into a fixed, stable surrounding culture. For one thing, there no longer is such a surrounding culture. Therefore, even the adolescents who wish to stay with tradition (the censors) must work actively on developing an identity that will allow them to cope with a world which changes at a dizzying pace and in unpredictable directions. The task is still to devise a workable formulation of that world. And it is here that adolescents divide themselves into two groups: one, the sensers, three times as large as the other, the censors. The sensers stubbornly stick to and further develop and sharpen their senses so that they can see the world and their lives as accurately as possible and eventually have an overall picture, a *gestalt*, of what is happening. The censors rely on the traditional views and deal with a changing world from that vantage point. To avoid confusion, they place their senses in the service of the views they have developed and thus interpret reality at all times before they deal with it. Whereas the sensers achieve a more accurate picture of the contemporary world, their censor peers provide continuity with the world as it was and also provide a moral commentary that brings in focus the choices we all are making or will have to make.

Notes:

[1]Singer Benjamin D: The future-focused role-image. In Toffler Alvin (Ed): *Learning For Tomorrow: The Role of the Future in Education.* New York, Random House, 1974, p 21.

[2]Maier Henry W: Adolescenthood. *Social Casework,* 46 (1): 3–9, 1965.

[3]Nesselroade John R, Baltes Paul B: Adolescent personality development and historical change: 1970–1972. Monographs of the Society for Research in Child Development. vol. 39, no. 1, serial no. 154, 1974.

[4]We do not know, nor do Nesselroade and Baltes, whether this was true in the past or will continue to be true in the future.

[5]In Nesselroade and Baltes study, "cohort" was defined as a group of people born at the same time or during an arbitrary period of time. They suggested that the term "generation" be reserved for reference to groups born during a larger time unit.

[6]Erikson Erik: *Identity and the Life Cycle.* New York, International Universities Press, 1959.

[7]Erikson Erik: Reflections on the dissent of contemporary youth. Daedalus 99 (1): 154–176, 1970.

[8]Without specifically stating so, Erikson thus also has fundamentally changed his definition of "ego identity," which in the past only included emphasis on an individual's meaning to himself and his meaning to others.

[9]Toussieng Povl: Changing sex roles in changing times. Sexual Behavior 1 (3), June 1971.

[10]Offer Daniel: *The Psychological World of the Teenager.* New York, Basic Books, Inc., Publishers, 1969.

[11]Mead Margaret: *Culture and Commitment.* Garden City, New York, Doubleday & Co, 1970.

[12]Fromm Erich: *The Revolution of Hope: Toward a Humanized Technology.* New York, Bantam Books, 1968, p 66.

[13]Offer Daniel: *The Psychological World of the Teenager.* New York, Basic Books, Inc, Publishers, 1969.

[14]Blos Peter: *On Adolescence.* New York, The Free Press, 1962.

[15]Douvan Elizabeth, Adelson Joseph: *The Adolescent Experience.* New York, John Wiley & Sons, 1966.

[16]Kris Ernst: *Psychoanalytical Explorations in Art.* New York, International Universities Press, 1952.

[17]McLuhan Marshall: *Understanding Media.* New York, New American Library, 1964.

[18]We found low correlations between openness to perception and Lois Murphy's Coping II (internal organization and equilibrium) ratings. Coping II, as defined, comes close to many definitions of "mental health."

[19]Toussieng Povl W: Mental health: in memoriam. POCA Press, 8 (2), June 1973. (Also published in: 1973 POCA Proceedings, University of Alabama Press, 1975.)

[20]Simmons JL, Winograd Barry: *It's Happening.* Santa Barbara, California, Marc-Laird Publications, 1966, p 46.

[21]Erikson Erik: *Childhood and Society.* New York, W. W. Norton & Company, 1963.

[22]Footnote, page 61. In Identity and the Life Cycle (see 6 above).

Chapter 12

So What?

> O, grant me, Heaven, a middle state
> Neither too humble, nor too great
> More than enough for nature's ends
> With something left to treat my friends.
>
> David Mallet (1705–1765)

As we attempt here to spell out the implications of our findings for parents, teachers, and future or present colleagues in the behavioral sciences, we are only too well aware of the limitations of our data. Our sample is small and is limited to white middle and lower middle class youngsters. The data are based on what our subjects were willing to tell us in the interviews or reveal in their test responses. Although we had contact with our subjects' families in the past, we were unable to interview the parents during this last round of the coping study. Finally, we have repeatedly had to ask ourselves whether we merely have been reading our own values into the data we accumulated. We can well understand those of our readers who at this point still view our data with skepticism and find it presumptuous to generalize from them.

Therefore, we would not have had the courage to add this chapter if we had not experienced how our findings applied to and changed our other professional activities. In other words: how much our subjects taught us and how much we were changed by our findings. Both authors were deeply committed to helping to finish the coping project, not only to complete the research in which we had had a major stake, but also as our personal tribute to Dr. Lois Murphy and our subjects after many years of intensive collaboration.

Given that focus and that set, the observations which many of our subjects already forced us to make in early interviews were by no means welcome. As a matter of fact, both authors for a long time felt so guilty about having our focus and attention diverted from what we had intended that we were unable to communicate our anguish to each other until we were well into the last round of data gathering. The eventual decision to change our research plans and to zero in on what became the substance of this book was also an agonizing one, as time and other considerations made us realize that we then would have to alter our original research design. Even in retrospect, we would not and could not have done this if our data had not also had major and useful implications for our professional activities elsewhere — and for our personal lives as well.

In our contacts with young people outside our research, we found ourselves having new avenues of viewing what was happening with and to contemporary youth. Both of us authors (AJM in her work as a consultant to the Topeka public schools and as a parent of teenage children, and PWT in his clinical work with teenagers and his contacts with medical students, coming from backgrounds at least as conservative as those of the young people in Topeka), found, independently, that our rapport with young people grew as our views began to change. From these contacts with many other young people we were also able, over and over again, to observe the usefulness of our spectrum. It applied in the "real" world as well as it did in our research group. Much of what we include in this chapter is based on an empirical application of our research data to parenting, teaching, and diagnostic and therapeutic activities. Our new conclusions were considered useful and stimulating by a number of parents, teachers, and other professional colleagues whom we had the opportunity to talk to. The encouragement enabled us to add this chapter without feeling presumptuous.

The most important lesson from our data is that young people's wish for change must not automatically be viewed as being synonymous with rebellion or a wish for revolution. What they are trying to do is to renew existing structures and fit them to a situation that they perceive as being drastically changed. This, then, is renewal in the sense of John Gardner[1]:

"Every individual, organization or society must mature, but much depends on how this maturing takes place. A society whose maturing consists simply of acquiring more firmly established ways of doing things is headed for the graveyard — even if it learns to do these things with greater and greater skills. *In the ever renewing society what matures is a system or framework within which continuous innovation, renewal and rebirth can occur."* (emphasis by John Gardner.)

Facing the concrete threats of atomic annihilation, worldwide pollution, overpopulation, greater competition for food, fuels, and raw materials, many young people find it important to see the situation as it actually is rather than as how they wished it were. Hence, they place greater emphasis on relying on one's own senses rather than on ideas. The problems to be solved are seen as requiring both an acceptance of man's dependence on nature and his fellow men and a greater emphasis on concrete action and different life goals. Our subjects consider it entirely possible to make these changes within the framework of existing society?

Even so, 72 percent of our subjects struggled with some pain stemming from their awarenesss that they were in certain respects disappointing and hurting their parents because they were not living up to their parents' expectations. We do not know how their parents felt about what was happening. We did sense, through their children, that communication between parents and children had suffered in many families. These parents had conveyed forcefully to their children that the fulfillment of the parents' lives depended entirely or greatly on the way their children's lives went. In this way they were, indeed, conveying the traditional purpose of parenthood: to seek fulfillment and perpetuation of themselves as men and women by having children, and to seek self-fulfillment via these children's lives by meeting their needs.

The coping study has taught us, however, that children can and will take responsibility for their own fulfillment, if given the chance. Developing this ability in turn helps them cope better with changing situations. In a rapidly changing world, then, parents too will be better off if they seek the sources of their own fulfillment within themselves. If they do this, there will be no need for mutual distance and sadness between them and their children, regardless of whether their children pursue traditional or untraditional lives. Between them they will be able to better sort out and cope with reality, without losing each other's support. An example will illustrate this.

In the last decade there have been many victims of changing economic conditions, such as the engineers in the aerospace industry in Seattle. There are many examples of people with Ph.D.'s from respected universities who are unable to find work. Overproduction of graduates in teaching, social work, psychology, and other professions affected by the federal cutbacks and the lowered birth rate has become a major problem. Knowing this, a number of young people have concluded that not hard work, an advanced degree, or even a college education any longer ensures a successful position, let alone a meaningful life, in today's world. Parents who have academic degrees or wish they had, on the other hand, may insist that their children acquire at least a college degree. They have the argument on their side that many bright young people do feel more fulfilled if they go to college. However, if the children do not feel that the schooling in any way is related to their lives, or if they question the need to learn a lot of patently useless things in order to get their degree in a field that does interest them, they may see no reason to go or may drop out of school. In reacting to this, parents need to ask themselves for whose sake they really want their youngsters to go to school and what it will cost their children to stay in school only for the parents' sake.

In some families we know, outside our research group, the situation we just described has led to a break between parents and children. The whole matter is seen in terms of discipline, in terms of who is in control of whom. Our subjects over and over made it clear to us how much they respected parents and other adults who really lived up to what they believed. When this could be done without being treated disrespectfully themselves, they particularly wanted contacts and dialogs with those adults. Consequently, in our professional and private contacts, we are learning to control those subtle but major needs we were fulfilling via the young people. We find repeatedly that the extension of real respect for the integrity and individuality of the young people is making it possible for them to reach out much more for us. For although the young people may see current reality more clearly and know what questions should be asked, we adults have a great deal more experience in problem solving. Together we make a good team, which surely can solve some of the major problems facing mankind today.

Invariably as we have discussed these ideas publicly, we have been asked whether we are advocating total permissiveness. Here again, we follow our subjects, who made it clear that they appreciated the firm limits their parents had set. They did not like teachers who were not in full control of their classes. By and large, they planned to be just as strict with their children as their parents had been, even though they also planned to foster more communication between themselves and their children than they had experienced with their parents. None of our subjects advocated total permissiveness, and they obviously viewed discipline, pain, and commitment as necessary ingredients of real freedom. We agree with their stand as we, too, think that painless learning, the lack of a demand for commitment, and the other things that characterize many so-called free schools really are a sham because they do not require or promote the development of coping mechanisms. Setting up a painless, fairy tale–like environment for children where there are no goals or demands and no reality consequences of any actions is just as disrespectful to children as subjecting them to the totally arbitrary "law and order" type of discipline now rampant in too many of our middle and high schools.

Our subjects value a form of discipline that lets them know exactly where the adults around them stand without being beaten over the head with it. They do not want issues forced down their throats, but they also do not want to be treated with the condescension implied in shielding them from hurt and pain. Our subjects had to cope with many minor and major hurts in their lives: sibling rivalry, the loss of friends through moves, the loss of parents through death or divorce, restrictions imposed on them by severe illnesses, financial crises for their families, and others. They grew by learning to cope with these pains, but only because they were surrounded by firm limits that allowed no escape. Some protested much more vigorously than others, and it seemed they had to overstate their protests to get attention. However, when they did get attention, they came through. We conclude from this that impersonal discipline, with a minimum of parental attention, does not create growth conditions for children. Attention and commitment from the adults are also necessary.

Another factor that affects the value of discipline is the degree to which the adults really live what they pretend to be. Too often the disciplining adults demand controls or behavior of youngsters which they themselves do not practice or live up to. If we adults under those circumstances can admit our own phoniness, we will appreciate more how hard it is for the kids to live up to our standards. However, we want to warn against the automatic assumption that only adults can be inauthentic. The obedient traditionalists in our sample have worked out a coping style that involves coping by making oneself completely dependent on a small segment of the total environment and by not facing reality oneself by borrowing the conclusions of approved others without examining those conclusions. The obedient traditionalists know only one way of living and are no longer able to improvise.

These findings raise a question that conservative parents will want to ponder: What fate is imposed on children if they are taught to adopt passively traditional lives in a constantly changing, more and more nontraditional world? Harriet, Calvin, Tony, and Douglas already have made substantial sacrifices to become the way they are today, particularly in terms of reality perception, but also in their restricted inner freedom and flexibility, and their inability to be truly close to others. None of them came from nature that way. They have become what they are today in families who, from a traditional standpoint, are fine and responsible. Having accepted their parents' values and life goals, these youths would be assured of success if they were entering the world their parents entered as young adults. Today, that success is less than sure. The plight of some of the engineers in Seattle we mentioned before in some instances seems to stem from their being shell shocked and unable to make changes which their current life realities cry for. Thus, the lack of preparation for making major changes if life circumstances change drastically can add further despair to a difficult situation.

These issues are equally important for teachers and other educators. Many of our subjects stubbornly refused to surrender their perceptions or to allow their schools to train artificial perceptual barriers into them. Teachers may not be aware that they are doing this while teaching their students only their version of reality or the one sanctioned by the school board. This, we believe, is why so few of our subjects experienced any of their teachers as important people in their lives. The great majority considered school and schooling as something entirely separate from their real lives[4]

In this context, it is interesting to observe the current debate as to how and what children need to be taught to help them grow. Drucker[5] has recently argued that the world is now so complex that direct experience has become an increasing unsatisfactory guide to reality. He proposes that we move from our empirical world into the concerted and deliberate acquisition of knowledge. Rather than to deal directly with the world around us, Drucker wants us to deal increasingly with scientific abstractions of that world. McLuhan[6] has insisted that electronic developments have transformed the world into one global village, where we increasingly must relate directly to concrete neighbors and no longer can keep the kind of sensory and ideologic distance from them which the colonialists could maintain from the "natives"

("natives" is an abstraction) in their colonies. It is in keeping with McLuhan's views, rather than with Drucker's proposal, that so many young people in the 1960s (and 72 percent of our subjects) have clung stubbornly to their own senses and particularly have resisted the efforts of their schools to make them view the world in a more detached, abstract manner. Over a decade ago Friedenberg[7] documented the intense efforts being made in contemporary high schools to suppress their students' own sensations and perceptions of the world around them.

While marrying emphasis on personal perception and sensation to Piaget's research findings, Kohlberg and Gilligan[8] recently concluded that schools must stress development rather than achievement if they are to help prepare their students for the world in which they will have to live: "If development rather than achievement is to be the aim of education, such development must be meaningful or real to the adolescent in his search for identity, and it must deal with life" (p.1083). On the basis of experiences both in education and psychotherapy, Carl Rogers[9] has come to the same conclusions, but warns that not all students want to, or can, be taught in ways that stress development rather than achievement. Our data underline Rogers' warning, in that 28 percent of our sample neither wanted or could have used stress on development.

Many adults today spend considerable time and effort to regain their own sensations. Growing up in another era, older generations were taught to disregard their own sensations and were rewarded for abandoning their perceptions of things. The tremendous interest of many contemporary adults in sensitivity training, encounter groups, the newer therapies, and the like reflects a wish to reclaim lost sensations and to achieve greater self-awareness. In discussing the changes he expects sociology to make as it takes the future into consideration, Bell[10] predicts that "it will distinctively add the cultivation of *awareness* as a central feature" (emphasis by Bell; p. 99.) Bell then quotes Polak[11]: "As long as the prophet-propitiator was acting only as a divine transmitter of messages from on high, man felt that he was accepting his ethics ready-made, with no alterations allowed. In a later stage man staggers under the double load of not only having to construct his own future but having to create the values which will determine its design." We note the underlying anxiety in these quotes from adults and compare them with the calm determination of our sensers, who never lost touch with the world in which they lived and yet were not afraid or apprehensive in any major way. With many educators, such as Kohl[12] and Summers,[13] who describe the remarkable success they had when they respected the subcultures of their students, we want to ask what the schools can possibly gain from ignoring their students' perceptions of the reality outside the school in favor of the "scientific" (and therefore "unreal" to the students) version of how reality is supposed to be.

When they graduated from high school, many of our subjects were hoping that they would find college more open, more responsive to their needs, more concerned about learning than about decorum, and, above all, more democratic. We have no answers to the questions they asked about why only guided discussions and not free interchanges are allowed in classrooms; nor why high school students may make decisions only about matters that have no importance anyway. Changes could be made immediately and would not require additional funds or equipment. However, a major change in the attitude in high school faculties, particularly in the administrative and counseling staffs, would be necessary: they would have to develop more respect for individual differences and for individual cognitive styles and realities.

In spite of many protestations to the contrary, schools are still expecting everyone to learn in the same way.[14] If a student happens to learn differently the officially sanctioned learning method is slowed down for that student but not changed in any other way. Furthermore, too often teachers expect that what fulfills (and fulfilled) them also will fulfill their students, even though these students may come from different backgrounds and are growing up in an entirely different world. For example, only the youngest teachers have grown up with TV — a factor whose influence on child development we have not begun to understand. Yet, many courses are still being taught (sometimes on closed circuit TV) as if TV had never been invented.

It is inconceivable to us that highly qualified and experienced high school administrators, counselors, and teachers in the long run can be satisfied to be cast in the roles of guardians and promoters of a life style which three-fourths of their students[15] consider to be irrelevant to their lives outside the school. Our nontraditional subjects stayed in school merely to get a ticket to go to college. They deeply resented having to spend years in a setting where they were not allowed to be themselves and where rewards could be earned only by giving up their individuality and by conforming, but never by what they could have contributed if anyone had ever cared enough about them as real persons to allow them to do so.

One of the reasons we have heard teachers give for discouraging real student participation is that they are afraid their own role will be reduced if they allow the students to contribute more. From the interviews with our subjects, we believe this fear to be totally unwarranted. Although wanting to be heard, these young people also wanted an opportunity to test their ideas in discussions with more experienced and knowledgeable adults,[16] provided this could be done in an atmosphere of mutual respect. As we already mentioned, almost without exception they preferred teachers who knew how to take charge of a classroom.[17] However, their respect for such teachers often evaporated when they found that the teachers could not admit that they were wrong even when this was patently obvious.

In dealing with today's youth, teachers need to be much more honest with themselves and with their students. They need to ask themselves seriously what their goals really are. Are they teaching merely for the next test, in reality merely requiring memorization of facts that may be obsolete or will be in the near future? Has what they teach been updated to fit the needs of the time, and does it also have meaning to the 3 out of every 4 students who are asking serious questions? Do they know their subject matter completely, or are they merely relying on their teaching techniques? Are they allowing real participation and input from the students, and do they allow themselves to hear what the students are asking? If the students express dislike for what is being taught, does the teacher dismiss this as student laziness, or is any effort made to find out whether course content is perhaps no longer relevant to the world the students perceive? Does the teacher love his subject? Our subjects hankered for teachers who conveyed their own enthusiasm for the subject matter to their students but allowed them the freedom of their own reactions. Do teachers extend the same respect to the students that they expect in return? The teacher can be a model of respecting other people for the student, but our subjects had found only a few such teachers in their schools.

We also want to warn teachers in grade and middle schools against making definite predictions about their students. During the prepuberty study many of our subjects looked shaky indeed, and we worried about their further development. This worry turned out to be quite unwarranted as we saw them again just before graduation from high school. Participation in a longitudinal study like the coping study has driven home to us time and again that crisis and symptoms, however dramatic they look on the surface, are rarely evidence of breakdown or of falling apart. To the contrary, they are much more likely to represent active attempts at growing up. Therefore, if we deal with growth disruptions from a cross-sectional point of view, as problems outside the context of the child's overall growth and development, we lose an opportunity to assist the child's growth efforts and may inadvertently undercut them.

Because they deal with 12 or more crucial years of children's lives, schools have an ideal opportunity to take a longitudinal view and monitor each child's growth in a helpful way. A number of children in the coping study turned to the project staff through the years not only because they knew we were available and interested, but particularly because they knew we would see things in perspective, understand that they were struggling, and not immediately rush in to "help." If school personnel would work toward earning the same kind of confidence from their students as our subjects granted to us, they would be amazed at how much growth support they would be able to extend merely by being available and by listening and understanding. This requires, however, that the adults share our faith in the children's ability to resolve their difficulties eventually. We developed this faith once we freed ourselves enough from our professional training to allow ourselves to also see children's strengths as clearly as their weaknesses.

Such efforts will not make much sense, however, unless teachers will heed our findings, and those of many others,[5,6,8] emphasizing that schools need to make a major effort to reflect, at least some degree, real pulsating life outside their walls. Our subjects complained repeatedly that the schools had no interest in teaching them about the world they lived in and only wanted to prepare them for jobs![8] Our brighter subjects clearly perceived that in their schools the so-called preparation for college, or the so-called vocational preparation, was directed to a society that existed 30 or more years ago. They were convinced that, for all practical purposes, that society no longer exists today. An example given related to which books were required reading in English, or any other courses for that matter. Our subjects were unable to see any connection between what they had to read and the lives they were actually living or preparing for. Consequently, reading was merely a meaningless chore to secure a passing grade. No wonder that practically all our students were achieving below their potential in school. They could not and would not be challenged by assignments they experienced as totally meaningless.

Those of our findings which have implications for parents and teachers will also have interest for youth directors in churches. A large number of our subjects[19] no longer saw the churches as fulfilling the needs of young people with strong religious yearnings. None of our subjects had turned to Far Eastern religions or any of the other alternatives that interested many of their contemporaries elsewhere. However, a fair number were in the process of leaving their churches in order to preserve their meaningful and personal closeness to God. This implies that churches will not become more attractive if they merely offer more or different youth activities or simplify their ponderous rituals. Churches need to allow and facilitate on active, direct, personal closeness to God. Like our subjects, churches also need to emphasize love which is not merely mouthed or prayed for, but lived and practiced. Emphasis on "we who have the Word" and "they over there who haven't found the only truth yet," attitudes which the youths we studied saw as characteristic of organized religion, repelled those subjects who displayed the strongest interest in love as a part of their religious strivings. The love these young people believe in is practiced at times other than Sunday morning. Most important of all, life and living people are loved rather than death and the hereafter, which our subjects believed the traditional churches are worshipping at the expense of life. Many of our subjects also disapproved of the stances taken by major religious denominations on issues such as abortion, contraception, illegitimacy, and divorce, because these stances were based on abstract theological considerations rather than on a hard look at the real social issues and situations in the contemporary world.

In an analogous manner, the pursuit of so-called scientific truths at the expense of the world of reality may haunt the fields of child and adolescent psychiatry today. In their diagnostic work, professionals in these fields may be the prisoners of the very developmental theories and schedules they have set up, as well as of a professional focus that sees growth disturbances as psychiatric illnesses or at least as evidence of poor mental health. A careful history is always taken but is related more to the time when certain skills were acquired — for example, walking, talking, toilet training, telling time — than to how a particular child has managed to cope with the inner and outer stresses of his life. Just as in the schools, in psychiatrist's offices the children are essentially evaluated cross sectionally rather than from a longitudinal developmental standpoint. Furthermore, strong pressures for conformity have persuaded child psychiatrists to assign diagnostic labels to more and more behavioral manifestations, with the tacit implication that these behaviors are more or less "sick."[20]

Marie Jahoda[21] stressed years ago that a concept of mental health was a human value and, therefore, would vary with the time, place, customs, and expectations of a cultural group. Hence, she urged anyone trying to define mental health to state clearly the underlying values that prompted them to single out this particular definition. In the recent revision of the American Psychiatric Association Diagnostic Manual,[22] as well as in the classification of childhood difficulties proposed by the Group for the Advancement of Psychiatry,[23] no one has attempted to spell out these underlying values. Our participation in a longitudinal study has taught us that individuals can mature at times and in ways never dreamed of by professionals in the field of psychiatry. The reason they have not dreamed about it is that they are tied, because of psychiatry's marriage with medicine, to an outmoded model of what goes on when people are physically diseased. Psychiatrists have not yet realized that more and more of their colleagues in physical medicine are focusing on the efforts physical bodies make to overcome disease rather than on the disease processes themselves. Similarly, we have found it far more productive and predictive to focus on our subjects' strengths and coping efforts than on their vulnerabilities and weaknesses.

We do not mean to imply, hereby, that these vulnerabilities and weaknesses are irrelevant. We merely see them in the larger context of the total youngster, who has strengths as well as weaknesses and who somehow tries to work out a useful mode of adaptation. For this reason one of us (PWT in his diagnostic and therapeutic work) invites the children to take a far more active part than in the past.[24] The results of this approach are encouraging and have driven home to us how many condescending biases have been trained into us, biases which we find to be entirely unrelated to real children. If, indeed, the children are ever allowed to be real in a diagnostic or therapeutic process which they cannot enter without first being declared a "patient" according to some form of abstract professional theology.

In their interviews a number of our sensers expressed appreciation for the opportunity to talk with a genuinely interested adult in a situation where they experienced total freedom because they could spell out their perception of reality without having to argue. In being used as a sounding board by these youngsters, we found ourselves induced to enlarge our research focus and to take a fresh look at the world we lived in, at what we considered "reality,"and at how we viewed our personal and professional roles within that reality. Thus, as we listened to our subjects, many of our most solid and cherished convictions came crashing down around us. Since then, everything we know, including what we have tried to crystallize in this book, has been in flux. Personal roles, sexual roles, professional roles, religious, social, and political attitudes — our own as well as those of many others — are changing. For as Levenson[25] has so cogently demonstrated, even the same words or concepts inevitably assume different meanings as the times change. Therefore, even though some people hold on to the same views, these views now operate in a different context and, therefore, are no longer the same. Where these changes will lead the world we do not know. Neither do we know how to judge the changes in terms of whether they are good or bad. We are convinced from the contacts with our research subjects that change is or can be an essential part of never-ending growth in life, and that change, even when it is extensive, by no means is necessarily bad or destructive. Change appears to be mostly a good experience for those who welcome it and find it meaningful. Change for the sake of change is meaningless. Those to whom change makes no sense or who have no desire for change will guard tradition and ensure that it will also be a part of the society of today and tomorrow.

Having allowed ourselves to see and experience a new, different reality and having changed accordingly ourselves, we hope that those of our fellow humans who also are changing or want to change will have found it as useful as we did to listen to what our subjects conveyed to us. For us, there is great hope in the well-considered, intelligent, deliberate, calm, almost diffident, way in which changes are being made by those of our subjects who see a need for change. Rather than allowing themselves to be swept by the tide of history, they are riding the crest of the wave, not totally without anguish or anxiety, but mostly full of confidence and hope. They illustrate to us what Camus[26] visualized when he wrote: "At this moment, when each of us must fit an arrow to his bow and enter the lists anew, to reconquer, within history and in spite of it, that which he owns already, the thin yield of his fields, the brief love of this earth, at this moment when at last a man is born, it is time to forsake our age, and its adolescent rages. The bow bends; the wood complains. At the moment of supreme tension, there will leap into flight an unswerving arrow, a shaft that is inflexible and free."

Notes:

[1]Gardner John W: *Self-Renewal: The Individual and the Innovative Society.* New York, Harper & Row, Publishers, 1965, p 5.

[2]In his recent survey for the John D. Rockefeller 3rd Fund, Daniel Yankelovich, Inc., found that only 8 percent of the college students they polled considered the existing American structures as "too rotten to repair." (Daniel Yankelovich, Inc.: The Changing Values on Campus. New York, Washington Square Press, 1972, p 68.)

[3]See Appendix.

[4]See Appendix.

[5]Drucker Peter F: *The Age of Experience.* New York, Harper & Row, Publishers, 1968.

[6]McLuhan Marshall: *Understanding Media.* New York, New American Library, 1964.

[7]Friedenberg Edgar Z: *Coming of Age in America.* New York, Random House, 1963.

[8]Kohlberg Lawrence, Gilligan Carol: The Adolescent as a philosopher: Discovery of the self in a postconventional world. Daedalus 100 (4): 1050–1086, 1971.

[9]Rogers Carl R: *Freedom to Learn.* Columbus, Ohio, Charles E. Merrill Publishing Company, 1969.

[10]Bell Wendell: Social science: the future as a missing variable, Toffler, Alvin (ed): *Learning for Tomorrow: The Role of the Future in Education.* New York, Random House, 1974.

[11]Reference given by Bell (see footnote 10): Polak Frederik L; The Image of the Future, vol 1. New York, Oceana Publications, 1961, p 56.

[12]Kohl Herbert: *36 Children.* New York, The New American Library, 1967.

[13]Summers Andrew: *Me The Flunkie.* New York, Fawcett World Library, 1970.

[14]Toussieng Povl W: Teachers and differences. Am J Orthopsychiatry 39(5): 730-734, 1969.

[15]See Appendix. In a "youthpoll" conducted in 1970 on a random sample chosen from one million students across the country by the American College Testing Program, 3 out of every 4 students were critical, some sharply critical, of their high school experience. Sabine Gordon A: When You Listen, This Is What You Can Hear. . .Iowa City, Iowa, ACT Publications, 1971, Chapter 2.

[16]As of now, close to half of our subjects have contacted the staff since the project ended. They were seeking the opportunity to discuss matters of concern with a more knowledgeable person before they made crucial decisions.

[17]This was also a major finding in Sabine's poll. See footnote 8.

[18]See Appendix.

[19]See Appendix.

[20]Dr. Lois Murphy made this point many years ago when she said: "Too often in these studies we have been burdened by rigid biases and assumptions about the role of more or less statically conceived genetic factors or by standardized criteria of developmental norms. When the child does not "behave" as adults demand, he is said to have behavior problems or "symptoms." Temper tantrums, thumbsucking, enuresis, and other behaviors have been seen as problems even at the ages of 3 and 4 years because their occurence deviated from the level of social conformity adults assumed the child should be able to meet by the age of 3 or 4 or 5." Murphy Lois B: *The Widening World of Childhood.* New York, Basic Books, Inc. Publishers, 1962, pp 2–3.

[21]Jahoda Marie: Current Concepts of Positive Mental Health. Joint Commission on Mental Illness and Health Monograph Series, No. 1, New York, Basic Books, Inc, Publishers, 1958, p. 80.

[22]*Diagnostic and Statistical Manual of Mental Disorders,* Ed 2. American Psychiatric Association. Washington, DC, 1968.

[23]*Psychopathological Disorders in Childhood: Theoretical Considerations and a Proposed Classification.* New York, Group for the Advancement of Psychiatry, 1966.

[24]Toussieng Povl W: Child psychotherapy in a new era. Am J Orthopsychiatry 41 (1): 58–64, 1971.

[25]Levenson Edgar A: *The Fallacy of Understanding: An Inquiry into the Changing Structure of Psychoanalysis.* New York, Basic Books, Inc, Publishers, 1972.

[26]Camus Albert: *The Rebel.* New York, Alfred A Knopf, 1954, p 273.

Appendix A

Data Collecting and Methodology

Initially, we proposed to interview and test each of our subjects in their senior year of high school. These sessions were taped, transcribed, and independently summarized by the two authors for each subject. The psychiatric session with Dr. Toussieng consisted of one 3-hour "in-depth" interview covering a selected set of topics (as shown in the appended outline) in order to secure uniform data. A free interview technique was used, and the items on the outline were covered, as far as possible, as they came up spontaneously. Wherever possible, question-answer types of interviews were avoided. For some of the subjects the outline was followed only partially because the subjects were at a crisis point in their lives at the time of the interviews and chose to use the interviews as vehicles to clear their minds.

Furthermore, subjects were not pressed to reveal about themselves or their families information they regarded as confidential or about which they felt uncomfortable or embarrassed. This was particularly true of material in relation to sexual behavior. Although our hesitancy to probe this area may have reduced the completeness of our data, it increased our subjects' commitment to the project and contributed to their willingness for continued participation over the 20-year span of the series of five studies. In fact, we had always tried to respect our subjects' and their families' wishes for privacy. This was particularly important in view of their conservative background and also a requirement set down by the NIMH as directed by congressional mandate. For these reasons, we sought indirect evidence of sexual behavior from expressed attitudes. In those few cases where subjects volunteered information about sexual behavior, this was a part of our confidential files, but we did not seek it if they chose to withhold it. Because of the limited quantity of this material, we have chosen not to summarize it for publication.

In two sessions, the psychologist (Dr. Moriarty) administered a variety of psychological tests (as indicated below) and also interviewed the subjects, focusing primarily on attitudes and feelings about school, community involvement, and future educational and vocational plans. Some of the material from these interviews duplicated the material obtained in the psychiatric interviews. This was deliberate, as we hoped to gain further depth and indices of reliability and validity in this way. We were also aware that our subjects might respond differently to the male psychiatrist and the female psychologist. As we anticipated, this did make a difference to some of our subjects, particularly in their freedom to express themselves. Furthermore, we obtained a cross check on our impressions and on the data obtained because each of the authors interviewed the subjects without knowing what the other had learned from the subject.

Although we had originally planned to use the Minnesota Multiphasic Inventory, we selected instead the California Personality Inventory, a shorter questionnaire similar to the MMPI but without the items about sexual information. We made this choice in response to congressional concern about violation of privacy during the years of our study.

We should also point out that financial and staff limitations during the period of the adolescent studies made it impossible to interview the parents during our subjects' senior year of high school. This meant that we necessarily saw the parents through the eyes of their children. However, these views were largely compatible with our backlog of family information from earlier interviews with parents during the children's infancy, preschool, latency, and prepuberty years. They were also reinforced by selected informal contacts with a few of the parents, suggesting that in these cases, by inference from cultural continuity, by and large the parents made up a group of responsible, concerned parents of predominantly conservative stance.

In addition, the psychologist offered, for those subjects who desired it, a "feedback" session to discuss the test results with the object of helping subjects use their knowledge and our assessment of their interests, skills, and personality traits in making future and vocational plans. All but 5 of our subjects availed themselves of this opportunity.

In the adolescent study, we were able to gather data on 54, or 83 percent, of the 65 subjects included in the latency and prepuberty samples. Six of the ones not included at this time had moved out of the state, and limitations of time and finances made it impossible to see these young men and women. The mother of 2 children objected to their continued participation. One subject had died before the start of the adolescent study.

We excluded two of the 65 subjects because they did not get close to graduation from high school. One of these two dropped out of school in his sophomore year because of severe emotional difficulties. A neurological work-up revealed that the other subject was suffering from major brain damage. Therefore, he did not meet the criteria for inclusion in our group.

Of the remaining 54, 52 had both a psychiatric interview and psychological testing. One had a psychiatric interview but refused to come back for the testing session. The other lives out of the state and was tested during a visit he made to Topeka relatives. Unfortunately, the psychiatric author had by then acquired new employment in Oklahoma and, therefore, did not interview him. These two subjects were included, nevertheless, because we had quite a wealth of data on them for the purpose of this book, even from the one contact.

We tried to see all of the subjects in their senior year, but in three it was necessary to schedule the testing and interviews before or after the senior year due to the timing of the project. We also found that our subjects' busy schedule, (participation in extracurricular activities and part-time jobs) made it necessary to schedule evening or weekend appointments. These were set up at the convenience of the subjects at a time when Dr. Toussieng was able to travel to Topeka. Our subjects' cooperation in arranging and keeping these appointments was an index of their continued interest in the project. Our ability to make these arrangements was also enormously facilitated by the interest and willingness of our project secretary, Mrs. Marie Smith, to make numerous evening and weekend telephone calls to coordinate scheduling. We are deeply appreciative of her help, as well as the cooperation and flexibility of our subjects in facilitating scheduling.

THE PSYCHIATRIC INTERVIEW

The psychiatric interview covered the following topics:

1. Did subject remember the interviewer or previous contacts with the project?

2. What was the subject's understanding of the purpose of the project and of this interview? (with explanation given, if needed, by interviewer).

3. How many years had passed since the subject was last seen?

4. Relationship(s) to parents: vicissitudes, changes, reasons for change, current view of parents, parents' characteristics, which parent closest, which parent pushed hardest for education, view of parents' child rearing practices.

5. Relationship(s) to siblings.

6. Relationships to other relatives.

7. Childhood: how did the subject view childhood in retrospect — happy or unhappy? Would he or she like to live childhood over again? How did the subject feel regarding approaching adulthood? Happiest and unhappiest moment(s) so far.

8. Friends: male and female, close or casual, influences on and of friends.

9. School: how did the subject like the education she or he had received? Academic performance, favorite subjects, least liked subjects, like or dislike for teachers, characteristics of an ideal teacher.

10. Church: relationship to and importance of religion, relationship to God, participation, desire to raise children in the church, personal values related or unrelated to religion, prayer.

11. Values: compared to parents' values, origin of values, nature of values (flexibility or rigidity, how well adhered to), values used to "shut out" or "include" people with different values, attitudes regarding smoking, drinking, and drugs.

12. Social interests: integration, Vietnam, politics, poverty and welfare.

13. Sexual attitudes: source of sex information, unwed mothers, abortion, "the pill," premarital sex, dating, going steady, engaged, been truly in love yet, criteria for love.

14. Marriage: age at which to marry, characteristics of "ideal" partner, how many kids, raise kids same or differently from own experiences.

15. Plans for future: college, vocation, draft, how to use training, remain in Topeka or move, see future as happy or unhappy.

16. Attitudes toward self: satisfied with looks and adult body performance, attitudes regarding clothes and grooming, what did the subject like best and least about self, how much trust in self in relation to future, degree of autonomy, reasons for any changes in view of self.

17. Death: had the subject been close to any deaths? Had any meaningful people died? Had the subject been to a funeral? If so, describe reaction. Should children attend funerals?

18. Family activities: activities as a family, family vacations, travel outside state.

19. Skills: had the subject learned to drive? How? How good a driver? Hobbies, sports, recreational outlets.

20. How did the subject feel about graduation?

21. Employment: what type, work record, income.

22. Money: sources, how did the subject plan to spend money, how important is money? If the subject had lots of money, what would he or she do?

23. Range and handling of emotions: how to handle anger, had the subject been in fights?

24. Major events caused by fate during entire life so far, but especially during adolescence.

25. How happy (unhappy) was the subject? If unhappy: source(s) of unhappiness, how did person view it? If happy: source(s) of happiness, how viewed?

26. Sleeping patterns: amount required, quiet or restless sleep?

27. Remembered dreams: happy ones, nightmares.

28. Relation to coping project: what did it mean to subject, advantages and disadvantages, why did the subject continue with the project?

29. Regarding this interview: how well was the person covered? How well did the subject feel the interviewer got to know him? What was hardest in the interview?

THREE SESSIONS WITH THE PSYCHOLOGIST

In the first two sessions, early in the senior year of high school, the following psychological tests were administered: Wechsler Adult Intelligence Scale, Rorschach, Thematic Apperception Test, California Personality Inventory, Gordon's Survey of Personal Values, Strong Vocational Interest Blank, and Elizabeth Drew's Ranking Procedure of Reasons for Occupational Choice. (As far as we know this last procedure has not been described in a publication. It was developed as part of a creativity study at Michigan State University. A copy of the form is included.)

In addition, the psychologist also used the testing session as an opportunity for further data collection about school activities over 12 years and subjects' feelings in regard to school.

Data obtained as part of the interview by the psychologist included information from the following questionnaire.

Age:
Birthdate:
Family constellation:
Parents' education:
Parents' occupation:

Schooling:
    1. Completed_____ Planned _____
    2. What have you most enjoyed?
        Subject?
        Teachers?
        Activities?
    3. What did you most dislike?
        Subjects?
        Teachers?
        Activities?
    4. If you were a high school principal given the task of establishing a school most meaningful for teenagers, what would you be most concerned with? How would you select your teachers?
    5. What changes would you suggest?
    6. What school clubs or activities have you been engaged in?
    7. Were you a good, average, or poor student? Were you pleased to do well?
        Did poor work bother you?
    8. Do you think you did as well as you could have? If not, why not?

Other activities:
    What other things do you do in the community or at home?
    Are your daily schedule and your use of leisure time exactly the way you think they ought to be, or the way you most prefer?
    How much and what do you read?
    What do you watch on TV?
    What movies have you liked?
    What is the most exciting thing you have ever done?
    How much time do you spend daydreaming? Is it all right to "loaf" or "goof off"?
    Do you like to have everything settled before you do anything? Or are you willing to take chances?
    Have you ever had a job? Describe.

Future plans:

1. What do you plan to do next? What are the reasons for your choice?
   Economic?
   Social prestige?
   Intellectual challenge?
   Interest in bettering the world?
   Helping people?
2. Who or what experiences in your life have most influenced your future plans?
   Parents?
   Teachers?
   Friends?
   Specific events?
   Specific circumstances?
   How do you choose your friends?
   What kind of people do you like best?
   Was it easy to choose and follow your own interests?
   How much pressure was there from others to take part in standard activities?
   How much did others interfere with your own wishes?
3. Describe the ideal life you'd like to have 10 years from now.
4. What besides a job and/or marriage will be important to you?
   Travel, home, continued learning?
5. What are the chances that it will work out this way?
6. What might interfere or help you have the life you want? (Personal factors? Hard work? World affairs?)
7. In your opinion,
   what is an educated person?
   what is an intelligent person?
   what is a well-adjusted person?
8. How much have you thought about your future?
9. Do you follow closely the standards of behavior set for you by parents or peers, or do you like to think things out for yourself? Do you think of yourself as a conformist or as an individualist?
10. How have you experienced being a part of the normal development project?
    Has it been interesting, boring, something you felt you

should but would have preferred not to do, helpful, a
nuisance?

The WAIS was administered according to standard procedures.
However, we used the context of the subtests to acquire information
about our subjects' self-evaluation of their cognitive skills. Thus, we
asked our subjects a series of questions about their performance on
each of the subtests as follows:

Information:
Do you like to acquire odd bits of information?
Do you consider yourself to be an informed person?
What value do you put on knowing facts?
Do you feel schools place too much value on facts? Should more
emphasis be put on understanding things and people?
Are you more interested in why things are true than in the fact
itself?

Comprehension:
Do you think of yourself as a practical person?
Do you like to figure out how to do things?
Given a puzzle or problem, do you hate to give up?

Arithmetic:
Do you see any useful reason for studying arithmetic?
Would you prefer to do problems stated numerically or those which
ask you to think through a problem in words?
Does it bother you to be timed?

Similarities:
Is it easy to see how things are alike?
Do you often find yourself making comparisons?
Do you find you like people better who seem more like you than
those who seem different?

Digit span:
Do you think you have a good memory?
Are some things easier to remember than others?
Do numbers automatically make you feel nervous or frustrated?

Object assembly:
Did you know in advance what the object would be?
Do you like puzzles of this type?

Vocabulary:

    Do you think you have a good vocabulary?

    Do you judge others by the language they use?

    Do meanings of words fascinate you?

    Do you try to be exact when you're describing something?

Digit symbol:

    Have you ever made up your own code?

    Is it challenging to you to figure out the meaning of symbols?

Picture completion:

    Do you think you have an eye for detail?

    Does it bother you to look at or think about things that are in some way incomplete?

Block design:

    Do you find this test hard or easy?

    Can you visualize how things will look?

    Do you get confused about directions when you are in an unfamiliar place?

Picture arrangement

    Is it easy for you to figure out a logical order?

    Do you find some of these funny?

    Do you agree that "one picture is worth a thousand words"?

Like the psychological interviews, each of the two testing sessions were taped and transcribed. In addition, test behavior, interaction with the psychologist, and test findings were summarized for each individual before discussion with the psychiatrist of any of his findings on individual subjects.

When we became aware of the different styles our subjects used to cope with their world we decided to rate and classify them individually (each author doing so on the basis of data from his sessions) as to their openness to their own senses and to the changing world. (See Appendix C.) We then devised and described the anchoring points on our continuum, as described in Chapters 2 and 5. The number of subjects in each of the five classes, interjudge agreement, and correlations with ratings on coping capacity, IQ, and grade point average are shown in Appendix C.

Case studies exemplifying each level of self-determination (Chapters 3, 4, 6, and 7) integrated findings from Dr. Toussieng's interview (one 3-hour session) and Dr. Moriarty's three sessions. (Two

testing and interviewing sessions and one optional feedback session.)
For greater readability and to protect confidentiality of the material,
we did not include test scores as such for individuals. These can be
made available privately for interested professional readers. In published form, they are available only for the group as a whole, without
individual identification.

Reasons for Occupational Choice

Name _____ School _____ Date _____

There are many reasons for deciding to go into a particular line
of work. Some of them we have listed below. Please rank from 1 to
9 the reasons listed as to how important they will be to *you* in choosing
your life's work. A rank of 1 is given to the most important reason,
2 to the next, and so on.

_____The work allows me to make new discoveries, to do creative
work.
_____It offers high pay.
_____It offers a stable, secure future.
_____It carries a high social prestige.
_____It presents straightforward, realistic problems for which an
answer can be found.
_____It will put me in the front lines intellectually — handling new
ideas or art forms, tackling crucial issues.
_____It will allow me to keep in touch with my parents and spend
time with my family.
_____It presents a challenge for me even though there may never
be any final answer to the problems.
_____It offers an acceptable position in our society.

Appendix B

Environmental Background

To understand the youth we have been studying for almost two decades, the reader may find it helpful to look at the ecological setting of the city and the state, especially the strong influences of its pioneer heritage and its basically conservative political, economic, and social values. It is also relevant, for considering the representativeness of our sample in this population, to describe some typical family values and relationships.

SOME FACTS ABOUT THE CITY

Topeka, a moderate sized city[1] and the capital of Kansas, combines some distinctly urban characteristics and some rural influences. Located in the geographical center of the United States mainland, Topeka is the seat of the state government, a regional insurance center, and a railroad distribution center. A city with growing industrial and commercial interests, it provides employment in railroad shops, steel fabrication, printing, meat packing, egg processing, flour milling, bread baking, and tire and cellophane manufacture. It is also an agricultural processing center for a major agricultural region. Although steadily increasing in population, Topeka is still a small city in some respects: the easy, quick accessibility of all parts of the city; its conservative

political stance; the availability of cultural and educational opportunities; and its relative lack of active participation in major social
changes.

In the 1950s and 1960s, the years during which our subjects were
growing up, Topeka was a city of relatively narrow socioeconomic range[2]
and the average yearly earnings were lower than those in larger cities.
Our families[3] fell into a similar narrow socioeconomic range, even
though they were slightly better off economically than the average
for the total city population. Having included no nonwhite or foreign-
born residents, whose deprivation was greatest, we probably came close
to the economic distribution for the white population in the city.

In our sample, few families were extremely poor; only 1 family
was occasionally on relief, although several others were economically
hard pressed at times as a result of seasonal unemployment, illness,
or both. Nor was extreme wealth typical; only 1 family lived in a
luxurious home, and only 2 families belonged to the local country
club. In a predominantly middle class, native born, white population,
largely of Anglo-Saxon descent[4] most project families, like the majority
of all Topekans, lived in modest, single-family dwellings[5] The contrast
between these homes and both the slum dwellings and the more affluent
residences was far less striking than in the larger cities of both coasts.
Furthermore, we believe that the city is relatively typical of a large
number of United States cities[6] suggesting that our findings have
relevance for a large segment of the national population. To justify
this assumption, we shall look somewhat more closely at the demogra-
phic characteristics of our sample.

In the infancy of the children in our sample, 2 families briefly
lived with grandparents; 3 families in small apartments; 1 family in
a duplex; and 1 family in a trailer. The last family, continuing to
live in a trailer throughout the series of studies, was the only family
who did not live in a single-family dwelling when the youths were
interviewed at adolescence.

Within modest limits, most families improved their living conditions during the project years, but there was also a good deal of stability
insofar as the majority lived in the same community, and in middle
class neighborhoods, which were also close to grandparents or other
relatives. During the two decades of the five studies, only 5 families
(each with 1 of our child subjects) lived in the same home throughout
the entire period; 42 families (with 47 subjects) moved to larger homes
within the community. Twelve families returned to Topeka before the
children's adolescence; one moved to another community in Kansas.

Several families remodeled their homes extensively, doing so over a period of years with parents and children contributing to the work. Furthermore, most of these single-family dwellings were located in comfortable residential areas with neat yards, for the most part attractively landscaped, and with ample play space and trees for climbing. Many were furnished with outdoor play equipment in the early years. Five families lived on the outskirts of town, where they maintained vegetable gardens and raised some animals as pets or for food.

Thus, in its size[5], as well as in a number of aspects of its composition and life style, Topeka could be seen as representative of a broad segment of middle American culture, and our research sample roughly reflected these aspects of the city, the state, and the nation.

GOVERNMENT AND POLITICAL AFFILIATIONS

As a first-class city with a charter from the state, Topeka selects a mayor and city commissioners for 2-year terms of office. These governmental agents are chosen at large on a nonpartisan ballot. However, there is no question that community voting patterns at a state and national level are predominantly Republican and conservative with little representation of radicalism of either the right or the left. Democratic candidates, although occasionally elected to office from personal preference for one man over another, tend to be more conservative than their national counterparts. In 1964, the Kansas vote went to Johnson over Goldwater, but in 1968 with a more moderate Republican candidate, the vote went to Nixon. Ten percent voted for Wallace. We never asked our subjects to identify their party preferences, but casual remarks on the part of the youth we interviewed suggested that the majority of parental voting patterns, and their own leanings, were consistent with the relatively conservative political stance of the residents of the city and of the state. Here, as in socioeconomic status, the families of our sample were typical of the majority of the local residents.

CRIME AND DELINQUENCY

In Topeka, 1960 census figures showed 1.78 major crimes for 1000 of the population[7]. Delinquency rates were at that time 1.47 per 100 in the adolescent years[7]. This compared favorably with national figures[8].

In our adolescent sample, no parent was known to have been charged with a major crime, although one father may have contributed to his wife's death. Only 2 of our subjects were, during the 20 years of our study, brought to the attention of the juvenile court. One of these dropped out of the sample before the adolescent phase of the study. Hence, both parents and children were essentially law abiding.

RACIAL CONFLICT AND STUDENT RIOTS

Racial conflict, which was present and in some respects smoldering in the 1960s (when our subjects were in their prepuberty and adolescent years), did not erupt into violence until 1970. Nor were there any student riots during out subjects' growing years. Hence, some of our subjects were concerned about racial equality and civil rights and the majority were distinctly opposed to the Vietnam War, but they were not in their own community experiences directly confronted with or forced to take a public stand on these issues. In the same way, parents, although frequently quite clear about their stance on matters of race, were not actively aligned with programs directed toward changing attitudes or promoting equal opportunities educationally or vocationally. We did not interview parents during our subjects' adolescence, but the relative stability of values over the preceding 12 years made it unlikely that there were substantial changes during the subjects' high school years.

RELIGIOUS AND ETHICAL VALUES

In a "Bible belt" city having over 100 churches of many different denominations, it is not surprising that at prepuberty 90 percent of our sample had, with strong parental encouragement, maintained active church ties and regularly participated in formal religious services? Only 1 mother and 2 fathers were opposed to church going. One-third of the families were Catholic; 59 percent belonged to conventional Protestant demoninations, and 8 percent were adherents of fundamentalist churches. Sixty-one percent of the Protestant youths regularly attended Sunday school.

For the majority of the families, religion was an important part of their daily lives and contributed vitally to parental views on child rearing. In the children's prepuberty years, two-thirds of the families held daily home devotionals, and 68 percent of the mothers, 36 percent of the fathers, and 42 percent of the children found religious teachings to be especially meaningful supports and guides. From informal contacts with a number of our parents, we believed they maintained these standards for themselves and their offspring in their children's adolescence. However, they apparently reduced demands for formal adherence to some religious practices.

By the adolescent years, the youths' church attendance and reliance on formal religious practices decreased. About half of the total sample (48 percent) still attended church regularly, and 20 percent were, according to their own report, deeply emotionally involved in formal religious practices. Many of our teenagers privately in their interviews described formal church activities as meaningless and not entirely relevant in a changing world. As one of our subjects said, "I'm against the church but I'm not against God." Their religious values were more directly expressed in their humanistic concerns. More than one half of our adolescent sample participated in church-sponsored activities to help the ill and disadvantaged.

Our families did not adhere to the "God is dead" philosophy, and they were not aroused to take an active stance in relation to the Pope's encyclical on birth control. Still, many of our teenage subjects later told us privately that they approved of birth control, and a few endorsed abortion. The latter indicated that these views were their own, not shared by parents, and not usually discussed with parents.

Compared to their contemporaries on the East and West Coasts, Topeka parents in the 1950s and 1960s were less tolerant of relaxation of moral standards in relation to sex, drinking, and social customs; more resistant to world involvement; and in their own behavior slower to adopt new styles. For example, bikinis and miniskirts were popular in Topeka only several years after they were commonly worn on both coasts. Although 22 percent confided that they had experienced some intense marital conflict and half of these considered separation, only 11 percent of the families went through with divorce proceedings. There was no reason to discuss drugs with parents since to the best of our knowledge there was no serious drug problem in the city as a whole during our subjects' high school years.

Our families were strongly influenced by their heritage of pioneer perseverance and practical needs for self-sufficiency. They were proud of their independence and capacity for hard work and responsibility.

They had been content with relatively modest goals of economic security and moderate material comfort which they chose to earn through their own resourcefulness and competence in dealing with practical problems of living. These views held by parents during the growing years of the youths in our sample were generally characteristic of values common to the community and to the state, and so far as we knew continued to characterize parental value systems in their children's adolescence. They were also characteristic of a broad national segment of solid, conservative middle class Americanism: Republican in politics; orthodox in religious practices; moralistic in adhering to the Protestant ethic; traditionalistic and self-restricting in thinking, feeling, and behaving. Our findings of qualitative differences in value systems between the two generations linked our subjects with youth throughout the nation.

EDUCATIONAL AND CULTURAL FACILITIES

Educational and cultural opportunities in Topeka are adequate and traditional. The city maintains 3 public high schools, 12 junior high schools, 51 public elementary schools, and a number of special classes for the handicapped. There are also 2 county high schools on the outskirts of the city and several special training facilities financed by the state for the child and adult retarded, the emotionally disturbed, the blind, and the deaf. Parochial education is provided by 1 Catholic high school, 12 Catholic junior high schools, 6 Catholic elementary schools, and 1 Lutheran elementary school. There are several private nursery schools. Head Start classes, although not in existence when we began our research, are now held in all sections of the city. Advanced education is available through a business college, a vocational school, and a municipal university. Several state universities and private colleges are within easy commuting distance.

The majority (69 percent) of our subjects attended the public schools in Topeka. Six had some preschool experiences through private nursery schools or church-sponsored activities. Eight graduated from the local parochial high schools. Six others completed public high school courses in other Kansas communities, and three in out-of-state public high schools. All of these schools were alike in the following of conservative policies and teaching methods and in offering traditional curricula.[10]

Comparing our subjects with their parents and the parent generation,[11] we saw increases in both educational aspirations and current achievement. Contrasting with the 20 percent of the parents who dropped out of school before completing high school, only 2 (4 percent) of the 54 subjects who were interviewed in the adolescent years had failed to complete high school.[2] Contrasting with 37 percent of the parents who enrolled in college, 41 (76 percent) of our adolescents, or more than twice as many in the current generation, were either already enrolled or definitely planning to enroll in college. However, we could expect that some of these would not finish college for various reasons. We know, for example, that in prepuberty 50 (93 percent) were planning to go to college. By the end of high school, 3 girls at least temporarily gave up their college plans after they became engaged. This was also true of 1 boy about to be drafted and of 5 other boys who decided to continue enjoyable summer work, a choice partly determined by their draft status. In the years of our study, Topeka differed from the larger cities insofar as it was less intellectually sophisticated, less aware of new or avant-garde movements socially, politically and artistically, and had fewer cultural and educational opportunities. In effect, the city's conservatism probably reduced potential intellectual stimulation and increased emotional restrictions on its youths. But at the same time, it protected these youths from some of the temptations, conflicts, and grosser emotional disturbances aroused by economic, social and political extremes of the larger cities. Yet, cultural and educational opportunities were not lacking to those who wished to take advantage of the municipal university, the nearby universities, three concert series, two amateur dramatic groups, and yearly opportunities to attend Broadway theatrical productions shown locally and in Kansas City. We had reason to believe that the families of our sample participated in such activities relatively little during our subjects' childhood, but the most recent interviews with our subjects suggested increasing interest in these cultural outlets by the young people.

HEALTH

Health facilities in Topeka were and have remained ample. There are 3 general hospitals, 3 psychiatric hospitals, and special diagnostic and therapeutic facilities for the adult and child physically, mentally, or emotionally handicapped and for delinquent youths. In addition, the State Board of Health and the City-County Health Department are located in Topeka.

The parents in our study were aware of these facilities and took advantage of them. All babies were born in hospitals, and many were first contacted for the study through Well-Baby Conferences. Our pediatrician was the state director of maternal and child health. No known physical problems were left untreated. All of the children in the sample were in relatively good health,[13] but they were not without a variety of physical stresses that were incapacitating at some time during their growth.

Parental health was also relatively good, although 5 fathers and 4 mothers suffered from some major chronic physical condition or had acute health problems[14] that involved hospitalization and some periods of unemployment.

As to mental health, most parents could be said to be relatively stable and generally optimistic and self-confident in caring for their children. Few sought advice through reading on health or child care. Ten of the mothers experienced periods of relatively severe acute or chronic depression; two of these were briefly hospitalized. Four of the fathers appeared to be distinctly unstable and alcoholic to a degree that created special family problems. In addition to these more serious emotional disturbances, about one-third of the mothers were at times functioning at a level less than optimal, in relation to environmental pressures. During the study, 2 fathers and 4 mothers died. There were also 2 accidental deaths among our subjects; one occurred in the subject's prepuberty years, the other in late adolescence.

Our data on extended families are incomplete, but the available evidence suggests that roughly 7 percent[15] of the members of all families (both adults and children) studied during the 20 years of our research at some time sought psychiatric help. More characteristic of these families was reliance on religion and on support from within the immediate and extended family. Hence, we feel that it is fair to say that our subjects were on the average healthy, stable, adequately functioning youths; that they were reared by relatively healthy stable parents; that they lived in a homogenous community in which family values were consistent with prevalent traditional standards of the community and not unlike those of nearly half of the United States white population.

With these generalizations in mind, it is important to look somewhat more closely at those aspects of family interaction that appeared to be typical of the sample as a whole.

COMMON CHARACTERISTICS IN OUR SUBJECTS' FAMILY INTERACTIONS

Infancy

During infancy, we saw a group of predominantly healthy, intellectually normal, perceptually alert, socially responsive babies, of which the majority were wanted and given competent physical care and a relatively secure emotional environment by reasonably healthy stable parents. This is not to deny that some of the infants from time to time suffered special vulnerabilities[16] that interfered with optimal functioning, and in a few cases may have reduced full mobilization of their native sensitivities.

During the infancy of our subjects, few mothers worked; hence, they were physically, and to a large extent emotionally, available to satisfy the needs of their infants. Most of the mothers, although not especially inclined to seek professional counseling about child rearing procedures and not avid readers of child guidance literature, were alert to individual differences, to the need to pace stimulation to the child's skills and disposition, and to adjust their own tempo to that of the children.

In most families, the mothers were distinctly dominant in home management. Fathers shared in the care and discipline of children, gave their wives a good deal of support, and in turn were respected for their earning capacity and their skills in building, repairing, and improving family homes and possessions.

Both parents were proud of their infants and were inclined to find time to play with the babies and to let the children develop as individuals. They enjoyed showing off their babies to relatives and friends and were likely to include the babies in whatever activities were planned for the family. That is, professional babysitters were rarely hired because relatives were usually available to care for the children in brief necessary absences of the mothers, and few parents took any vacations or trips without their children. Almost as soon as the baby was brought home from the hospital, it was assumed that he or she would be taken to church with the family. There was from the beginning a cohesiveness and continuity in living and growing together which included the extended families and provided opportunities for many shared activities and outings.

Preschool

In the preschool years, most mothers regarded formal learning experiences outside of the home as unnecessary because they felt an adequate number of playmates and opportunities for learning were available within the family and in the neighborhood. These feelings were justified by the fact that only 2 children had no siblings (family size varied from 2 to 8 children, with an average of 3.5); most lived in neighborhoods where there were other children of the same age; and nearly all the children were given freedom to explore the immediate neighborhood. It was taken for granted that they could, without much danger to themselves and without neighborhood objection, wander unrestrained through unfenced yards, and that adult neighbors would be as available as the mothers to give help or offer information. Children were encouraged to learn to care for themselves, to admire older siblings, and to help younger ones to grow in independence. Physical activities and skills were especially prized, but, in addition, most parents read to their children, were proud of their learning, and gave considerable opportunity for self-expression. Relatively few mothers were too busy or too preoccupied with personal problems or interests to take time from daily household duties to talk and play with their children. In short, the autonomy and individuality[17] allowed at this period provided sound bases for the self-respect, sense of identity, reflectiveness, initiative, sincerity, and responsiveness we observed in the majority of these children at adolescence.

Important in this process was the tolerance on the part of many families for periods of unusual dependence or withdrawal in some children, for slow development of motor and sensory skills in a few children, and in nearly all an appreciation of the need for pacing demands and expectations to the children's requirements for rest, delay, and recognition. This does not deny the facts that: nearly half of these children, at preschool or later, showed mild deviations in speech;[18] one-quarter were unclear or inaccurate in perceptual intake as registered on projective tests; one-third were incapable of age-adequate integration cognitively; and nearly all were at some times or in some circumstances acutely anxious and fearful.[19] Nor were sibling rivalry, severe oedipal problems, physical stress, or developmental crises uncommon. However, these normally expectable stresses were at least in part counter-balanced by parental, and especially maternal, expectations that the children would "grow out of" transitory difficulties, and by parental lack of anxiety about serious, permanent, or unusual damage of any sort. Parents' pride and pleasure in their children and their efforts to help their children constructively with whatever problems existed contributed to a sense of adequacy in the children that was and has for the most part remained impressive. In other words, our subjects with few exceptions never experienced a sense of total defeat. In addition, parents were on the whole capable of supporting positive growth and controlling negative aggressive feelings. In their own behavior, they provided consistent models of adequacy, responsibility, and commitment to high standards of honesty, directness, and loyalty to the family, church, and community.

Latency

By latency, the balance between firm, definite controls and loving support was even more impressive. Almost uniformly, parents demanded cooperation, expected responsibility, set limits, and provided opportunities for appropriate sublimation of childish energies. Respect for personal property and for people at all levels of society were required ("talking back" and breaking things were strictly taboo), but in turn, children were allowed to express opinions and encouraged to talk over their troubles with both parents and older siblings. As a last resort, half of the parents dealt with disobedience by spanking, but 77 percent preferred verbal reprimand or restriction of privileges, along with constructive suggestions. Children were shown how to repair, make amends, or satisfy needs for competitive and aggressive physical activity in sports and games. Verbal disagreement with family members was assumed to be par for the course (77 percent), but hitting was immediately reprimanded and restricted. The children did not protest vigorously because they tended to feel they were treated fairly. Looking back on their childhood in the adolescent interviews, most youths felt their parents were never overly harsh.

We learned from both children and parents that children were expected to complete their chores, including homework, but getting "good grades" did not have high priority.[20] Both emotionally and intellectually, there was a good deal of tolerance for individual preference, provided basic values of honesty and responsibility were met. If this produced relatively conservative, traditional, and perhaps mildly constricted latency-aged children in some cases, it also contributed to internal security on the part of the children, to fairly comfortable introjection of a definite scheme of values of right and wrong, and to a willingness to tolerate a range of behavior in others within these limits.

Prepuberty

By prepuberty, learned modulation appeared to be firmly anchored by an inner disposition toward conformity and containment of feelings in an environment that encouraged such a mode of reactivity.[20] [21] Our mothers considered most important and encouraged in their children such values as good manners, tolerance, loyalty to the church, and frankness.

Of relatively low value were desires for the children or themselves to make a name in the world or to obtain good grades. In the children's attitudes as expressed in the prepuberty interviews and in their school performance, they seemed to have satisfied the mothers' requirements quite well. Families remained close, but shared activities decreased somewhat as the youths reached out for new peer experiences socially, intellectually, and emotionally. Traditional religious backgrounds, as we have already indicated, continued to have strong influence on the thinking and behavior of the majority, but participation in formal church activities declined. Family outings were still frequent for a third of the sample, occasional for another third, and rare or never for the final third. In the boys, we found modest correlations between level of family interaction and grades.

On the face of it, the reduction in the time spent with the family was in many of our subjects a function of cognitive growth, of new interests, of greater attraction to peers, and of increasing involvement with special academic or social interest groups. But the level of participation in extracurricular peer activities (in contrast to interests pursued individually) appeared to be higher in the more stable, more adequately functioning individuals. Thus, we felt that activities served defensive needs for sublimation in a period of maximal developmental stress as a result of the onset of puberty, status changes with matriculation into junior high school, and conflicts and ambivalence about their own urgencies and adult demands for greater independence. Projective tests given in the prepuberty years, as well as retrospective reports by the adolescents, testified to the emotional stresses the majority experienced in their prepuberty years, and to more comfortable self-perception in the high school years.

One of our cautious modifiers vividly describing her uncertainties and self-doubts at this period in her life, captured the pressures the majority felt.

"I would like to forget that time ever, ever existed. . . .Through junior high, I had such a terrible inferiority complex, and I was scared to death of other people and I thought it was a sin to like boys. I was afraid to talk to people. . . .I knew that everybody was talking about me behind my back. Everybody thought I was horrible and in reality I'm sure they thought I was a snob because I wouldn't speak to them. I was afraid of them. And it just is the most horrible, horrible way to live. . . .My ninth grade year, I realized that something was wrong but I didn't know what it was. I guess toward the end of the year, I began to realize — just a little bit — that it was me instead of the other people that was wrong. . . .In my sophomore year things were just all changed . . . .I still have trouble with it, but it gets better every year. That summer was the first summer I ever had a date and it helped tremendously. And really — in my whole outlook — it's different and everything is so much more meaningful. Before that I was so much afraid of people I could never have helped them, and now I want to help them, and do all that I can to help them. I've made a lot of friends that basically agree with me. . . .And now I'm friends with the kids that I think are really sharp kids. The kids that will really go some place in life. . . .before that I was scared to death of them. Oh, I was so scared of them!"

Another cautious modifier described his change of perspective about himself as follows: "Some of the grades I didn't like and some of the teachers — particularly having a teacher the whole day really made a difference. . . .I didn't like the idea of going to junior high, but I guess it was all right; I mean there wasn't much choice. I just couldn't, you know, stay back in time. It was kind of scary at first, thinking of having all those big kids around you — you know they were only eighth graders — I look down upon that now. . . .Then once you are a senior you realize that they really weren't that big." As he went on to talk about his high school experiences, he explained that he felt more adequate as he became involved in student activities, particularly working in and setting up a youth center.

An ideological, conservative had a similar story to tell. As he thought about his feelings in relation to junior high school, he said,

"Well, I don't know. I just didn't have a good time with the kids particularly in junior high. I don't know whether I should attribute that fault to me or to them. It just happened. I know there was a radical change in high school, either in me or in the kids. I know for one thing the crowd that I went with changed. . . .It was expanded and. . . .I chose different elements of the crowd to associate myself with, and things just happened better." Both boys experienced increasing self-confidence and satisfaction as they found some new interests and further developed already existing interests. For a few, academic success was rewarding; for a larger number, recognition by peers and adults for competence in sports or the arts increased confidence and provided new social outlets.

For a cautious modifier, self-esteem and social prestige grew concomitantly out of experienced success on a high school debating team. Shy and without many friends in junior high school, she found in high school that her peers liked her for herself. In turn, she was more able to appreciate herself and to enjoy her individuality. "I love to talk to people and I just walk up and talk to them. . . .and you just meet people and you try. . . .I tried for a long time, you know, just to put on a show, but then I decided you can't do that; you've just got to be yourself, so that's just it. . . .I'm just myself."

The frequency with which similiar comments were made to both authors, separately, on different occasions and in different contexts, emphasizes the painful stresses most preadolescents experienced. Yet, the majority were able to weather these pressures by chosing to participate in activities which they found personally and socially rewarding and/or by taking stock of themselves and by seeking through their own experiences to reformulate their ideas and feelings. While they did this with the help of families, siblings, and peers, their urgency to seek out their own sensations and to integrate a variety of experiences helped them formulate their own viewpoints by the time they were adolescents. These viewpoints, although similar to those of their parents, often seemed to have moved beyond them.

Adolescence

In the adolescent years (in most cases the semester before graduating from high school) our subjects were independently interviewed[22] by our psychiatrist and by our psychologist, who also gave them a variety of psychological tests. These two assessments, independently summarized by the two authors for each subject, were on the average in remarkable agreement that these teenagers showed unusual sober thoughtfulness, stability, and seriousness of purpose, and an openness and responsiveness beyond that often attributed to teenagers (and different from the usual stereotype of the conservative midwesterners). Our subjects' aspirations for continued education, their increased involvement in living, and their overall adequacy in dealing with their personal lives all pointed to coping adequacy and stability on the part of the majority. In this, they resembled the teenagers other authors have described. However, in the longitudinal context of long association and intimate acquaintance with our families over our subjects' entire life span, there were identifiable new value systems emerging, and these differed qualitatively from those of the parents. A possible criticism of subjectivity was rejected because these impressions were supported in a wide variety of psychological tests as well as independent interviews with the teenagers. In their verbal comments as well as in the projective tests, the majority expressed new appreciation of themselves, broadened and refined interests in nuances of feeling, and more tolerance of differences in others than their parents or they had voiced in their prepuberty years. They looked for relevance in a world which, although stressful, is challenging and exciting.

These independent assessments and their remarkable clinical consistency led us to develop a continuum of perceptual openness and to make the following hypothesis: all adolescents, whether strictly identified with parental standards or seeking to develop new moral and ethical standards, in some ways and to varying degrees share the impact of social and technological world change.

Alienation and lack of commitment, so often reported in current discussions of modern day youth, were contradicted by subjects' cooperative and often enthusiastic responsiveness to the time-consuming requirements of our research. Eighty-two percent of the prepuberty sample continued to participate in the research; and of these, an overwhelming majority (87 percent) expressed feelings that the research was pleasant, meaningful, and helpful. Furthermore, about half of those seen at adolescence initiated further contacts after the research was terminated for additional counseling in relation to school, vocational guidance, or personal problems. The flavor of these feelings is suggested by some typical comments, ranging from mild pleasure to deep commitment, from interest to a sense of pride. For example, a cautious modifier said, "I thought it was fun. I thought it was really neat. I'm really glad I'm a part of it. . . .I tell some people about it because I think it is interesting."

With somewhat more depth of feeling, another cautious modifier saw project participation as helpful in sorting out personal feelings. She said, "I found it interesting. . . .I have liked it real well. . . .I've always been proud of it. . . .You think that somebody knows my past, and if you ever really wanted to find out, you could." In the same vein, and with marked enthusiasm, one of ideological conservatives remarked, "This has been the most interesting thing in my life. I feel that it's — you really stop and think! You really do. Man, I tell you! [He elaborated for some time on possible meanings of violence in others and then examined his own behavior in this regard.] Oh, it makes me stop and wonder why I'm doing something. . . .You kind of diagnose yourself there. . . .You are your own psychiatrist, you know. . . .You sit there and clear your mind of it." (That is, in regard to whatever problems happen to be bothersome at a particular time.) This was true, too, of another ideological conservative who pointed out both the value of contributing to a scientific study and the rewards of gaining self-knowledge. "It feels good to have contributed, to be part of something that is research. . . .Well, you get to talk to people. You learn how to express yourself. . . .You start thinking about these things. . . .Somebody kind of gives you a little shove to start thinking about being educated and adjusted. It kind of brings them out in front of yourself."

Some felt particularly gratified by the unique opportunity to talk about personal aptitudes and interests in relation to making further educational and vocational plans. "I do appreciate it. I am enjoying it. . . .Anything that makes you different, you enjoy. . . .I've always enjoyed it because it is something quite different than every day. . . .I feel happy that I'm in it because it has given me an insight into psychology. . . .And, naturally, I feel that I know more than the majority of people about that kind of thing. (This boy was planning to major in psychology at one of the state universities.)

A number of subjects saw their part in the project as something special, which not only increased self-knowledge but which in some ways contributed to self-esteem. For example, one of our brightest ideological conservatives said, "This experience was mostly positive indeed. It helps me to know myself for one thing. . . .And if I am contributing something, by golly, there is nothing wrong with that at all, and I am proud to do it. Apparently, it is not something that everyone is in on, and I like the bit of uniqueness within myself. I've gotten to meet you fine people and I'm glad for that. . . .It is probably my own association really with the Menninger Clinic, and since the city is — well, world famous for it, I am pretty proud to have a small part in it and some knowledge of it."

Several subjects contrasted feelings at different times or in relation to specific demands. A shy cautious modifier who did not communicate readily said, "It is pretty good on the whole, but there were some times when it was boring and some of the things I had to do that I didn't like." (When she was asked specifically what had been boring or unpleasant for her, she could remember only the projective tests, in contrast to the structured tests which were "kind of fun.") Another girl who had experienced a good deal of physical stress while growing up remarked, "When I first started it, I liked it because you could play with all the little toys. (The Miniature Life Toy Sessions with one of the psychologists.) Then in junior high and the first couple of years in high school, I just hated it and I just dreaded coming. My mother had to order me to do it. Sometimes all of those questions got me kind of embarrassed. But in the last couple of years, I've kind of been interested in it and I wanted to come."

A few subjects participated despite negative comments from relatives and associates. Most common was mild embarrassment from kidding by friends; 8 of our adolescents mentioned this. Two experienced jealousy, one from a sister and another from a boyfriend. The former said, "I don't know why she is always jealous when I get to come out here. She always wants to come out here. . . .I don't understand it." The latter, feeling some responsibility, kept an appointment even though her boyfriend objected to her doing so. "I've really enjoyed it. . . .I want to be a part of it and try to help. . . .What really tore into me was when he said he didn't want me to come here and tell everything about my life, and I said they had been researching on me for this project since 1950 and I'm not going to say I'm not going to go because I don't think it is right."

Impressive, too, was the typical willingness of 12 subjects to keep evening or Saturday appointments and for 6 subjects to travel a considerable distance from out-of-state homes. Only 5 subjects who kept an initial appointment failed to return for the second; of these, 2 girls were about to be married, 1 boy was in service, 2 boys who lacked firm plans for their future apparently felt unable to discuss the issues involved. But for the majority,[23] project participation appeared to have been experienced as interesting, often helpful, and a source of pride and pleasure in contributing to and gaining knowledge of social sciences and about one's self.

Indicative of the active, responsible life styles of most of our subjects were their projected future academic plans and the range of activities in which they engaged. Eighty-two percent of our subjects sought some kind of advanced training, with seventy-six percent enrolled in or planning on college. With 2 exceptions, school grades were average or better, but roughly half of the sample earned grades inferior to those that might have been expected from their measured intellectual ability, and therefore this was possibly a measure of some underachievement. Still, their academic performance was not inconsistent with parental expectations and not a true measure of achievement if we consider the extent to which they were involved in community and school affairs.

In the senior year, 90 percent were actively involved in extracurricular pursuits, and nearly half of these held leadership positions in the organizations to which they belonged.[24] In addition to participation in sports, dramatics, music groups, and special interest clubs in school, 53 percent were engaged in church or other community service activities such as a volunteer work in local institutions.

During high school, 93 percent supported themselves partially with semiskilled or part-time jobs. However, 6 youths were after college enrollment employed fulltime, or had received academic awards that made them completely self-supporting. Thus, if we consider achievement as reflected by participation in extracurricular activities in school and in community affairs, employment, and the maintenance of average academic work, 75 percent of the sample were leading well-rounded, productive lives.

These data suggested that most of our subjects were using their opportunities and skills, resiliently dealing with expectable stresses, and appeared to be headed toward productive and stable futures. Nearly all saw their lives as similar to those of their parents, but at the same time they were able to accept differing from their parents in thinking, behavior, or both without feeling real alienation or guilt. The ambivalence about dependency, so prevalent in the preadolescent years, was in most of our subjects close to resolution, or at least considerably diminished. In one-tenth of the sample, resolution was still incomplete; and in a few of these, more serious maladjustments appeared likely to continue well into the adult years. But on the average, these adolescents justified the faith of their mothers who at preschool felt they would "grow out of" the difficulties they experienced in growing up.

Notes:

[1] In 1950, the population of Topeka and the surrounding urban area was 105,418. By 1958, the population had increased to 129,600. These figures were released by the county assessor and reported in *Know Your City*, published by the League of Women Voters, 1959. By 1970, the population figure reported by the United States Bureau of the Census was 135,000.

[2] According to the official United States Government Census for 1960, 15.46 percent of Topeka's residents earned less than $3000 a year, the figure usually given as poverty level for a family of four; 20.94 percent earned between $3000 and $4000 yearly; 26.5 percent between $5000 and $6000; and 37.45 percent more than $7000.

[3] Although we did not ask our families about their yearly earnings, we knew that 8 percent of the fathers were unskilled, 19 percent semiskilled, 25 percent skilled, 20 percent employed in white collar jobs or small businesses, 25 percent in the professions, and 2 percent in career army positions.

[4] In Topeka, as reported in the Unites States Government Census for 1960, 90.82 percent of the residents were of Anglo-Saxon origin. In our sample, two families were of Germanic background; the rest were of Anglo-Saxon origin.

[5] As reported in the 1960 United States Government Census, 78.16 percent of all Topekans lived in single-family dwellings.

[6] In 1950 (when our subjects were between 1 and 3 years of age), 40.9 percent of the American people lived in urban areas with a population of less than 250,000. In 1960 (when our subjects were between 9 and 13 years of age), nearly half (47.9 percent) of the American people lived in urban areas of less than 250,000 people. These figures are reported in the United States Government Census for 1960.

[7] Reported in the United States Government Census for 1960.

[8] According to a 1965 Childrens' Bureau report, 91 percent of all young people at some time commit a delinquent act. Most are never arrested. However, for all youth in the United States, 1 in 9 is referred to the juvenile court. For males, this figure is 1 out of 6. These figures were reported in The Challenge of Crime in a Free Society, U.S. Government Printing Office, 1967, p 55.

[9] Practices and feelings about religion on the part of our subjects in early adolescence are described more fully in Adolescent Religion by Charles William Stewart, Abingdon Press, Nashville, Tennessee, 1967. Also see Chapter 3.

[10] Some further thoughts about the effects of traditional schooling are expressed in Toussieng Povl: Teachers and Differences. Am J Orthopsychiatry 39 (5), October 1969.

[11] According to the 1960 United States Government Census, the median number of school years completed in the United States was 10.6 grades. In Kansas, the median number of school years completed was slightly higher (11.7 grades); in Topeka, this figure was still higher (12.1 grades). In Topeka, 46 percent of the present adult population dropped out of school before finishing high school; in the present 15–19-year age range,

4 percent dropped out before completing high school. Of the adolescents who completed high school, 50 percent went to college.

In our sample, 20 percent of the parents of our 54 subjects dropped out of high school before graduation. 37 percent began college training; 21 percent finished college; 13 percent took graduate training. Breaking these figures down by sex, we found our fathers more likely than our mothers to drop out of school prior to high school graduation, but if they completed high school and enrolled in college, they were more likely to complete college and more likely to pursue graduate work.

[12]One of these later finished high school. The other was accidentally killed in late adolescence just before completing plans to take the high school equivalency test.

[13]We have been unable to obtain health statistics reported in exactly the same terms or covering exactly the same period of time, but representative findings suggest that our sample in most cases resembled or surpassed the national level of health for 1950–1960. The statistics we obtained for comparative purposes were reported by the United States Department of Health, Education, and Welfare, either in *Illness Among Children,* published by the Children's Bureau, 1963 (IAC); or by Public Health Service, National Center for Health Statistics for 1965–1967 (NCH).

In the 20 years of the study, almost 50 percent had accidents or illnesses requiring stitches, casts, or both. (IAC reports that 30.7 percent of children under 17 are injured annually.)

Nearly all had the usual childhood diseases, but few were seriously ill. (As of 1961, NCH reported that for children under 15, there were on the average 3 episodes of acute illness per year.) Twenty percent had been hospitalized at some time during the 20-year span for such relatively serious illnesses as rheumatic fever, hepatitis, pneumonia, scarlet fever, mononucleosis, osteomyelitis, and diabetes. Fourteen percent underwent surgery for such conditions as hernia and appendicitis. (Between July 1958 and June 1960, IAC reported that 54.6 per 1000 children between 5 and 14 years were hospitalized. Of these, 52.5 percent had major surgery.) Half of our sample had tonsillectomies. (In 1959–1961, IAC reported that 47.1 percent of the hospitalized children under 15 were treated for respiratory problems, primarily by tonsillectomy.)

Nearly half had some visual problems, primarily myopia, and one-third of the sample wore glasses by the time they were adolescents. (In 1960, the Children's Bureau reported that more than 10,000 children between 5 and 17 years were known to have refractive errors. In the 1960 United States Census report, it was reported that 30 percent of the population of 20 years and under wore glasses.)

Three children or 4 percent of our sample were known to have some hearing loss (2.9 percent, IAC). In this case, our sample was slightly higher than the national average, but probably not significantly so.

Three, or 6 percent, required orthodontia (9.2 percent as reported by IAC).

Upper respiratory infection was common, and one-quarter had allergies. (Respiratory conditions accounted for 55 percent of the acute conditions in children under 15 in 1961. In the 0–16 age range, 10.8 percent had hay fever; 11.4 percent, asthma; 10.6 percent, other allergies. These figures were reported in IAC.)

Sixteen percent had unusually sensitive skin with such problems as eczema, infectious reaction to insect bites, or sunburn. (Of the 0–16-year age range, 3.6 percent were reported in 1959–1961 by IAC to have skin infections and/or disease, and an additional 10.6 percent to have allergic reactions.)

Chronic nausea, ear infections, limited energy, and diffuse neurological problems were relatively rare, each occurring in less than 9 percent of the subject population. (From July 1959 through June 1961, 18 percent of the population under 17 were reported to have at least one chronic condition by IAC.)

[14]In our parents, major chronic physical conditions included diabetes, heart trouble, and cancer. Acute health problems included pneumonia or accidental injury. In all, 17 percent had some major health problems. (In 1966–1967, 59.2 percent of the population age 25–44 had one or more chronic health conditions; 29.4 percent were hospitalized; 29.5 percent were injured; 45.9 percent suffered some acute illnesses. These figures were reported by NCH.)

[15]Between July 1963 and June 1964, 7.3 of every 100 persons in the United States sought either inpatient or outpatient psychiatric care. (This was reported by NCH.)

[16]Heider Grace: Vulnerability in Infants and Young Children. Genetic Psychology, Monograph, 1966, 73, pp 1–216; and Murphy LB, Moriarty A: Development, Vulnerability and Resilience. New Haven, Conn., Yale University Press, 1976.

[17]Murphy LB: Widening World of Childhood. Basic Books, Inc, Publishers, 1962.

[18]See Rousey Clyde L, Moriarty Alice E: Diagnostic Implications of Speech Sounds. Springfield, Illinois, Charles C. Thomas, Publisher, 1965.

[19]Moriarty Alice E: Normal preschoolers' reactions to the Childrens' Apperception Test: some implications for later development. J Projective Techniques and Personality Assessment 32 (5), 1968. Also see Moriarty Alice E: Coping patterns of preschool children in response to intelligence test demands. Genet Psych Monographs 64: 3–127, 1961.

[20]Eighteen percent of the parents considered grades important. Higher education was not pushed; only 32 percent of the parents of the latency-aged children expected their offspring to attend college although an additional 29 percent viewed college positively and were willing to help financially if the children were inclined in that direction. These findings and others were obtained through interviews with mothers in 1964 by Miss Diana Dolgoff and Miss Beth Koropsak, research assistants.

[21]Gardner Riley, Moriarty Alice: Personality Development at Preadolescence, Seattle, University of Washington Press, 1968.

[22]See Appendix A for content of the interviews, tests given, and special procedures to tap student self-assessment and provide feedback to the students in regard to their skills and personality traits as we assessed them through observations and tests.

[23]In view of their pleasure in participating in the project, we wondered whether contacts with the staff contributed to some of the changes made by so many of our subjects. However, the very facts that the subjects were seen only once or twice by each of the interviewers and that the staff itself changed in composition over the years made the development of any real identification with individual staff members less likely. Furthermore, nothing the young men and women said about their changed values gave even a hint that the subjects credited these changes in any way to their participation in the project. One mother complained that her son's excessive self-preoccupation was due to the introspection which the project had encouraged. We agree that the continuity of contact over the years made it easier for our subjects to talk openly and perhaps to reflect about themselves.

However, it is difficult to see how a few interviews with up to 5-year intervals between them could have influenced value change. In this one case, the son did not in any way blame his difficulties on his contact with the project staff.

[24]Their total involvement with these activities was in marked contrast to their frequently negative assessments of the relevance and vividness of the academic aspects of school.

Appendix C

Identifying Data and Group Findings

Table 1
Religion, Occupational Level,* Ordinal Position, and
Number of Children in Family.

Case Number	Sex	Religion	Occupational Level	Ordinal Position	Number of Children
1	F	Protestant	1	2	4
2	F	Protestant	1	3	4
3	F	Protestant	4	4	4
4	M	Protestant	4	3	4
5	F	Protestant	1	3	4
6	M	Protestant	1	4	4
7	M	Protestant	4	1	2
8	M	Protestant	3	1	2

*Based on August B. Hollingshead's Two Factor Index of Social Position, Yale University, 1955, unpublished.

1. Higher executives, proprietors of large concerns, and major professionals.
2. Business managers, proprietors of medium-sized businesses, and lesser professionals.
3. Administrative personnel, small independent businessmen, and minor professionals.
4. Clerical and sales workers, technicians, and owners of small businesses (value under $6000).
5. Skilled manual employees.
6. Machine operators and semiskilled employees.
7. Unskilled employees.

Table 1 (Continued)

Case Number	Sex	Religion	Occupational Level	Ordinal Position	Number of Children
9	F	Protestant	1	1	2
10	M	None	4	1	1
11	M	Protestant	1	1	1
12	M	Catholic	5	2	4
13	F	Catholic	4	3	5
14	M	Catholic	5	1	4
15	F	Protestant	4	1	2
16	F	Protestant	4	4	6
17	M	Protestant	7	3	8
18	M	Protestant	7	4	8
19	F	Protestant	5	2	5
20	M	Catholic	5	3	5
21	F	Protestant	4	5	5
22	F	Catholic	3	1	6
23	F	Catholic	3	2	6
24	F	Catholic	7	3	6
25	F	Catholic	6	1	3
26	M	Catholic	4	3	3
27	M	Protestant	1	1	2
28	M	Protestant	5	2	3
29	M	Protestant	6	3	5
30	F	Protestant	4	3	7
31	F	Protestant	1	2	2
32	M	Catholic	3	1	3
33	M	Protestant	5	3	3
34	F	Protestant	6	5	5
35	M	Protestant	4	1	2
36	F	Protestant	4	2	2
37	M	Protestant	5	2	3
38	F	Protestant	3	2	2
39	F	Protestant	6	1	2
40	M	Protestant	6	1	5
41	F	Protestant	1	2	4
42	M	Protestant	1	2	2
43	M	Catholic	3	1	4
44	M	Protestant	5	2	2
45	F	Protestant	1	1	3
46	F	Protestant	5	2	2
47	M	Protestant	5	2	2
48	M	Protestant	5	2	2

Table 1 (Continued)

Case Number	Sex	Religion	Occupational Level	Ordinal Position	Number of Children
49	F	Protestant	3	3	3
50	F	Protestant	5	3	3
51	M	Catholic	1	3	4
52	M	Catholic	5	2	5
53	F	Protestant	1	1	2
54	F	Protestant	2	2	5
55	M	Protestant	6	3	3
56	F	Catholic	5	3	4
57	F	Catholic	3	2	3
58	F	Protestant	7	2	4
59	M	Protestant	4	2	4
60	F	Protestant	1	2	4
61	M	None	1	2	3
62	F	None	1	3	3
63	F	Protestant	2	3	3
64	M	Protestant	1	2	3
65	M	Protestant	2	2	2

Some Additional Facts

1. With two exceptions (cases 10 and 11), all subjects had at least one sibling.

2. Our sample included 5 sibling pairs (1 and 2, 5 and 6, 17 and 18, 20 and 52, 22 and 23). With the exception of 1 and 2 who moved out of the state, all sibling pairs participated in the adolescent study.

3. Our sample included two sets of cousins (17 and 18, who were brothers, and 16, a girl; 20 and 52, brothers, and 24, a girl who died before the adolescent study).

4. Six sets of parents (or 11 percent) of the adolescent sample of 54 subjects were divorced by the subjects' adolescent years (8, 10, 40, 45, 49, 65). The parents of cases 5 and 6 were also divorced, but these subjects did not participate in the adolescent study.

5. We saw 54 subjects in the adolescent study. Eleven of the subjects included in earlier studies were unavailable at adolescence. These included 5 and 6, siblings whose mother objected; 1, 2, 13, 25, 27, and 56, who moved out of state; and 35 and 37, who were unable for physical and emotional reasons to enroll in the senior year of high school.

Table 2

Adolescent IQs and Grade Point Average*

Case Number	Age (yr-mo)	WAIS† V.	P.	F.	Grade Point Average
1	20-5	126	106	118	3.07
2	19-2	116	111	115	1.94
3	19-2	110	104	108	1.57
4	19-1	137	143	144	3.60
5	19-0	131	123	129	2.67
6	18-9	107	115	111	3.05
7	18-8	96	110	102	1.74
8	18-8	108	106	107	2.76
9	18-6	121	105	115	3.46
10	18-6	109	127	117	2.36
11	18-5	115	120	119	2.43
12	18-5	121	124	124	2.50
13	18-3	123	114	120	2.90
14	18-3	139	133	139	3.76
15	18-2	108	123	115	2.16
16	18-1	114	119	117	3.54
17	18-1	119	119	120	2.15
18	18-1	122	116	121	3.09
19	18-0	102	103	103	1.60
20	17-10	117	129	124	3.41
21	17-9	105	116	110	2.16
22	17-9	107	96	103	3.14
23	17-9	108	104	107	2.50
24	17-9	110	120	115	2.10
25	17-9	123	122	125	3.09
26	17-9	123	103	115	3.09
27	17-8	126	124	127	2.25
28	17-8	120	116	119	3.25
29	17-8	120	111	117	3.00
30	17-8	102	111	106	2.83
31	17-7	104	109	107	3.35
32	17-6	114	120	118	3.13
33	17-6	112	100	108	1.78

*Letter grade equivalents: A = 3.6 – 4.0; B = 2.6 – 3.59; C = 1.6 – 2.59; D = 0.6 – 1.59.

†Mean IQ on WAIS for boys were verbal 117.01, performance 115.89, full scale 117.68. Scores for girls were 112.50, 114.65, and 114.35, respectively.

Table 2 (Continued)

Case Number	Age (yr-mo)	WAIS†			Grade Point Average
		V.	P.	F.	
34	17-6	132	134	135	3.09
35	17-6	124	121	124	3.54
36	17-5	98	106	102	2.31
37	17-5	107	108	108	2.55
38	17-5	106	125	115	2.56
39	17-4	121	124	124	3.25
40	17-4	109	121	115	3.15
41	17-4	121	115	119	2.50
42	17-3	106	108	108	2.87
43	17-2	114	112	114	3.21
44	17-2	106	112	109	2.44
45	17-2	108	116	112	2.28
46	17-1	112	111	112	2.14
47	17-1	120	112	118	3.25
48	17-1	120	123	122	3.25
49	17-1	119	120	121	2.43
50	17-0	120	115	119	2.75
51	17-0	117	109	115	3.37
52	16-1	116	125	121	3.30
53	15-11	101	100	101	2.65
54	15-10	110	107	109	2.72

Table 3

Intercorrelations Between Openness* and IQ, Grade Point
Average, Coping Capacity,† and Family Interaction‡

Boys	N	GPA	Openness	Coping I	Coping II
WAIS					
Verbal IQ	28	0.6423§	0.2037	-0.0973	-0.1722
Performance IQ	28	0.5522‖	0.2509	-0.0134	-0.3188¶
Full scale IQ	28	0.6562§	0.2508	-0.0791	-0.2667
Family Interaction					
Fun	22	0.2509	0.3865¶		
Work	22	0.0476	0.2345		
Communication	22	0.3920¶	0.0972		
Understanding	22	0.4572#	0.0070		
Average	22	0.4423#	0.2582		

*Openness to value change.

†Coping I, as defined in the series of 5 studies, is a rating based on clinical findings and observations of children's problem-solving skills in everyday problems. It reflects their capacity to use their resources constructively to meet the demands, expectations, and challenges from the environment. These ratings were made at each age level; here coping I is an average of ratings made independently by the two authors during the subjects' adolescence. Coping II is a similar rating of our subjects' internal equilibrium at adolescence. Hence, it reflects the balance or internal integration within individual subjects.

‡Family interaction, divided into four parts — shared fun, shared work, interfamily communication, and understanding among family members — was rated by two staff members on their observations of and interviews with parents in the prepuberty years. For each individual subject, these ratings were averaged to assess overall level of family interaction. Because of time and economic limitations, we could not repeat these family assessments in the adolescent years. Hence, they represent our best estimate of family interaction in the adolescent years. Insofar as family interaction, as judged by our subjects' verbal communication with us in their adolescence, was of similar level, these assessments can be assumed to be an accurate measure of family interaction in our subjects' adolescence. This assumption is supported by our impression, from living in the community, that cultural influences in Topeka remained stable in these years, before drugs were a significant problem. We cannot, of course, estimate how much the drug culture might have affected our families, nor do we have data on our subjects in this period. Our estimate of family interaction is that obtained closest in time to the period in which the reported interviews and psychological tests were taken.

§Correlations significant at the 0.001 level.
‖Correlations significant at the 0.01 level.
¶Correlations significant at the 0.10 level.
#Correlations significant at the 0.05 level.

Table 3 (Continued)

Boys	N	GPA	Openness	Coping I	Coping II
Openness	28	0.1500			
Coping I	28	0.1482	-0.1736		
Coping II	28	-0.1980	-0.0870		
Girls					
WAIS					
Verbal IQ	26	0.3616¶	0.3300¶	0.1462	-0.1078
Performance IQ	26	-0.0818	0.1477	0.0971	0.0450
Full scale IQ	26	0.2122	0.2965	0.1395	-0.0518
Family Interaction					
Fun	23	-0.0377	-0.1748		
Work	23	-0.0656	-0.1693		
Communication	23	0.2400	-0.3270		
Understanding	23	0.0519	-0.1484		
Average	23	0.0612	-0.2468		
Openness	26	-0.2349			
Coping I	26	-0.0969	0.1128		
Coping II	26	-0.1531	0.0120		
Total Sample					
WAIS					
Verbal IQ	54	0.4954§	0.1837	-0.0506	-0.2039
Performance IQ	54	0.3168¶	0.1880	0.0157	-0.1611
Full scale IQ	54	0.0534	0.2120	-0.0362	-0.2151
Family Interaction					
Fun	45	0.1118	0.0956		
Work	45	-0.0322	0.0093		
Communication	45	0.2459	-0.1641		
Understanding	45	0.2226	-0.1060		
Average	45	0.2014	-0.0523		
Openness	54	0.0308			
Coping I	54	0.0812	-0.0147		
Coping II	54	-0.1285	0.0342		

IMPLICATIONS OF TABLE 3

1. Openness was not significantly correlated with IQ in boys. In girls, some relationship was suggested (0.10 level) between openness and verbal IQ, but this was at such a low level (0.33) that no predictive value could be attached for individuals.

2. Openness was not correlated with coping I (problem solving) in either boys or girls separately or in the sample as a whole.

3. Openness was not correlated with coping II (internal equilibrium) in either boys or girls separately or in the sample as a whole.

4. In the sample as a whole, and in girls, no relationship was found between family interaction and openness. In boys, openness was related to shared fun in the family. However, correlation was low (0.39) and significant only at the 0.01 level. Hence, this relationship had no reliable predictive value for individuals.

5. Openness was not related to grade point average for either sex or for the sample as a whole.

6. For boys, grade point average was significantly related to WAIS IQ (0.64, $p < 0.001$; 0.55, $p < 0.01$; and 0.65, $p < 0.001$, respectively, for verbal, performance, and full scale IQ). However, these correlations do not warrant individual prediction, and at the level at which they exist, they account for less than half of the variance in school achievement. Clearly, other unmeasured factors determine achievement.

7. For girls, grade point average is modestly associated with verbal IQ (0.36) at a suggestive level of association ($p < 0.10$). Apparently, girls' school achievement is dependent almost entirely on other factors.

8. For the sample as a whole, grade point average is somewhat more clearly and more reliably related to verbal IQ (0.50, $p < 0.001$) and to a lesser degree (0.32 $p < 0.10$) with performance IQ. Hence, grade point average for the group may be predicted with some accuracy from verbal IQ; in individuals, predictive relationship may be distorted considerably by other factors.

9. Openness appears to be a distinct aspect of functioning, not determined to any great extent by IQ, problem-solving skills, internal stability, or family interaction. In Chapter 10, we discuss other factors that may be related to level of openness to reality.

Table 4

Smoking Habits in the Senior Year of High School
(N = 54; 28 Boys and 26 Girls)*

Never Smoked	Boys† Tried, Gave-up	Habitual	Never	Girls‡ Tried	Habitual
1. Peter	1. Otto	1. Everett	1. Harriet	1. Martha	1. Edna
2. Barney	2. Albert	2. Horace	2. Elaine	2. Flora	2. Evelyn
3. Frederick	3. Douglas	3. Manuel	3. Beatrice	3. Cheryl	3. Rose
4. Lionel	4. Avery	4. Carl	4. Selma	4. Agnes	4. Marilyn
5. Paul	5. Irving	5. Terry	5. Eva	5. Eleanor	5. Edith
6. Calvin	6. Floyd	6. Alan	6. Cora	6. Phyllis	
	7. Clinton	7. Luke	7. Faith	7. Shirley	
	8. Neal	8. Lester		8. Viola	
	9. Matthew	9. Henry		9. Celeste	
	10. Earl	10. Arthur		10. Irma	
	11. George	11. Victor		11. Dora	
				12. Amelia	
				13. Eunice	
				14. Estelle	

*In the entire sample, 13 (24 percent) never smoked, 25 (46 percent) tried smoking and quit, and 16 (30 percent) were habitual smokers at adolescence.

†Of the 28 boys, 6 (21.4 percent) never smoked, 11 (39.3 percent) tried smoking and gave it up voluntarily, and 11 (39.3 percent) were habitual smokers at adolescence.

‡Of the 26 girls, 7 (27 percent) never smoked, 14 (54 percent) tried and quit, and 5 (19 percent) habitual smokers at adolescence.

Table 5
Drinking Habits in the Senior Year of High School
(N = 54; 28 Boys and 26 Girls)

Never Tried	Rejected for Self and Others	Moderate; Tolerant of Others	Heavy
Boys			
1. Paul	1. Peter	1. Horace	1. Everett
2. Calvin	2. Otto	2. Manuel	2. Alan
	3. Albert	3. Carl	3. Irving
	4. Douglas	4. Byron	4. Luke
	5. Avery	5. Lester	5. Henry
	6. Frederick	6. Floyd	
	7. Lionel	7. Victor	
	8. Clinton	8. Matthew	
	9. Neal	9. George	
	10. Earl	10. Arthur	
	11. Barney		
Girls			
1. Faith	1. Harriet	1. Edna	1. Evelyn
	2. Flora	2. Martha	
	3. Agnes	3. Cheryl	
	4. Eleanor	4. Phyllis	
	5. Elaine	5. Shirley	
	6. Celeste	6. Viola	
	7. Irma	7. Beatrice	
	8. Eva	8. Rose	
		9. Marilyn	
		10. Selma	
		11. Dora	
		12. Cora	
		13. Edith	
		14. Amelia	
		15. Eunice	
		16. Estelle	

SUMMARY

1. By their senior high school year, only 3 (6 percent) of our subjects had never tasted alcohol of any kind.
2. Nineteen (35 percent) did not use alcohol, disapproved of its use by others, and tended to avoid friendships with those who drank.

Table 5 — SUMMARY (Continued)

3. Twenty-six (48 percent) drank moderately in social situations and were tolerant of drinking in others.
4. Six (11 percent) were heavy drinkers at some time in their high school years. However, by their senior year, most of these had moderated their drinking habits.

Table 6
Religious Beliefs and Practices (N = 54; 26 Girls and 28 Boys)

	Regular Participation						Irregular Participation					
	Habit			**Conviction**			**Mild Doubts**			**Rejection**		
	Girls	Boys	Total	Girls	Boys	Total	Girls	Boys	Total	Girls	Boys	Total
Catholic N = 12; 22% of the sample (4 girls, 8 boys)												
N	1	2	3	1	0	1	2	2	4	0	4	4
%	25	25	25	25	0	8	50	25	33.3	0	50	33.3
Protestants N = 42; 78% of the sample (22 girls, 20 boys)												
N	7	6	13	5	4	9	8	6	14	2	4	6
%	32	30	31	23	20	21	36	30	33	9	20	14
Totals by sex:												
N	8	8	16	6	4	10	9	8	18	3	8	10
%	31	29	30	22	14	19	35	29	33	12	29	19

Totals for entire sample:

N–26	N–28
%–48	%–52

Summary findings about religious beliefs and practices.

1. Twenty-six or 48 percent, of our subjects still attended church regularly in their adolescence.
   a. Sixteen, or 29.6 percent of the total sample, went to church primarily out of habit; they did not question religious beliefs and practices.

    b. Ten or 18.5 percent of the total sample, had strong personal convictions that religion played an important part in their lives.

2. Twenty-eight, or 52 percent, of our subjects attended church irregularly and expressed mild to serious doubts about the value of religion in their lives.

    a. Eighteen, or 33 percent of the total sample, expressed some mild doubts about religious practices and were irregular in church attendance.

    b. Ten, or 19 percent of the total sample, expressed serious doubts about religious beliefs, rarely or never attended church, and did not anticipate that religion would play a major part in their lives. In effect, these subjects rejected religion altogether.

3. Among the 12 Catholic youths: 25 percent attended church regularly, primarily out of habit; 8 percent attended church regularly out of strong personal convictions; 33.3 percent expressed mild doubts and were irregular in their participation in formal religious practices; and 33.3 percent had serious doubts about the value of organized religion or tended to reject religion altogether.

4. Among the 42 Protestant youths: 31 percent attended church regularly, primarily out of habit; 21 percent attended church regularly out of strong personal convictions; 33 percent expressed mild doubts and were irregular in their participation in formal religious practices; and 14 percent had serious doubts about the value of organized religion or tended to reject religion altogether.

5. Among the 26 girls: 31 percent attended church regularly, primarily out of habit; 22 percent attended church regularly out of strong personal convictions; 35 percent expressed mild doubts and were irregular in their participation in formal religious practices; and 12 percent had serious doubts about the value of organized religion or tended to reject religion altogether.

6. Among the 28 boys: 29 percent attended church regularly, primarily out of habit; 14 percent attended church regularly out of strong personal convictions; 29 percent expressed mild doubts and were irregular in their participation in formal religious practices; and 29 percent had serious doubts about the value of organized religion or tended to reject religion altogether.

Index